Rediscovering the Himalayas

As narrated by
Shambhu Nath Ghosh

Chandan Ghosh

Srishti
PUBLISHERS & DISTRIBUTORS

Srishti Publishers & Distributors
Registered Office: N-16, C.R. Park
New Delhi – 110 019
Corporate Office: 212A, Peacock Lane
Shahpur Jat, New Delhi – 110 049
editorial@srishtipublishers.com

First published by SRISHTI PUBLISHERS & DISTRIBUTORS in 2004
Copyright © Chandan Ghosh 2004

ISBN 9788 1885 75220

Typeset in AGaramond 11pt. by Suresh Kumar Sharma at Srishti

Cover design by Creative Concept

This book is dedicated to my elder brother
Sri Shambhu Nath Ghosh.
Rightfully this book belongs to him only.

PREFACE

My elder brother, Sri Shambhu Nath Ghosh, is perhaps the most well known music theoretician of Bengal. He fell in love with the Himalayas at a very early age and has returned to the mountains at every opportunity. He made it a point to travel, trek or walk to the most exotic places of the Himalayas again and again. Even at the ripe age of 71 he does not miss a chance to go to the Himalayas at least once a year. A well-known writer, he has written extensively about his experiences in the Himalayas. His book on **Pancha Kedar and Sapta Badri** was first published in Bengali in the early seventies. The second book entitled **"Kailash and Mansarovar – A Pilgrimage** was published in the late eighties. He personally narrated anecdotes about his visits and trekking adventures to me. I have consolidated the entire effort to present it to the lovers of the Himalayas. Though I am also fascinated by Himalayan beauty, I have not had the vivid experiences that my brother has had. So I have seen through his eyes all the places that I couldn't visit myself.

The reader will be fascinated by the mythology behind each hill and temple in the Garhwal region, which has been incorporated vividly in the book. Unless a visitor knows about these, he will not be able to understand the exquisiteness of the Himalayan journey. He will never be able to feel the pulse and the attraction of thousands of ascetics who left the material world behind and made the Himalayas their permanent home.

They were in search of God for thousands of years. The book may provide some answers for an enthusiastic and enquiring mind.

I acknowledge the great sage Swami Pranavanada for his stupendous work on Kailash and Mansoravar and have drawn heavily from his book "Exploration in Tibet" to make the chapter interesting and informative. I also thank the Indian Institute of Travel and Tourism for providing me with details on the Himalayas.

I hope this book will be a guide for people who wish to undertake a Himalayan pilgrimage or a pleasure trip through that monumental work of Nature.

ABOUT THE AUTHOR

Dr. CN Ghosh is a fighter pilot who joined the Indian Air Force in 1964 and retired in the rank of Air Commodore. He participated in the 1971 Indo-Pak war and was injured while attacking a Pakistani troop position. He was part of the Indian training team to Iraq which trained the Iraqi fighter pilots at a crucial time in Iraq's history, and was deputed to participate in the training programme at the US Air War College.

Apart from being a fighter pilot Dr. Ghosh has excelled in many other fields. He is an accomplished musician who plays the Sarod and has acquired prestigious degrees like Sangeet Visarad and Sangeet Pravin in Hindustani classical music. With a PhD degree in Military Science under his belt, he acquired proficiency in languages like French, Russian and Arabic. Being a prolific writer, he has also published books in the field of computer education, an Encyclopedia of Sports and Games and a few creative works in Bengali.

He has had a long love affair with the Himalayas and has delved into their mysteries whenever he could take time out of his busy schedule. He has also undertaken the task of translating his brother's tremendous enthusiasm about the Himalayas into readable form for the benefit of a larger audience.

CONTENTS

Himalayas:
The Abode of The Gods

The Himalayas (snow-abode), also known as Himavat, Himachala, Himadri and Giri-Raja are the highest mountain ranges in the world, though the youngest, and extend for 1,600 miles. along the Northern border. This is fittingly called the Lord of the mountains. Animated by divinity as its soul and internal spirit, it stands as it were like the measuring rod of earth" No Alpine gorges can seriously compare with the majestic, almost incredible, gorges of the Himalayas. On these mountain ranges, there is habitation even at a height of 17,000 feet above sea level. In beautiful scenes and exquisite panorama, the Himalayas excel even the best part of the Alps of Europe and Rockies of America. Kullu, Lahaul,Kumaon, Nepal, Sikkim and Bhutan, all Nature's beauty spots, are situated in the lap of the Himalayas. Thus, explained Swami Pranavanand about the Himalayas.

Lord Krishna in the Bhagwad Gita has said, "*Of the Great rishis, I am Bhirgu, of words, I am the syllable, of immovable things, I am the Himalayas.*" Kalidas called the Himalayas Devastatma. To the people of the South, a thousand and five hundred miles away, to the men of the sea coast, to the dwellers of the desert land of Rajputana, no less than to the inhabitants of the Gangetic Valley, the Himalayas have always been the symbol of India. The majesty of the snow clad peaks, visible from afar, the inaccessibility of even the lesser ranges, the mysteries of the gigantic glaciers and the magnificence of the great rivers that emerge from the gorges have combined to give the Himalayas a majestic status which no other mountain range in the world can claim.

In the past, only hermits and sages in quest of divine solitude explored the mysterious Himalayas. For mystics, the Himalayas had always been a source of inexhaustible mystery. For explorers, the Himalayas are intriguing. Pilgrims trekked only as far as the sacred Kedarnath and Badrinath.

Nestling in the foothills of the Himalayas is Garhwal the El- Dorado, the land of rishis, sages and ashrams a traveller's delight and a naturalist's paradise. Encompassing scenic locales along the Himalayan range, Garhwal is redolent with mythology and includes some of the holiest places of Hindu pilgrimage. Once upon a time Kashmir used to be the 'heaven on earth' but not any more. The terrorists have managed to paint this paradise with blood. But Garhwal maintains its heavenly characteristics, despite the invasion by an ever increasing population and the presence of security forces. All the major Hindu deities have their shrines in Garhwal, and the two great rivers, the Yamuna and the Ganga, originate from the Garhwal Himalayas. Thus, Garhwal is 'Dev Bhumi' the land of the gods and down the ages, the world-weary and the truth-seekers of this troubled universe of man have found tranquillity and peace in this land of Gods. The four traditional retreats for the pilgrim in Garhwal have been the 'dhams' or holy places of Yamunotri, Gangotri, Kedarnath, and Badrinath. Today, tourists and trekkers not only from India but also from different parts of the world join the pilgrim in his journey to

3

these abodes. Even a short visit to the Himalayan mountain ranges touches a chord of contemplation and wonder in a naturalist's heart, giving him glorious satisfaction.

The Shiwalik range, which is in the foothills of the Himalayas, forms the first barrier between the plains and the actual Himalayas. These lesser peaks of the Himalayas lead ultimately to the towering heights of the eternal snows and peaks such as Nanda Devi, the highest in India. The other great peaks of Garhwal — Trishul, Shivling, Neelkanth, Bhagirathi, Sri Kalilash and Swargarohini — all have myths associated with them for the Hindus, as well as unmatched allure for the mountaineer.

Shivling

Garhwal owes its fame to the holy Pancha Kedar, Sapta Badris and Pancha Prayagas. The Pancha Kedar is the collective name for five great temples of Lord Shiva-Kedarnath, Madmaheswar, Tungnath, Rudranath, and Kalpeshwar. The Sapta Badris comprise seven great temples devoted to Lord Vishnu- Badrinath, Yogdhyan Badri (at Pandukeshwar), Bhavishya Badri (near Tapovan), Vridha Badri (near Animath) and Adi Badri (Between Ranikhet and Karanprayag). The Panch Prayagas refer to the five places of confluence of the holy Alakananda with its tributaries.

Garhwal also abounds in high altitude lakes such as Sahastratal, which is a collection of more than twenty known lakes in an area of ten kilometres in the district of Tehri Garhwal. Masertal is situated near Sahastratal. Roop Kund is a mysterious lake where the mountaineers have reportedly found skeletons of animals and human beings. Dodital[1] is a beautiful high altitude lake in Uttarkashi district. Deoriatal is situated in Chamoli district near Okhimath. Vasukital is the high altitude lake near Nandanvan, Gaumukh. Chori Bara Lake and the Kedartal are also famous for their location in the snow-clad locales. Gandhi Sarovar near Kedartal[2] is well known as the bone ashes of Mahatma Gandhi were immersed here. The high altitude meadows of Garhwal are breathtaking. After the winter snow and cold give way to spring showers, followed by the summer heat and monsoon deluge, the meadows come alive with flowers. The Valley of Flowers is world famous and Har-Ki-Doon[3] is equally beautiful.

---

1 DODITAL TREK. Another picturesque hike through high mountains and beautiful valleys. The trek begins at Bhatwari, a small marketplace which has a PWD Inspection House. Trekkers will have to camp at Dayara, and can enjoy stunning Himalayan views from here. Dodital has a beautiful lake and is excellent for trout fishing. Both Dodital and Agoda have Forest Rest Houses to stay in. From Dodital, there is another exciting trek route to Hanuman Chatti in Yamuna Valley. As there is no accommodation between Dodital and Hanuman Chatti, trekkers are advised to carry their own alpine tents, or be prepared to spend the night in a shepherd's shelter.

2 KEDARTAL. This spectacular and enchanting lake is situated at a distance of about 18 kilometres from Gangotri, negotiable through a rough and tough mountain trail. The trek is very tiring and there are testing moments even for a hardy trekker. There is no facility of any kind on the way and one has to make all arrangements in advance. A local guide is a must. The lake is crystal clear with the mighty Thalaysagar (Sphatiki-ing) peak forming a splendid backdrop. The place is about 4000 metres above sea level and is the base camp for trekking to the Thalaysagar, Jogin, Bhrigupanth and other peaks.

3 HAR-KI-DOON. At an elevation of 3566 mts. it is surrounded by glittering peaks and dense forests. The forests are rich in wildlife and are a veritable paradise for bird-watchers and nature lovers. The trek from Netwar to Osla is through dense forests of chestnuts, walnuts, willows and chinars. The trek from Osla to Har-ki-Doon is through terraced mountain fields, lush green grassy land and conifer forests.

These meadows provide pasture to the wandering herds of sheep, brought up to the high altitudes in the summer by the nomads.

This entire area is a paradise for both the religious pilgrim and the discerning naturalist. A substantial degree of tourism in this part of the Himalayas comprises pure pilgrimage, the remaining proportion being related to the so-called bourgeois tourism and social tourism.

History

According to the *Skanda Purana,* Lord Vishnu was incarnated in the form of the *Kurma* or tortoise at Champawat in the Kali river and this region came to bear the name of *Uttarakhand* or *Kedarkhand.* In fact, every rock and rivulet is dedicated to some deity or saint, with an appropriate legend attached to it. Recent excavations carried out in Pauri Garhwal district in 1976 and 1977, give us a picture of the history of Uttarkhand during the 5ᵗʰ and the 6ᵗʰ century BC. These excavations have brought to light the remains of three periods, embedded in a three metre deep layer. The earliest period of the 6ᵗʰ to the 4ᵗʰ centuries BC, is characterised by the use of distinctive pottery known as red-ware consisting mostly of dishes, while the other items discovered were iron and copper objects such as arrowheads and fish hooks, which show that the people of this period knew the art of smelting copper, and consumed meat in large quantities. The other important objects found of this period are a terracotta plaque of Lord Krishna and another of Lord Buddha which belong to the Maurya and Kushan periods respectively. All this proves that Uttarkhand was a part of the Mauryan Empire. These discoveries are considered significant as they push back the history of this region by at least 1000 years.

Permanent settlements existed in these regions since 3000 BC (Indus Valley Culture). The excavations at Harappa and Mohenjodaro testify to the extraordinarily high level of culture that the people of this area had developed. Around 1500 BC, nomadic Aryan tribes intruded from the north-west and drove out the original settlers. The existing urban culture was thereby completely overrun. The single source for gaining insights into the Aryan culture are the Vedas, a collection of religious hymns, which, in later centuries, were written on the basis of oral recitations. The Vedas were the source of a new religion called Hinduism, which was, however, in the course of only a few centuries, made so complicated by the Brahmins that by about 550 BC, the great reformers Buddha and Mahavira felt the urge to counteract this development. Through Buddha's enlightenment, a new religion, Buddhism, was born which, between 250 BC to approximately 600 AD, dominated the religious life of the Himalayan Valleys. Thereafter, Hinduism regained some of its former importance. Mahavira's Jainism did not spread so fast. It retains, however, till today, a minority of followers all over India perhaps which may be due to the fact that it closely resembles Hinduism in its main features.

In 327 BC, parts of North India were conquered by Alexander the Great and around 300 BC, the Macedonians were thrown out by Chandra Gupta, the founder of the Maurya dynasty. He established the first large North Indian empire, which was considerably expanded by Emperor Ashoka (273-323 BC), his grandson, a devoted Buddhist, who promoted the spread of Buddha's teachings.

Between the 4th and 7th centuries the Guptas founded the second big empire in North India. This was also the time when classical Indian art flourished and found its main expression in painting and sculpture, made in and outside the temples. After the 7th century AD, the Muslim raids began, the famous ones being in Kangra led by Mahmud Ghazni, who seized the temple treasures of Bajreshwari. Around 1200 AD, the Mongols followed. For centuries there was turmoil in this region, which was followed by Muslim influence.

It was in the 16th century that Raja Ajaipal integrated the 52 fortresses (garhs) and their associated territories into Garhwal (fort-integrated territory). The Kiratas, Khasas, Seythians and Mongoloid elements also contributed profusely to the culture complex of the Garhwal region. During the Moghul Empire, Portugal, France and England entered the Indian theatre, and after Aurangzeb's death in 1707 AD, the British East India Company gradually seized power over the whole of India following a prolonged period of battles and wars. After the major Indian uprising in 1857, the Indian administration was directly taken over by the British Crown. Thereafter, the history of Uttarkhand flows very much with the history of the rest of India.

People and Economy

Before the adventurers take on the task of understanding the Himalayas, they need to understand the people of this exotic place and how they manage to survive despite living in adverse conditions. From times immemorial, ethnic groups migrated here for various reasons and, in the remote past, Uttarkhand was peopled by the Khasa race, and Indo-Aryan or possibly Indo-Iranian people, who spread from Kashmir to Nepal. It seems that these Khasas settled in Kumaon in remote antiquity, after subduing the aborigines of this terrain. In later stages, other ethnic groups also migrated here for religious or commercial reasons or to escape Muslim tyranny. This intermixing resulted in a remarkable convergence of social and cultural influences of different kinds.

Races and tribes have mixed more in the valleys of the north than in other parts of India. One can roughly distinguish three races: the light-coloured, tall Aryans; the shorter stocky original inhabitants; and people with Mongolian features from the North East. Whereas the first two races settled in the plains as well as in altitudes upto 2500 metres, the Tibeto-Mongolian people isolated themselves in the higher mountain regions, and have maintained, till today, their connection with the north, which is specially obvious in Lahaul and Spiti. These people live mainly as peasants in villages and cultivate, through hard labour, their terrace fields. A lesser number work as cattle breeders or shepherds. The valley people have, till today, preserved their skills as craftsmen, which were acquired during the course of many centuries.

Wheat is the most important crop of the southern Himalayan valleys. Rice, barley, millet, maize, fruits and tea are also grown here to some extent. All the valleys lie in a moderately warm climate, with an average rainfall of between 500 and 1,500 mm. The harvests are, therefore, ample, and surplus can be exported to other States. Goats, sheep and, to some extent, cows and yaks are raised. The region has started its own industry and its handicrafts are becoming extremely popular.

Festivals. In Garhwal the majority of the people are Hindus; Sikhs and Jains form a minority. It is here, near the holy cities of Hardwar and Rishikesh that the important routes of pilgrimage lead to Kedarnath Badrinath. The various ashrams around Hardwar, Rishikesh and to their north are centres of Hindu philosophy. Here one encounters the great gurus, prominent yogis and yoga schools. One of the biggest ever Hindu festivals, the Kumbh Mela, takes place at an interval of 12 years in Hardwar on the banks of the Ganga.

The most important festivals of this area are: Shivratri, Holi, Dusshera, Diwali and Janamashtami.

Mountaineering

The mountainous terrain of the U.P. Himalayas, consisting of pyramid like lofty and hoary headed peaks appears to crown the State of Uttaranchal. The mighty Himalayas standing on

10

the northern frontier of U.P. are highly rugged and have difficult and precipitous slopes, horned peaks, serrated crests of high ridges, cirques and glaciers, snow clad slopes, hanging valleys, cascades of sparkling water supplied by melting ice, torrential rapids, deep canyons, roaring streamlets, huge boulders and glistening lakes.

The environs of the Himalayan peaks of UP arouse a deep hidden longing to reach upto those awe inspiring wonder and dizzy heights that exude a magnificence of their own. The region and especially the peaks are abundantly referred to in historical literature, indicating that great saints, travellers and kings frequently visited this part of the Himalayas. In fact, every peak, rock and rivulet is dedicated to some deity or saint and has an appropriate legend attached to it. These lofty Himalayan peaks have a complex physiography falling into three regions: Himadri, Himanchal and Shivaliks. The topography of the rugged land and dangerous slopes has often beckoned the spirit of the adventurers. No wonder, many of the peaks have been successfully scaled by mountaineers from all over the world. Details of some important peaks of the Garhwal region are given below.

Nanda Devi (7,817 Metres). Nanda Devi, which literally means 'Blessed Goddess' is the highest of the Garhwal peaks. It is considered to be the pearl of the Himalayas because of its beauty. The graceful symmetry of its double peaks, the main and the east, thrusting up to the sky, is indeed a visual treat, a rare example of perfect twin peaks. It would perhaps be strange if a mountain of such beauty were not an object of worship. In fact, since ancient times, the inhabitants of the region have revered this mountain as the dwelling place of the Gods. The names of mountains and passes in the area often have religious meanings.

Nanda Devi refused for years to yield to the many climbers who tried to overcome her. It is extremely difficult to even approach her foothills, the entrance to which is guarded by long, deep gorges. After several failures, one party finally succeeded in crossing these gorges in 1934 and entered the south foothills of the mountain. The Nanda Devi East peak, 7,434 metres high, is the third highest peak in this region.

Bander Punch West (6,316 Metres). This peak lies to the South West of Kalanag. In June 1950, JTM Gibson along with Tensing Norgay (of Everest fame), attempted to scale it from the south. They were defeated by the vertical walls of ice gullies. Ascent to the corniced top, after avoiding the crevasses, reveals a view of the steep drop to the southern valley, the adjoining ridge of Bander Punch and the distant Swargarohini peaks.

Kamet (7,756 Metres). Kamet taken from the word 'Kangrie' which literally means 'lower snows' in Tibetan, attracted the early mountaineers. The Kamet peak is the second highest in Garhwal and was attempted ten times before it was conquered. The eleventh and victorious climb was headed by F.S. Smythe of Britain. One of his companions to the top, R.L. Holdsworth, wore skis up to the col, 7025 metres high. In

1848, Richard Strachy determined its height, followed by Schlagintweits. In 1855, they went over the Mana Pass and attempted it from the North, reaching 6,745 metres on Abi Gamin. In 1874-77, the Survey of India under E.C. Ryall and I.S. Pocock set up a plane table at 6,700 metres on the slopes of East Abi Gamin – these are now identified on modern maps as Mukut Parbat, Kamet and Abi Gamin respectively. In fact, in 1931, it was while returning from their successful Kamet expedition that Frank Smythe and Holdsworth stumbled into the Valley of Flowers.

Neelkanth(6,597 Metres). Nilkanth is a pyramidal snowy peak towering above Badrinath. It is popularly known as 'Garhwal Queen' because of its dramatic sight. No history of Central Garhwal would be complete without a detailed mention of this majestic peak. It is a name of Lord Shiva, presiding over Badrinath, and is worshipped by millions of pilgrims. It is a tough and challenging proposition for mountaineer though forbidden by custom.

Nandkot (6,861 Metres). This 'Fort of Nanda' is an imposing peak dividing the Gori and Pindari Valleys. It was scaled by Dr. Longstaff in 1905 and in 1936, the Japanese made the first ascent. An Indian team climbed it again in 1959. In 1986, an Indo-Japanese team made another ascent to celebrate the fiftieth anniversary of the first ascent.

Chaukhamba. One of the most majestic looking peaks of the Himalayas it has four peaks, the highest being 7,138 metres.

Shivling. 6,543 metres in height, this is one of the most challenging peaks of the Himalayas. The base is at Tapovan near Gomukh

Abi Gamin at an altitude 7,355 metres, it is the fourth highest peak in the Garhwal region.

Bhagirathi I, II & III. Close to Shivling is the Bhagirathi group of peaks. The heights are 6,856, 6,512 and 6,454 metres respectively.

Changbang. This massif is one of the hardest to climb. Its height is 6,864 metres.

Shivling

Satopanth. Close to the Gangotri group of peaks, this peak is 7,075 metres in height. It has the toughest trail to its massif. Only a few climbing expeditions have been successful in conquering it.

Sudarshan Parvat (6,507 Metres). Sudarshan Parvat has beauty as well as challenge. It is a sight for the Gods. Situated above the Gangotri temple, it has been seen by millions of pilgrims and mountaineers through the ages. It gets its name from *Sudarshan,* the weapon which Lord Krishna or Vishnu holds in His hand.

Tourism

It is needless to emphasise that the development of tourism in the Himalayan macro-level region must be integrated with the socio-economic development at the micro-regional level. Such a multipurpose, integrated model needs to be formulated so that the entire local population is involved in the development process. In such a process, the maintenance of the recreational features of the landscape, both physical and cultural, is inter-linked with patterns of socio-economic development. The retreats of the Himalayan poets like Sumitranadan Pant, scholars and Manishis (saints and sages) have to be developed as academic resorts, even for a longer duration in special cases, for improving the quality of life of the local people while enlightening the country as a whole. The Governments, State as well as Central, and the voluntary organisations have made coordinated efforts in this direction. It may be advisable to organise a working group to evolve a feasible model for such integrated development, at both national and international levels. It is further suggested that the Garhwal region may be adopted as a case for preparing such a model of tourism-cum-socio-economic development. It needs to be emphasised that though this is one of the most under-developed regions at the micro-level, the peoples' perception and faith have made it the most sacred region of the Himalayan habitat.

Pilgrimage or other types of tourism is not new to the Garhwal Himalayas but there has been a great upsurge in the annual tourist influx since the opening of new roads and the formulation of liberal policies by the Government. With a sizeable number of tourists visiting this locale, the environment here is bound to be affected in various ways. The present communication is an endeavour towards enumerating the beneficial as well as detrimental aspects of mountain tourism with special reference to the vegetation wealth. Remedial measures have also been suggested to improve the deteriorating environmental conditions.

Tourism and its Impact After independence, the Indian Government started promoting tourism in the public sector on a large scale. As a consequence, various plans and strategies were formulated to encourage tourism, particularly in the Himalayas. New roads were constructed, obviously resulting in indirect benefit to this region. Only 50,000 tourists visited Badrinath prior to 1968 when the road was extended to this holy shrine. The number of visitors increased to over 1,00,000 just after this and to over 2,43,000 in 1982. Encouraged by these figures, an extensive plan was prepared to access the various eternal shrines of the Garhwal region. This has undoubtedly helped the local populace that would have remained ignored at least for some more years. Local transport has also been facilitated and the people are now able to get in touch with areas previously inaccessible to them. The opening of tourism in Garhwal in 1974 has greatly influenced the economic scenario of this region and has indeed proved to be fundamental in the economic upliftment of the society. The roads, constructed for encouraging tourism, helped in starting the process of urbanisation. There has been a new impetus in the socio-economic environment. Tourism has transformed the life style of a sizeable number of people dwelling in the remote areas in and around the places of pilgrimages. People have shifted from the unproductive agricultural and pastoral practices to small businesses related to tourism, e.g., small huts and stalls have been opened at places where no one could have imagined such facilities. Selling of local craft items is also a profitable business dependent almost entirely upon tourism. The porters, pony owners, and local guides are among those who have benefited in these areas.

Tourism brings a number of positive cultural and social changes too. Cultural consciousness, reawakening, social renovation and preservation are good symptoms of modern tourism. It has resulted in the restoration of architectural monuments and buildings, and preservation of the landscape. Without tourists, these may have been allowed to slowly decay. The UP Himalayas comprise the best example of this cultural process. Here, every pilgrimage centre, scenic spot and historical, religious, and cultural centre is being remodelled and refashioned to give them a new and fresher look so that they may attract a larger number of tourists. Cultural renovation, increased tourism and economic growth have become a cyclic process in most of the regions. The hill people have become fully conscious of this culture and they are preserving it to harvest money and thereby push their economy far ahead.

However, the adverse impacts are even more important than the beneficial ones, owing to their long term and far-reaching side effects. Taking road construction, for instance, one cannot deny the necessity of roads but, at the same time, what this process harms is no less than what is gained. Plants are the direct sufferers of road construction, as trees need to be felled when a road is proposed to be constructed. The construction of roads changes the slope angle of the rocks which automatically tends to destabilise and while doing so, results in landslides. The 'blasting method' used at first for breaking and then removing very hard rocks is even more disastrous as it creates cracks in the surrounding rocks also. Water easily percolates through these cracks during the rains, thereby enhancing the phenomenon of landslides.

Apart from the indirect effect on plant life through road construction, plants are directly affected by the tourists in several ways. A tourist comes to the Himalayas to enjoy the enchanting beauty of the natural heritage but he returns after contributing a little towards the deterioration of the ecosystem. Forests particularly are destroyed since they comprise the only easily available fuel in the remote areas. Tourists burn wood for cooking, for warmth and sometimes also for protection against wild animals. In this way, a large quantity of wood is extracted from the forests in every tourist season. According to a rough estimate, about 100 tons of wood is burnt at Ghangria per month from May to October in order to meet the requirements of the pilgrims and tourists visiting Hemkund and the Valley of Flowers. Tourists sometimes set fire to Juniper bushes as these burn easily. Such acts provide amusement to some misguided travellers. A point to be remembered here is that the juniper is a very slow growing plant and takes a long time to reach adult size. As far as the small herbaceous vegetation is concerned, it is adversely affected by being trampled upon by the tourists and this results in diminution of the plant cover besides destruction of the species themselves. Such problems arise in the meadows of sensitive areas like the Valley of Flowers, Har-Ki-Doon, Rudranath Bugyal, Tapovan, etc.

The colourful flowering herbs fall victim to tourists who love these beautiful gifts of nature but do not really know how to admire them. One can often see the tourists returning from Hemkund with bunches of Brahma Kamal in their hands. Such practices have resulted in damage to the environment. If this exploitation of valuable flora is allowed to continue, it will lead to threatened conditions. In many religious places, forest fires occur because of the pilgrims staying in the adjoining forested areas due to the lack of lodging facilities, resulting in heavy losses to the forest wealth. The rhododendron is a well known and beautiful species with a range of flowering shrubs and trees and most tourists to Garhwal pluck these flowers, endangering their very existence.

Sticks of Zanthoxylum are sold at religious places as these are considered holy and useful for various religious rituals. Chimonobambusa and Thomnocalamus are also being extensively depleted from their natural habitats since these are used in preparing various handicrafts which are mostly purchased by the tourists.

The trekkers also contribute to the deterioration of the ecosystem while camping. The ground vegetation is totally destroyed at the campsite. Often , there are chances of a fire spreading while raising a 'bonfire' in a thick forest. These fires sometimes prove highly disastrous.

In parts of the Himalayas, the soil, bio-mass, flora and fauna, water, etc. have suffered loss due to heavy and unplanned encroachment into the deep interior. Flora and fauna have been badly affected by tourism development projects in the region. The Ramganga Dam has submerged a vast area comprising the natural habitat of the tiger and other animals species, and the Tehri and Jamrani Dams may be cited as other examples in this respect. Increasing construction at Gangotri is causing great loss to a number of plant species like the chir, fir, birch (Bhojpatra), etc. Heavy human use of open space adversely affects the biomass. Trampling directly kills plants, and causes soil compaction. Increased use of an area changes the microclimate and water balance and thus kills plants. Increasing use of wood as fuel and timber in a number of industrial products (including the souvenir industry) also leads to felling and cutting of trees. These initial changes in the local biotic community can lead to the eventual loss of other species.

The animal species are also badly affected by the proximity of human beings. Musk deer – a rare Indian species – is almost vanishing due to excessive human interference and deforestation. In addition to the physical loss of animals, human pressure increases the incidence of disease. Over-harvesting of fish is a special problem in Ramganga and Alaknanda near Tehri. Contamination due to washing, bathing, drinking, and sewage treatment has also increased at different watering places in the Himalayas.

The social or environmental impacts are not always positive; sometimes they become even negative. Tourists not only bring money to a region, but also a strong and visible life-style. Their dress, food habits and merry-making manners all bring some newness in the region of their travel. The locals get impressed with their life-styles and are tempted to adopt them. This can cause a strong cultural shock which may prove to be an antithesis to the very spirit of tourism.

Tourists visiting countries, especially with backward economies, leave behind a life-style and spending pattern that has many demonstrative effects. The residents of the host countries are tempted to follow these unthinkingly and with negative results. A number of vices like prostitution, gambling, drinking, smoking, drug addict and juvenile delinquency may be attributed to foreign tourists. The pouring in of a number of tourists from foreign countries has had a serious impact on the social life in Hardwar, Rishikesh, Dehradun, etc. The traditionally religious atmosphere of these regions is being disturbed by such encroachments. The tremendous influx of visitors during the summer season results in overcrowding, traffic congestion, noise and inflated prices of goods and services, especially in Dehradun and Mussoorie.

In the hill areas specially Mussoouri, all the men or workers, engaged directly or indirectly in different sectors of tourism activities, take full advantage of tourists coming from outside. Gradually, they are discarding the simplicity and humility of their behaviour – a unique feature of the hill people. Modern tourism has made them cunning and clever, leading to clashes within their own community. Further, in order to develop tourism and attract tourists from outside, the culture of the land is often commercialised. Religious beliefs, traditional dress, secular celebrations and other modes of life are reduced to tourist commodities in the search for marketable tourist products. It ultimately results in the loss of self-respect among the residents, and becomes an insult to them; often violence may be sparked off at the slightest provocation. Xenophobia, the fear of strangers, can also result from some typical social changes due to the influx of foreign tourists.

The influx of pilgrims leads to demands for facilities for a comfortable journey to their destination. Sometimes forested lands are destroyed to facilitate the pilgrims, for constructing luxurious lodges, encampments, electrification, telecommunications, etc. These are being subjected to gradual destruction as has been experienced in the Bhyundar Valley in the Garhwal Himalayas where trees have been destroyed for telecommunications, and forested lands cleared for the construction of magnificent lodges, etc. to provide amenities for the pilgrims and tourists.

Tourism in the Himalayas was developed in order to reduce socioeconomic disparities along with promotion of an aesthetic sense in the visitors but it has widened the gap and affected Nature adversely, in the long run. An equilibrium needs to be maintained between the ecological and economic aspects and this can be achieved by giving adequate thought and consideration to the environment from the very beginning while formulating any such plan.

On Our Way to Kedarnath

Panch Kedar
Sapta Badri

In the first chapter we have already learnt that Garhwal owes its fame to the holy Pancha Kedar, Sapta Badris and Pancha Prayagas. The Pancha Kedar is the collective name for five great temples of Lord Shiva – Kedarnath, Madmaheswar, Tungnath, Rudranath, and Kalpeshwar. The Sapta Badris comprise seven great temples devoted to Lord Vishnu-Badrinath, Yogdhyan Badri (at Pandukeshwar), Bhavishya Badri (near Tapovan), Vridha Badri (near Animath) and Adi Badri (between Ranikhet and Karanprayag). The Panch Prayagas refer to the five places of confluence of the holy Alakananda with its tributaries.

I paid my homage to Badrinath and Kedarnath but could not travel to the seven badris and five kedars, hidden in mythology. I wanted to dig them out of the mythology. I wanted to reach that shivering height which couldn't be touched by civilisation and could be older than the Sumerians.

The nectar that was swallowed brought a particular vibration to my hungry mind which seeks beauty in ugly stone caricatures lifted by the unknown Godmen in the Himalayan wilderness. I prayed to those Gods whom the Hindus revere for their blessing with those divine eyes. Yes, I wanted to be the Sanjay of the great epic Mahabharata.

I had to avoid the summer rush because the hordes of pilgrims had created disharmony in my tranquillity during my previous visits to Kedarnath and Badrinath. As a result, I undertook this journey on 16th September along with two other pilgrims. Niloy and Brahamachari, a young boy of 24, and Dadu, the grandpa, but not so old, joined us on our way to Badrinath, later.

Dadu had a long beard and hair like that of a meditative Hindu monk. At Joshimath, I distinctly remember, we threw our tired selves onto meagre mattresses provided in the Kalikamli Dharamsala. It was about 5 p.m. All of a sudden, a lady walked into our room much to our chagrin, and without paying any attention to us, prostrated herself in front of Dadu and offered him some money.

Dadu was shocked at this case of mistaken identity and pleaded with her to take back the money, which was immediately misconstrued by her. She decided that the greatness of this sage had made him refuse her offerings. She was almost in tears and refused to believe otherwise, even though we tried to console her.

I remarked, "I hope you will patronise saffron clothes from now on, so our pilgrimage may be on the house."

Ajit never failed to join us in our lighthearted banter. Once he said, "We are like five Pandavas and Dadu is Yudhistira among us, being the eldest."

Dadu quickly retorted, "I do not have any intention to walk into the heaven".

Niloy went further, "But where is Draupadi? The five of us can't leave her behind at least."

"I thought it was your department dear. Don't we call you Arjuna?" Dadu looked back and smiled at Niloy.

Niloy didn't expect such a rejoinder. After all, he couldn't forget that innocent face of Rukmini. What was it? Infatuation? Niloy didn't know himself. He wanted to confide about this chance meeting with the attractive girl. He first saw her at Joshimath, in peculiar circumstances. The journey had been heavy, the tired body and soul tried to rest, hut a sweet voice floated through the closed doors. Niloy woke up, looked at his companions, and surreptitiously left the room in search of that female voice. It didn't take long. The door was ajar, the voice was that of a young girl who was singing the immortal songs of Mirabai for her beloved, the Lord Supreme. The mother of the girl sat in mediation and he was no doubt charmed by that tune. No doubt, Lord Krishna blessed Mirabai.

The singer sang, oblivious of time and space. He did not know when she stopped singing, but the tune was his, before he returned.

At around 9 o'clock, we reached Hardwar[1] , but missed the Hrisikesh connections which forced us to go to the bus stand.

---

1 **Hardwar** (Altitude 294 Metres) Literally means the gateway of God Hardwar, formerly called Kapila, is one of the holiest of Hindu places situated on the south bank of the Ganga. Amongst a multitude of temples, a part of which were built in the 13th century, the most outstanding one is the Daksheswara Temple with the Har-Ki-Pauri-Ghat. The Ghat and temple enjoy special worship because Lord Vishnu left a footprint on a stone there. Other temples are: Bholagiri ashram, Bilkeshwar Mahadev, Chandi Devi, Gauri Sankar, Gita Bhavan, Guru Gorakh Nath mandir, Hanuman Mandir, Mansa Devi, Maya Devi, Neeleshwar, Pashupati Mahadev, Shrawan Nath and Shri Ayyappa. The most important ashrams are: Sapt Rishi Ashram, Arya Banprashth Ashram and Parmarth Ashram with beautiful statues of gods, and a branch of the Ramakrishna Mission.

It is only 24 kilometres from Hardwar to Hrisikesh[2] from where a number of buses ply between these two towns. Hardwar may be called the gateway of the Himalayan pilgrimage though the foothills begin at Hrisikesh. I may be wrong but whenever I have come here, I feel in my bones that I am not far away from the Himalayas. At Hrisikesh, we found shelter at Kalikamli Dharamsala.

On Sunday the 19th September we boarded a bus for Adi Badri, only 18 km from Karan Prayag[3]. To reach Adi Badri

---

2 **Rishikesh.** 43 kilometres from Dehradun and 24 kilometres from Hardwar, at an altitude of 355 metres, the celebrated spiritual centre of Rishikesh is situated amidst a calm environment, impressive waterfront, dense forest and hills. Virtually a town of saints, sages and scholars. Rishikesh is a large religious centre located on the right back of river Ganga. There are a number of ashrams (hermitages) where religious discourses are held. The place is also a renowned centre for Yoga teaching.

3 **Prayag,** literally, is a confluence of rivers. In Hindu mythology, rivers are personified as goddesses and even today, they are held in high reverence by Hindus. The water of a holy river is supposed to wash away all sins. The confluence of two or more rivers makes them much more sacred. The most important Prayag or confluence of rivers is at the Triveni Ghat, Rishikesh. The Panch Paryag (five confluences) rank next to it.

Deoprayag. Situated on the confluence of the Alakananda and Bhagirathi rivers, it is commonly believed to be the birthplace of the Ganga. It comprises the oldest route to Badrinath and Gangotri. The famed Raghunath Math and Shiva Temple are situated here.

Rudraprayag. Named after Shiva (Rudra), it is situated at the confluence of the Alakananda and Mandakini rivers. Sati, the first wife of Shiva, is believed to have meditated here. It is also said to be the place where Shiva humbled Narada. Temples include Rudranath and Chamunda Devi. The road diverts to Kedarnath excavations from here.

Karnaprayag. Situated on the confluence of the Alakananda and Pindar rivers. Archaeological excavations 6 kilometres from here, at Simpli, have revealed pre-Gupta period statues, further confirming its importance since earlier times. This place is also famous for the Karna Temple and Uma Devi Temple. The road from here diverts to Ranikhet, Almora and Kausani and Gwaldham and Kund.

Nandprayag. Situated on the confluence of the Alaknanda and Mandakini rivers. It derives its name from Nanda, the Yadav king and foster father of Lord Krishna. There is a very famous Gopalji Temple here.

Vishnu prayag. Situated on the confluence of Alaknanda and Dhauli Ganga rivers. An ancient temple stands here beside a pool called Vishnu's Kund.

29

one has to change buses at Karna Prayag. As the bus crept up the hilly track, one of my co-pilgrims fell sick. He vomited out the fried food and slumped into his seat. We were distressed to have a sick passenger at the onset of our journey into the hills. We couldn't abandon him and had to help him to change the bus, and we reached the ancient temple at 3.30 p.m.

Ancient badri or Adi Badri justifies its name because way back in history, the pilgrims who couldn't reach Badrinarayan, crossing the hostile terrain, used to pay their homage here instead. That is why this place acquired its popular present name. During his pilgrimage, Sankaracharya established an idol in the temple. We found a kind hearted and religious man in the present priest. We paid our homage and prayed for our safe conduct through this unusual pilgrimage and returned to Karan Prayag by nightfall.

Badrinarayan

It was not difficult to find accommodation for the night. We hired the ordinary charpoys at an extremely low price. But the midnight drama explained the price. The straps of the charpoys refused to bear our weight and slowly took the shape of hammocks due to gravitational force, almost touching the cold stony surface. In the middle of the night, the charpoy owner couldn't be traced through that hilly darkness. Finally, we gave up the unequal battle and slept.

When the mild morning sun rays caressed my face, I woke up in that suspended state. My movements would have put a gymnast to shame if he had have only seen my body contortions to get out of that ropy mess. We ate a simple breakfast and took the earliest available bus for Joshimath. Our destination was Adha-Badri and Vabishya Badri. The route is through Joshimath and Tapovana.

We reached Joshimath within four hours well before lunch time, and found a place to stay. We had our baths and lunch before we took to the road to visit the famous temples of the place.

At first, we visited Acharya Shankaracharya's Joshimath. This great sage established four ashrams or maths in four corners of India. In the North, Joytirmath; Sringeri Math or Sringerii Rishi Math in Mysore; Gobardhan Math at Puri; and Sarda Math at Dwarka. All the titular heads of these maths are known as Shankaracharyas. And these four maths are termed as four dhamas. Hindus believe that a visit to these four dhamas concludes the pilgrimage for ever.

We went to pay our homage to Swami Santananda Saraswati of Joytirmath but were disappointed to learn that he had gone to Allahabad. The math was situated in a picturesque area. We had to climb a little distance to reach the temple of Lord Jyotirisher which was built by Acharya Shankara inside a natural flower garden. Also we found among these unknown flowers a place like Panchavati where Shankara had meditated.

From Joytirmath, we left for Vasudev Narayan, Naba Durga, Mahalaxmi, Vabishya Kedar and Nrisimha temple. Some historians add Nrisimha temple among the list of Badris.

During the winter when Badri Narayan becomes inaccessible, and the Lord Narayan is worshipped at Joshimath instead.

We boarded the 3 p.m. bus and reached Tapovan by 5 p.m. at a distance of 16 kilometres. The morning bus leaves at 9 a.m.

We didn't know that at this not-so-hostile height of 6,500 feet (1976 Mtrs) there was no place to stay other than the Government inspection bungalow. We looked up at the sky but saw no hope for the cold night. But the God manifested himself through a local businessman, who willingly offered us our much required shelter for the night in one of his empty shops.

The businessman, Sri Gopal Dutt Sharma, was an employee of the Border Security Force and was posted at Barrackpore and Krishnanagar during his 11-year long tenure with the organisation. He came to our help. We kept our luggage in his safe custody and asked him if he knew about any noble holy man around. He informed us most respectfully about a sage who lived in a cave across the tiny stream at Tapovan and also didn't fail to tell us about the hot spring nearby.

We were told that the name of this Mahatma was Gujri Baba and he hailed from Ludhiana. He had lived at Bhabishya Badri for a number of years before coming to Tapovan. No one knew his actual age. It could be anything between 110 to 125 years. He was widely respected by the local population, and his supernatural powers were a part of folklore. By now we were getting engrossed by this extraordinary story.

Sri Sharma continued earnestly, "Once a man went up to the cave, and after paying due homage sat down in front of him without speaking a word. He thought that this great man must be able to read his thoughts so he need not trouble him by opening his mouth unnecessarily. Contrary to his belief, the sage refused to speak. He sat in deep meditation for more than an hour The man then left and returned with some doubts in his mind about the folklore.

"The disappointment did not leave him throughout the day. He slept uneasily. All of a sudden, he saw a bright trail of blue light rushing towards him. He became panicky. As the light entered through the window, he jumped out of bed to escape from such an unusual meteorite. But he stopped in his tracks as he saw the light coming to a halt and gradually taking the shape of a human being.

"It was none other than the sage from the cave.

"In a soothing voice, he asked, 'Have I passed your test my child? I know you felt despondent when I refused to speak to you. Have faith, my dear, every day repeat the mantra at least one lakh times, you will be cured of your incurable disease, No sooner he said that, the ball of blue light rushed out of the window.

"The man couldn't believe his eyes or ears. The next morning he ran and fell at the sage's feet to seek forgiveness. The sage opened his eyes and smiled at him."

We couldn't wait to see the great sage and almost ran up the distance to meet him. As we reached the cave, we saw him sitting next to a small fire along with two of his disciples. We offered the apples we had brought for him and paid our homage. We wanted to photograph him but he refused. He read the Gita for about an hour and distributed prasad. We wanted to stay longer and seek his blessings but the journey's schedule forced us to leave.

The next morning we started for the village Subayan where stands Adha-Badri and little further up the temple of Bhabishya Badri. One could take a bus to cover the five kilometres. But we decided to walk as the bus timing didn't suit us, and covered this distance easily. Thereafter, the climb began. We had to climb to a height of 3040 Mtrs from 1948 Mtrs along a hilly track through thorny shrubs and jungle.

The climb was tedious and we couldn't see the end anywhere. I have climbed the rocks to cross the Mahagunas salient on the way to Amarnath but this was much more difficult.

We had no idea about the terrain to be traversed to reach the

On Lay to Bhabishya Badri Shambhunath

34

destination. As such, we ate a light breakfast, hoping to arrive early for lunch. Within a few hours, we were proved wrong because the stomach protested, it wanted food. The hostile surroundings didn't provide anything to eat till such time we staggered into the village Subayan. The villagers were extremely hospitable. No sooner did they come to know about our hunger, they offered us a sumptuous quantity of apples. One of the villagers went to an extent of inviting us to share his meagre lunch. Such simplicity and hospitality were unknown to us.

We paid our homage to Adha-Badri, and began our climb through another (456 Mtrs) covering a distance of only three kilometres to Bhabishya –Badri situated at a height of (3496 Mtrs).

The density of the air reduced appreciably which made my poor heart work overtime. My God, it was tiring. We almost crawled to a house but there was no sign of life. We yelled to draw attention. We yelled for help. Finally, a voice replied from an orchard below. There we met Mangal Singh, who was the caretaker of the orchard owned by the Government. We asked him about our destination.

He replied, "Not very far. Just over there."

A standard answer from any villager in the hills. They do not understand the problems of a city dweller, for whom climbing even a few hundred feet is difficult. I became suspicious and tried to find about the actual height and distance to our destination.

He didn't bother to answer. Instead, he invited us for a cup of hot tea. We grabbed the offer immediately and began to feel better after the hot cup of tea. Mangal Singh volunteered to be our guide for the rest of the journey. The route was through the jungles but there was no back breaking climb involved. We followed him upto a temple like structure in a small clearing in the jungles. A small flag had been hoisted by someone in front of it. Mangal Singh showed us the deity and told us about his self-creation which was commonly believed to be Bhabishya-Badri or Badri of the future. Mythology speaks about this future Badri where the offerings will take place once the road to Badri-Vishal gets destroyed and the temple becomes totally unapproachable. We saw the abandoned hut of Gujari Baba next to the temple.

It was Mangal Singh again who informed us about the apple orchard and the foreigner, and invited us to have lunch with him. Soon we reached the orchard and Mangal Singh brought varieties of apples for us to eat, as promised. Here we met young Patrick from France.

We learnt a little bit about this recluse. He was attracted towards the Hindu religion and philosophy when he met an Indian monk in France. Gradually, discontentment with the material world and the luxuries of the West drove him to the Himalayas in quest of the self. He travelled the length and breadth of India and finally came to settle down at Badri of the future. He readily agreed to pose under an apple tree as we wanted to photograph him.

36

We bid farewell to Patrick and Mangal Singh who happily treated us to a lunch where both the first the last courses consisted of varieties of apples. I could eat no more. When we reached Subayan on our return journey, we met the villager who had invited us to lunch. I was surprised to notice his disappointment when we politely declined and cited the picnic lunch as the cause of our loss of appetite.

We began our steep descent along the hill slope. We slipped a couple of times but managed to keep our limbs together. By the time we reached Tapovan, it was four in the afternoon.

We had to spend one more night at Tapovan. In the morning, Mr. Sharma came to bid us farewell. He was apologetic about our inconvenience in his not too spacious shop where we had rested for two nights. We expressed our gratitude. He forced some apples on us which we couldn't decline. We could never forget his hospitality. The rarefied air of this surcharged place where the Gods only seek refuge must have cleansed our hearts.

We boarded the bus for Joshimath. No sooner did the bus begin to move, my mind raced back to Niloy and Rukmini.

Niloy said, "After I listened to that charming tune I returned to the room like one possessed. It began to haunt me. I could not forget the notes as they rippled through the air. We reached Badrinath. A particular happiness engulfed me. I found a quiet place and sat down. The silence was overwhelming. The bhajan came to my mind, the lips began to pronounce the lyrics clearly.

I sang the song of Rukmini. The sun went behind the Western snow-peaked mountains, I began to feel cold. Suddenly the voice of a girl startled me. I looked back and found her standing gracefully against the setting light of the Western sky.

"She asked, 'Where did you learn this song?'

"I was too startled to speak, I whispered, 'It is you, who have taught me, my dear.'

"Nonsense she responded, she smiled.

"I felt a peculiar sensation as I looked into her eyes and said, 'I have stolen it from you.'

"She didn't believe me. I told her the story of Joshimath and my adventure of the night.

"She looked pleased but ran away into the darkness as she heard her name being called by her mother. That is how I learnt her name.

"Before leaving, she caused a powerful explosion in me. I heard her saying as she departed, 'I have caught a thief, Ha Ha. I shall tell mummy."

From Joshimath, Gobind Ghat is only 8 kilometres away. We decided to visit Nandan Kanan because it remained snow covered during May. The flowering season of Nandan Kanan is between July and end August. Now in the third week of September, we hoped to see some flowers for which this natural garden is famous throughout the world. We boarded the bus and arrived at Gobind Ghat to be greeted by a sizeable Sikh population at the Gurudwara. The Sikhs had travelled all the way from the plains to pay homage at Hemkund, situated at 14,200 feet.

No accommodation. We were dismayed when we were told on a cold rainy day that we won't find a place to sleep. As a last resort, we approached an old Sikh gentleman who looked at our distressed faces and offered his own room to us, though he had refused many others. Kartar Singh was one of the members of the management committee of the Gurudwara. If he had not helped us, we would have been on the road that night. We felt as if the Lord himself had extended His hand through this kind gentleman to help us. He lodged us in his room and became busy making us comfortable much to our embarrassment. Gobind Ghat is at a height of (1824 Mtrs) Ghangria is 8 kilometres away at a height of (3040 Mtrs). Therefore, a steep gradient of (1216 Mtrs) lies between Gobind Ghat and Ghangria.

From Ghangria, Nandan Kanan is about five kilometres and Hemkund is at a height of (4316 Mtrs).

We left our non-essential items with the Sri Kartar Singh and set course in the morning for Ghangria. The ascent was not as difficult as the one we had faced on our way to Bhabishya Badri. We slowly climbed through forests of innumerable beautiful plants and trees which were a botanist's delight. But for me it only brought joy. I didn't want to dissect them. I enjoyed their beauty, I enjoyed their colours. It seemed as if Nature had sprinkled colour in abundance with a set pattern.

The two of us progressed as quickly as possible and reached Ghangria by 11 o'clock to find accommodation for the night.

It was cold at 3000 metres and we needed a few blankets for survival. We stood in a queue and could manage to get only

Ghangria

three, for the three of us, and were disappointed when we thought about the dark cold night ahead of us.

I tried to console myself because we knew that a journey like this couldn't provide us with all the comforts. The famous philosophy of a traveller shouldn't be forgotten. "Eat whatever you get, sleep wherever you find a place." Yes, we were comfortable and found a place for ourselves in a corner of the covered verandah.

After having our lunch, the two of us waited for the third member of our small team to arrive but he was not to be seen. We became anxious and at 3 p.m. decided to walk down. After covering a certain distance we found our sick friend on the way. It is generally not advisable to climb high altitudes without acclimatisation because of hypoxia.

I hoped my friend had not become a victim of it.

A Sikh gentleman was helping him to walk up the slope and we found his bag hanging on his shoulder. The kind-hearted doctor had seen our friend lying unconscious on the wayside just 3 kilometres short of Ghangria. He administered first aid and helped him walk up. We expressed our deep gratitude when we heard the acts of kindness of this unknown relation.

We couldn't sleep well. One blanket couldn't provide us with sufficient warmth in the cold night at 3000 metres. An uncomfortable, sleepless night forced us to commence our journey early in the morning. We struck road at 7 a.m. for the Valley of Flowers. After covering a little distance from Ghangria, the road bifurcates. The Easterly route goes to Hemkund whereas the Northerly route goes to Nandan Kanan[4].

We took the Northerly route, which was much easier to negotiate than the others we had trekked already. The steepness of the gradient and other obstacles on this road do not bother a traveller as he looks at the beauty all round and does not concentrate on his feet.

---

4 VALLEY OF FLOWERS. East of Badrinath is the exotic Valley of Flowers in a conical shape with the river Pushpawati flowing through it. This valley has been declared as a National Park to regulate camping. cooking, grazing etc. which disturb environmental conditions and endangers a number of endemic flora.

This valley is a 19 kilometres trek from Govindghat. The base camp is Ghangharia, 14 kilometres from Govindghat, where lodging and boarding facilities are available. It was in 1931 that Frank Smythe and Holdsworth stumbled into this valley while returning from their successful Kamet expedition. Their subsequent writings on the valley evoked a great deal of interest among people, both at home and abroad.

The twists and turns of this track ended at the valley enclosed by high mountains on all three sides, and every inch was covered with various flowers. I don't know what heaven will look like, but I know this garden could compete with that heavenly beauty. The springs in this garden made by Nature only added to its grandeur.

In 1931, Mr. Smythe stumbled on to this natural garden during the Kamet expedition. The length of this garden is

Rhododendron in the Valley of Flowers

kilometres and the width about 1 ½ kilometres. He named this garden the Valley of Flowers. During full blossom, more than three hundred varieties of flowers can be found here. We reached Nandan Kanan on 24th September. By the flowering standard we were late. Yet it took almost three hours for us to

Flowers on the rocks

look at the receding beauty of the blossoms. The stream from this valley joins the river Bhunder.

The plants had begun to shed their leaves. The flowers couldn't face the cold anymore. Yet we were mesmerized. I wish the people of plains may come and visit this unparallel beauty on top of the world.

I wanted to see the famous lotus of Brahma (Brahma Kamal) which couldn't be grown anywhere else in the world and was disappointed because I couldn't see any. I made a mental note to see what this flower looks like at Lokpal Hemkund. We were late coming to Nandan Kanan, as a result of which the Brahma Kamal deluded us.

We were reluctant to turn our backs on such beauty, but time and circumstances forced us to return to Ghangria Gurudwara.

Thereafter, we planned to go to Gobind Ghat via Hemkund.[5]

Guru Gobind Singh the tenth Guru of the Sikhs, in his previous birth had attained Nirvana in the name of the sage Medhas near Hemkund which made this place sacred for the Sikh pilgrims.

Again mythology dictates that Lakshman did 'tapasya' on the banks of the Hemkund for a long time, that may be the

Hemkund Sahib

reason why the river originating at this place is called Lakshman

---

5 **Hemkund Sahib.** Situated at a height of 4,329 mtrs., near the Valley of Flowers, is the holy lake Hemkund, associated with Guru Gobind Singh. Encircled by seven snow clad peaks and their associated glaciers, the crystal clear serene waters of the lake reflect the surroundings enchantingly. The glaciers from Hathi Parvat and Sapt Rishi peaks feed the lake and a small stream called Himganga flows out of this lake. According to the holy Granth Saheb, it is believed that Guru Govind Singh, the 10th Guru of the Sikh faith, meditated on the banks of this lake in one of his earlier births. It has not only become a place of pilgrimage for the Sikh community but also for the Hindus and people of other faiths. There is a Sikh Gurudwara and a Lakshman Temple built on the bank of the lake.

Ganga, and meets the Alaknanda later in the hills.

From Ghangria upto Hemkund is constantly upslope. We climbed upto (4563 mtrs) while traveling through these five kilometres. As we struggled up to the lake, the scenic beauty captured us. The lake was filled with the cleanest water and next to it we saw the Sapta-Sringa mountain. We sprinkled that super cool clean water on our faces, which refreshed us immediately and made us forget our arduous climb.

We began our search for the Brahma Kamal (Lotus of Brahma) which we couldn't find in the Valley of Flowers.

Brahma Kamal

Hemkund didn't disappoint us. We found large numbers of this rare flower in full bloom on a hillside. The flowers are large in size with white petals stained with blue. We knew it was not correct yet collected a good number of these flowers to offer at Kedar and Badri.

By evening, we reached our room for a good night's rest.

The path in front of the Gurudwara leads to the temple of Yoga-Badri in Pandukeswar. A pilgrim can take a bus from Gobind Ghat to go to Pandukeswar. The distance is only three kilometres. Mythology

45

tells us that, Panduraja worshipped Lord Vishnu for a long time for atonement after he was cursed by a sage. The place Pandukeshwar has been name after him.

Another story from the Mahabharat tells us that the Pandavas on their final journey from mortality to immortality arrived at Pandukeshwar and decided to build a temple to be dedicated to Lord Vishnu. The temple was built but a suitable idol of the God couldn't be found in that remote place. Lord Indra came to their rescue. He gave Yudhisthira the much wanted idol which was given to him by Lord Brahma. Such an incident may have led to the naming of this place.

Perhaps it had been given by God himself. The idol could be the envy of any sculptor. I had not seen such flawless beauty created by any master sculptor. The priest informed us that the idol was made out of eight metals. Two hands held the conch shell and the eternal wheel. The other two hands were empty. It was in deep meditation. For whom was the lord was meditating? I wish I knew the answer. We paid our homage and climbed the hill to reach the bus route.

The distance to Badrika-Ashram from Pandukeswar is (22.5 km) miles, from Joshimath, (43.44 km) and on foot over hilly tracks, 19 miles. The bus had to ascend from (1852 mtrs) to (3116 mtrs). As the bus picked up speed, I thought about our previous trip on this route.

Dadu taunted, "Brother Arjuna, how about picking up little speed?"

Niloy quickly retorted, "That may force you to run behind

me. At your age, that may be harmful."

"Can a unwilling horse win a race? I have my doubts," Dadu wanted to be evasive.

Niloy stopped in his tracks and said, "What do you mean Dadu?"

"The magnet behind may be the cause, isn't it?" He pointed towards the back.

Niloy blushed. He didn't expect a direct attack like this. He knew that his intimacy with Rukmini and her mother was known to all. He couldn't reply as quickly as he wanted to.

He sarcastically said, "I hope it has not created jealousy?"

Dadu laughed out loudly and said, "Ha! Ha! I like that. No brother, not at all. You go ahead but be careful."

The bus jerked to a stop. I woke up. I didn't realise that 14 miles had gone by. The time on the clock indicated 1 p.m. I

---

7 **Badrinath.** Situated in the lap of Nar-Narayan Parvat, with the towering Neelkanth peak (6,597mts.) in the background, Badrinath is one of the most revered Hindu shrines of India. It has been said that "there were many sacred spots of pilgrimage in the heaven, earth and the other world but neither is there any equal to Badrinath not shall there be one." It is believed that to revive the lost prestige of Hinduism and to unite the country in one bond, Adi Guru Sri Shankaracharya built four pilgrimage centres in four corners of India. Among them were Badrikashram in the North, Rameshwaram in the South, Dwarkapuri in the West and Jagannath Puri in the East. Badrinath is considered to be amongst the most holy sgrines.

Altitude	:	3,133 mts.		
Area	:	3 sq. km.		
Climate	:	Month	Max. Temp.	Min. Temp.
April		3°C		0°C
Dec-Mar		Snow-Bound	Snow-Bound	
Rainfall	:	1460 mm		
Best Season	:	May to October every year the temple usually remains open from first week of May to 2nd week of November		
Clothing	:	June- Sept. - Light woollens Oct.- Nov. - Heavy woollens.		

47

was a surprised man when I saw the new ugly look of the mini township that had mushroomed around Badrinath.[7] It pained me to see the uninhibited trespassing into the sanctity of this pure place of religion. It took time for me to adjust to the reality. I picked up my luggage and thought, "Oh God what have you done to yourself?"

We found accommodation in the Sri Banana Brahmchari Guest house. At 3000 metres, winter had already set in, which is why during September it was easy to find suitable accommodation. We dumped our luggage, quickly finished our lunch and began our exploration of this unknown township, though I had visited this holy shrine long ago. I had time till 4 o'clock when the temple doors would be opened.

The clock struck four and I jumped out of my reverie as a loudspeaker at the entrance of the holiest of holy shrines Badrinath sprang to life and blared out an old Hindi film song. My heart bled to find that the glory of God had to be loved through loudspeaker at a place which is not easily accessible to a man from the plains. I have visited

Badrinath Temple

48

many well known temples in India but I have yet to notice such noise pollution.

Lord Shankaracharya dreamt about the present idol and recovered it from Narad Kundu. Initially, he placed it in the Garuda cave for the daily worship, or under the badri tree. The idol was brought into the temple after it was built by the king of Garhwal in 1420.

I heard another story about Badri Narayan. This was the abode of Lord Shiva and his divine consort Parvati who saw an abandoned child weeping helplessly. She requested Ashutosh to take the child along with them. But Lord Shiva, however, was not convinced. He thought that it was a trick by Lord Narayan, who could have disguised himself and appeared as the child, for some purpose. He was not sure, yet he gave in to Parvati's request and picked up the child. The next day, as they returned to the temple after their evening walk, they found the temple door closed, which surprised them.

They began to speak to the child from outside and requested him to open the door. Instead a heavenly voice filtered through the closed door. The child said, "I am Narayan, I want to stay here, I request your Lordship may go to Kedar." Mahadeva was proved correct. They left for Kedar, leaving Badrinath to be the future abode of Narayana.

In the Puranas, we find another story about this place. During Satyayug, the religious land was in trouble due to the tyrannical Kabacha rakhshasas. They desecrated the temple and stopped the smooth flow of religion. The sages approached the God to help them to save the religion. The God smiled benignly. He took birth as Nar and Narayan, under the parentage of Dharma (one of the eight Basus) and his wife Murti.

Nar and Narayan instead of declaring war, decided to accentuate their power through tapasya and destroy the demons. For a number of years, they sat in meditation on top of the mountain Gandhamadan. Gradually, their power through tapasya began to manifest through the destruction of the demons. Only one was able to escape the fury of the powerful destructive rays and run away to Suryaloka. He was born as Karna during Dwapar Yuga and was finally killed by Nar and Narayan born as Arjuna and Lord Krishna.

During the years of their penance, Goddess Lakshmi saved Nar and Narayan and spread her branches over them as the badri tree. That is why the place is called badri or Badrikashram and the God is called Badri-Narayan. Purana further explains, "He who can see here the Goddess Lakshmi as the Badri tree he reaches the omnipotent. Even better is the person, who can live on this tree and immerse himself, meditating about Lord Vishnu."

More than one Purana talks about the holiness about this place and calls it the supreme place for pilgrimage. When the Pandavas were thrown into the wilderness for 12 years, they came to Badrikashram. Bhima (second senior Pandava) met Hanuman while he was searching for the Saugandhik flower for Draupadi. King Janmejoy came to Badri Narayan for penance. Even Lord Sri Krishna advised his dear disciple Udhava to go to Badrikashram for tapasya. The great sage Sukhdeva got his Nirvana at this holy place. Mythology explains, "From Kanwashram till Nanda Devi is particularly holy to a person seeking religion."

Badrinarayan is called Badri Vishal in the 46th chapter of the Varaha Purana. The Surya dynasty King Vishala, after losing the throne of Ayodhya, came to this place and engaged in severe penance. Narayan was pleased and offered his kingdom as the boon, thus, the place came to be known as Badri-Vishal.

The Skanda Purana gives another meaning to Vishal (great). This holy place was the abode of the Gods and sages which is why it is called Vishal.

The main temple is situated on the Southern bank of the Alaknanda. After climbing a few stairs, a pilgrim has to enter the temple through the entrance door that is of 14 mtrs height. On the side of the entrance, one sees the treasury of Kuber, and in front there is an idol of Garuda. On the left of the entrance, there are Shankar's room, the temple of Goddess Lakshmi, and the prasad room. On the right is an idol of Ghanta Karna.

Swamiji entered the room. We found in him a dedicated, kind person who could make you comfortable in a few seconds. He wanted to know about our dinner. When he heard that the food was to be brought to us by the hotel bearer, he was satisfied. He informed us that a bigger guest house was being built to accommodate the summer rush. He requested us to collect a few more blankets considering the bitter cold at that altitude. We readily acceded to his suggestion and made a beeline for the store. No sooner I had closed my eyes, the thoughts of the Niloy-Rukmini episode surfaced from nowhere.

During our last visit we had found accommodation in the house of the priest-guide (Panda). Rukmini and her mother were also there. We were tired but our spirits were high. Fatigue could never overcome the desire to travel. A little rest has always brought back the energy to travel again. It was dusk. The light was fading across the Western sky.

Dadu asked Niloy, "Dear singer, will you sing a devotional song for us?"

Niloy was a good singer. He hesitated for a while but agreed and began to sing a devotional song of that famous devotee, Mirabai. The singer and the song cast a spell on us and we failed to notice the presence of Rukmini at the door. She was starting at the singer intently. As the song came to an end, she whispered to Niloy, "Mummy, wants to talk to you. Will you come?"

As Niloy stepped outside the door, she whispered in his ears, "The thief was supposed to be arrested and dragged to the high priest."

"Ha! who minds being arrested by such lovely female police," Niloy retorted quickly.

He failed to see the rise of crimson from a shapely throat.
Rukmini felt the heat on her cheeks.

Dadu's parting request was left hanging in the air. He wanted
to be present in a duet concerto.

As Rukmini's mother saw him enter, she came forward to
welcome him and said, "Please come in dear. I have heard a lot
about you from Rukmini. I was eager to hear a few devotional
songs. Will you oblige?"

Niloy was surprised at this request from a lady he hardly
knew.

He stammered, "But I don't sing too well. In any case, I am
not in the class of your daughter."

No protestations helped. Niloy finally sat down in front of
the photographs of Lakshmi and Narayan. The smell of incense
hung heavily in the room. The atmosphere was intense as he
sang. He forgot the time. He didn't remember how many songs
he sang. When he finished, he looked at Rukmini, who quickly
lowered her face to avoid the searching eyes.

The old lady sighed and said, "Lovely. You sang exactly the
way I taught ...."

Niloy quickly picked up the thread. "Oh that means you
have taught her," he said as he pointed at Rukmini.

She nodded. She had taught Rukmini everything.

Niloy quickly glanced and said, "If she can sing the way she
looks, then you must be a teacher par excellence. If you consider

me fit, will you teach me a few of those immortal Bhajans, Madam?"

She tried to refuse but Niloy persisted. Finally, she had to give in to an eager disciple.

Morning brought the cool freshness. We went to the temple at 9 a.m. I worshipped the lord with the Brahma Kamal I had brought from Hemkund. I sat down to mediate in a somewhat empty shrine. Last time due to summer rush, I couldn't see the deity properly, I could only have a fleeting glance. Now the desire to see Him was fulfilled. There were only about 25 to 30 pilgrims in the shrine.

After the rituals, we left the temple for Vyas cave, Ganesh cave, Bhima bridge and Vasudhara. On our way to village Mana, we saw the eye of Sesh Nag on top of Nar mountain. Mana is only three miles from Badrinarayan, where one can find the famous Vyas and Ganesh cave.

An anecdote from the Puranas has made these two caves famous. When Vyas Deva decided to compose the Mahabharata, he wanted a writer to write down his thoughts but was unable to find any. In desperation, he approach Lord Brahma. He suggested the name of Ganapati, who alone had the capability. Vyas Deva went to Ganapati and requested him to be his writer. He agreed but on one condition. Vyasdeva would have to compose incessantly. He would discontinue writing if Vyasdeva stopped even for a moment. In turn, Vyasdeva requested, "My lord, I agree to your proposal but please do not write anything which you do not understand fully." The composition of the epic began in heavenly surroundings. Whenever Vyasdeva got stuck with his thoughts, he uttered something difficult in Sanskrit. Which made lord Ganapati stop and think. The time gap was sufficient for Vyasdeva to recollect his thought. The two caves are next to each other. We left the caves behind and began walking towards Vasudhara. We found a bridge over the river Saraswati which was called Bhimpool. The Mahabharat tells us that Bhim built this bridge on the Pandava's final journey to heaven. Nakul and Sahadeva died close to this bridge and Arjuna succumbed at a place called Chamtoli, about a furlong from here. Vasudhara is five miles from Badri Narayan and only two miles from village Mana. The road to Vasudhara from Badrinarayan can be negotiated easily. At certain places one has to be careful about tripping over loose stones.

The waterfall at Vasudhara roars down the hills from a height of 400 feet with white froth on its bosom. The beauty is captivating.

There is a rock near the waterfall. We were told that Lord Shankar came upto Vasudhara and rested on this rock. If a pilgrim with virtuous deeds to his credit stands on this rock, water droplets will bless him, but for a sinner they will not.

The Puranas tell a story about Vasudhara. On listening to the greatness of this holy place from Devarshi Narada, the Eight Vasus carried out tapasya for 30,000 years which pleased Lord

Narayan and Vasudhara became a holy place for pilgrimage. The Satopanth glacier is a stone's throw from Vasudhara.

We returned to the guest house before lunch. After having our food, we went to see Panch-Shila, or Panch-Tirth consisting of Narad, Nrishimha, Varaha, Garuda and Markendaya-Shila. The Skanda Purana says that Hrishi-Ganga, Kurma-Dhara, Narad, Prahlad and Tapta-Kunda make Panch-Tirtha.

The large stone at the centre of Tapta Kunda and Narad Kunda is known as Narad-Shila. Narad sat on this stone and carried out tapasya to please the Gods. He survived only on air. Lord Vishnu was pleased and offered to give him anything as boon. But the Devarshi only asked for Bhakti (devotion). Mortals can achieve Nirvana on seeing and touching this particular holy stone.

After destroying the demon king Hiranya–Kashyap, Narayan in the form of Nrisimha (half lion above and half man) came to his abode, Badrikashram. The Gods came forward to welcome him and requested him to abandon such a ferocious form. Nrisimha, thus being requested, dissolved himself with the stone situated just above Barad-Kunda, which is called Nrisimha-Shila.

Lord Vishnu, in the form of a wild boar, killed another demon king, Hiranyaksha, and sat on the stone called Varaha-Shila to control his destructive anger.

Garuda wanted to be the mascot of Lord Vishnu and to free his mother Vinata from the slavery of his stepmother. He sat down for penance on Garuda-Shila. He succeeded in pleasing Narayan to seek his blessings.

Near Narad Kunda, in the centre of the Alaknanda stream lies Markandeya-Shila. Sage Markandeya did tapasya sitting on this stone and received a boon which enhanced his life from only four years to 14 kalpa.

After visiting Panch-Shila, we set course for Panch-Tirtha.

The stream that has originated from Nilkanth mountain[8] is known as Hrishi-Ganga. In the past, the sages performed pujas in the valley and on the shores of this stream which has given it its present name.

Kurma-Dhara is a cold stream near Tapta Kunda. The Purana says, "Before incarnation, the God created himself in the shape of a tortoise and lived in this stream for a while."

Narad Kunda is natural cold water lake from where Sri Shankara recovered the present idol of Badri-Narayan.

Prahlad and Tapta Kunda, are both hot water springs. A pilgrim is supposed to bathe here before going into the temple to pay homage.

Tapta Kunda also abounds with mythological stories.

"During the absence of sage Bhrigu, a demon stole his wife.

---

8 Nilkanth (6,597mtrs). Nilkanth is a pyramidal snowy peak towering above Badrinath. It is popularly known as 'Garhwal Queen' because of its dramatic sight. No history of Central Garhwal would be complete without a detailed mention of this majestic peak. It is a name of Lord Shiva, presiding over Badrinath and is worshipped by millions of pilgrims.

Before departing, the demon left Agni (Fire God) as the witness. On his return, sage Bhrigu, not finding his wife, enquired about her. Agni was worried, yet he told him the truth. The sage became annoyed, he cursed Agni for allowing her to be taken away. Agni ran up to Vyas Deva and told him about his predicament. Vyas Deva consoled him and advised him to carry out penance to please Lord Vishnu as the only way to clear himself from the curse. He acted accordingly for many years. Narayana was pleased and appeared before him. The almighty emancipated Agni and said, 'Anyone who will come here will find me.' He also asked Agni to be present here to relieve the mortals from all bondages.' That is why Tapta Kunda is also known as Agni-Tirtha.

Being in close vicinity to the temple, we completed our tour of these places and set course for the temple of Mata-Murti, two miles away.

The name of Narayan's mother was Murti or non-violence. She asked to be allowed to live close to Badrikashram along with her daughter-in-law Goddess Lakshmi. Narayan agreed and arranged for them to live here and promised to meet them once in a year in the human form of Udhav. Respecting his wishes, each year Udhav returns to this temple on the twelfth day of the moon (popularly known as Vaman Dadasi).

We returned after paying our respects to Mata-Murti. I looked around and saw those famous mountains with snow-covered peaks. Behind the temple is the Narayan mountain with a height of 19,800 feet and on the other side lies Nar mountain. Behind them, one can see the snow covered Nilkanth mountain peak at (7174 mtrs).

Narayan and his brother Nar began their serious tapaysa which made King Indra uneasy because he was not aware of their identity nor was he sure of their intentions. He misconstrued that they may be seeking blessings from God to unseat him. He decided to disturb their meditation by sending beautiful dancing girls from the heavenly court. But it was in vain. To belittle these beautiful women, Narayan rubbed a flower on his knee and created the most beautiful woman in heaven and earth. The dancing girls felt their insignificance in front of this exquisite beauty and went to report to Indra about Urbashi.

Indra understood his folly and being repentant, sat down to worship Nar and Narayan till such time they excused him. The divine sages knew everything. They excused Indra and handed over Urbashi to be another court dancer of heaven.

We returned to witness the evening worship of the God with lights.

There was no crowd in the temple, so we could spend our time in the shrine peacefully. I saw clearly for the first time the exquisite idol of Lord Narayan, sitting in a particular posture of a yogi, as if in deep meditation. On his right were Kuber and Ganesh. On the left , Goddess Lakshmi and Nar Narayan. Below him, Garuda, Udhava and Narad.

Like on our last visit, this time also we decided to stay for three nights maintaining the common belief of religious Hindus. During this stay, we were also introduced to Rukmini and her mother through Niloy and become a part of the audience at the evening Bhajan sessions. I could see tears in Dadu's eyes whenever Rukmini sang those celestial songs. He could be a light hearted walking partner in the hills but I wasn't aware of the depth of his devotional feelings till Rukmini sang. He must have loved the God deeply.

After completing our tour of Badri Narayan we again hit the road for Kedarnath[9]. En route we planned to visit two other Badris and four Kedars[10] to complete our pilgrimage.

We returned to Joshimath, found a place to stay, picked up

---

9 **Kedarnath.** The Kedarnath shrine, one of the 12 Jyotirlingas of Lord Shiva, is a scenic spot situated, against the backdrop of the majestic Kedarnath range, at an altitude of 3,581metres. It is a 14 kilometre trek from Gaurikund.

Kedar is another name of Lord Shiva, the protector and the destroyer. Shiva is considered the embodiment of all passions,love, hatred, fear, death and mysticism which are expressed through his various forms.

There are more than 200 shrines dedicated to Lord Shiva in Chamoli district itself, the most important one being Kedarnath. According to legend, the Pandavas, after having defeated the Kauravas in the Kurukshetra war, felt guilty about having killed their own brothers and sought the blessings of Lord Shiva for redemption. He eluded them repeatedly and while fleeing took refuge at Kedarnath in the form of a bull. On being followed he dived into the ground, leaving his hump on the surface. The remaining portions of Lord Shiva appeared at four other places and are worshipped there as his manifestations. The arms appeared at Tungnath, the face at Rudranath, the belly at Madmasheshwar and his locks (hair) with the head at Kalpeshwar. Kedarnath and the four above-mentioned shrines are treated as Panch Kedar. The best season to visit is May to October.

10 **Panch Kedars.** They are the five different forms of the Hindu God Shiva, and are known as Kedarnath (3584 metres); Madmasheshwar (3,289 metres.); Tungnath (3,810 metres); Rudranath (2,286 metres); Kalpnath (2,134 metres). The mountain scene from each temple is fascinating, the valley full of rich fauna and flora and the people hospitable.

knick-knacks for a night halt and set course for Helang temple at Animath near Helang. After paying homage to Buda-Badri we had to go to Urgam, where the temple of Dhyan-Badri is situated. A mile away from Urgam is the temple of Kalpeswar or Kalpnath, one of the five Kedars.

On the bus conductor's advice, we got down a little short of Helang to shorten our journey to Animath where lies the temple of Buda-Badri. The hill track through the village was exquisite. The land on this hill seemed fertile because we saw cultivation all around. Away from the pilgrimage route, a small temple was situated under a peepal tree. The priest had to work elsewhere to earn his living. He opened the temple door only during the morning and evening for the daily worship. On our arrival, we requested the priest to allow us in, and he promptly opened the door for us. We prostrated ourselves before the black stone idol holding a conch shell and chakra in his hands.

The old Badri was installed by Devarshi Narad. Lord Vishnu was pleased with his penance, and appeared before him in the guise of an old man. Narad didn't have time for this old man, his yearning was to meet his Lord Vishnu. The old man vanished in front of his eyes and he heard a heavenly voice say "Thou hast lost the chance to see Him." He became repentant and decided to install the idol of Lord Vishnu and name the holy place old Badri or Buda Badri.

On the right side of this temple, there is another small

temple containing the idols of Shiva and Parvati. Mythology tells us a story about this God and his heavenly consort.

"Lakshmana was lying unconscious on the shore of Lanka. Mahavira had to collect a particular herb called Vislaya-Karani from the Drona-Giri area. He could recognise neither Gandh Madan nor Visalya Karani. As a result, he broke a mountaintop full of various plants and trees and began his journey to Lanka. On his way, as he sat down to rest, he noticed Lord Shiva and Parvati in deep meditation among the branches. He realised his mistake and replaced the mountaintop quietly."

Since then, Hara and Parvati have been worshipped.

I felt sad that I had to leave this heavenly place, yet I had to move on. I had to proceed to Urgam to pay homage to Dhyan-Badri and Kalpanath before I could return to Joshimath. We retraced our steps to Helang by noon. I started feeling hungry. Luckily there was a shop selling milk and biscuits, and we commenced our journey to Urgam, along with three guides who knew the short cut well enough to reduce our distance to our destination considerably. It was a tiring journey, the villager took pity on us and began to walk slowly, yet we had to stop at number of places before we could scale the height of (1915 mtrs).

The Himalayan journey can be pleasant only if the traveller loves Nature and the mountains. Otherwise it can be painful. The difficulties are too many. The ascent on a hilly track may be back breaking and the descents are not easy either.

Mangal Singh accompanied us all the way from Helang to Urgam. He was a Government servant, helping the local populace with their agricultural activities. He was a teacher from Joshimath but had left the job to join the Government department which forced h'·. to live in the beautiful surrounding of Urgam. This kind-hearted teacher agriculturist offered us some apples to eat, fresh from the orchards. It was 3 p.m. We exchanged

Dhayan Badri

pleasantries with Sri Mangal Singh and hurried to Dhayan-Badri. It was an ordinary neglected temple and it is commonly believed that the idol was installed by Sri Shankaracharya.

Nama Shibay Shantaya Karantraya Hetabe

Nibedayami Chatmanang Gatistang Parameswar.

Our next halt was at Kalpnath only a mile away. A few years ago, a permit had to be obtained from Joshimath to visit Urgam because the Tibet border is not far from here. But the procedure has been discontinued. We walked for 15 minutes on a plain road but couldn't locate the temple. We left behind a few old temples on our way and finally passed the last of the village houses also but there was no sign of Kalpnath. As per Sri Mohan Singh's directions, we were to cross a hanging bridge over Kalpa Ganga to reach the temple, which we couldn't locate. We had to retrace our steps back to the village. As we didn't find any one around, we began to yell for help. The noise was deafening in the quiet surroundings. However, it worked. A boy of about eight or nine appeared and happily agreed to escort us to Kalpanath. The road to Kalpanath was quiet and one could have a sense of meditation in the air. The ethereal beauty was unparalleled. Such an atmosphere could convert even an atheist.

By the time I finished my last song, we reached the dangerous hanging bridge over a fast flowing river. The planks on the bridge didn't inspire confidence. We crossed the bridge and at last reached the doorstep of Kalpanath. Anyone who wants to see heaven must come here.

I remembered an anecdote from mythology. A famous heavenly court dancer, an Apsara presented a garland to the sage Durbasha, who in turn presented it to Indra, the King of Gods. Indra, who was riding his elephant Eirabat, placed it on his head and forgot about it. The elephant didn't know the significance of the garland, and quickly brought it down with his trunk and trampled on it mercilessly. Sage Durbasa was known for his violent temper. Before Indra could retrieve the situation, Durbasa saw the garland under the feet of the animal. He immediately flared up and cursed Indra with the loss of kingdom.

The Gods went to Lord Vishnu for his advice for Indra, so that he could be absolved. The Lord said, "Let him worship Mahadev. Only he can rescue him and help him to return to his kingdom." Indra heard the dictum and went out in search of Ashutosh. But it was in vain. No one could tell him where he was. He had hidden himself after the untimely death of Sati. As Indra was about to give up the quest, he heard a voice from heaven, "Go thou to Kalpnath, and feel his presence." Indra quickly returned to Kalpnath and sat down to do his penance. The Lord was pleased, absolved him of his sins and presented him with the tree of boon (Kalptaru). This holy place is also known as Kalpa-kedar-khanda. Many sages have meditated here and have attained Nirvana by the grace of God.

We got busy arranging flowers to worship the God in a natural cave. To us it was nothing more than a piece of stone, similar to Kedarnath. Our little guide in the meantime went out to collect flowers for us to perform puja. We found some water in the cave. The priest was not there. We showered flowers on Him, poured a little water and prostrated before the Almighty, who sees the worshipper's mind and does not bother about his offerings. He is ever satisfied and present in a pure soul. I felt a current of happiness flowing through my body. I love Thee, my lord, yet I have to go away from you.

We spotted a monk nearby. With his permission, we went and sat in his small shelter which was full of smoke. Our eyes started burning as we waited to speak to him. He spoke Hindi and said his name was Sri Ajaynath. When we asked him about his preference for Kalpanath, he told us an amazing story.

Ajaynath, like many others wanted to live peacefully in his familiar material world, but it was not to be. His relatives persecuted him. They wanted to grab his property, and went to the extent of poisoning him.

He became seriously ill. Well-wishers lost all hope for his life. He was lying unconscious when he heard a voice telling him to go to Kalpa-Khetra in the Himalayas. When he regained consciousness, he began to think about the voice. He was not sure where this Kalpa-Khetra was, who Baba Kalpanath was. He also thought about his physical weakness and incapacity. At night, again he heard that voice, ordering him to go to Kalpanath. He gathered his courage and left home under the cover of darkness for an unknown destination. I couldn't understand how he had travelled such a difficult path in his feeble physical condition. Yet managed to get there and was cured by His grace.

Ajaynath asked me, where I had come from. I answered, "Calcutta."

He got up and asked me to follow him. At a little distance, he pointed to a stone. I was surprised to see an etching which resembled the known face of Mahadeva.

He went back to his shelter. We, along with our little guide, began our return journey to Urgam. On reaching Urgam, we dumped all our loose change in his small palm much to his surprise. He looked at the money once and then at me, surprised at such an unexpected gift. When he saw me smiling, without a word he ran away.

We began to descend as quickly as possible to reach Helang by sunset. In this hurry, we took a wrong hill track and found ourselves in a forest. We carried on, relying only on our sixth sense but it was time consuming. When we finally located Helang it was well past dusk. The last bus for Joshimath had already left. There was no place to stay in on that cold night. We went to a teashop and had our dinner — tea and biscuit's — and requested the shopkeeper to allow us to spend the night on his covered verandah. He agreed and also provided us with three blankets to fight the cold. Lord bless the soul of that kind man.

The following morning we journeyed to Joshimath and on to Gopeswar. From Gopeswar , we had to cover a distance of 15 miles to Rudranath on foot.

There is a difficult route to Rudranath via Urgam and Kalpanath, covering a distance of 30 miles. Pilgrims do not prefer that route due to the lack of travel facilities. Instead, they travel to Rudranath via Gopeswar.

During the winter, Rudranath is worshipped at Gopeswar. When we arrived (4000 feet) it was dusk. Therefore, we decided to spend the night there and begin our trek to Rudra Nath on the following day at 6 a.m.

Before we could visit the temple of Mahadev at this place, we found suitable accommodation for our night's stay. Lord

Shiva is known as Gopeswar at this place; in Varanasi he is called Viswanath; at Kedar, Kedarnath; at Kathmandu, he is worshipped as Pasupati Nath; and in Kashmir, he is Amar Nath. Among the Hindu trinity, he is perhaps the most worshipped God in every part of India.

On the right of the entrance to the Gopeswar temple, we found a large trident and at the bottom of the trident there is a metal axe like object. It is believed that this axe belonged to the famous Parasurama who destroyed the Khastriyas (the warrior race) twenty-one times on this earth. If a sinner touches the axe, it remains stationary but if a virtuous man touches it, he can feel a vibration through it. Apart from the trident and the axe, there are various other idols in the temple.

I heard an interesting story about Gopeswar. Many years ago, this place was full of jungles and the shepherds used to bring their cattle and sheep to the grazing ground around the jungle. Once a shepherd noticed that one of his cows would regularly disappear into the forest and return on its own after a while. One day he decided to follow it. A big surprise was awaiting him. He found the cow following a known path. It went to a particular spot and as soon as it stopped, its milk began to flow out automatically. Being curious, he started digging and discovered the stone symbol of Lord Mahadeva, which is worshipped at the Gopeswar temple.

We began our trekking in the morning with very limited luggage and food. It is not easy for a man from the plains to scale the distances in the hills. While climbing a slope, one tends to get out of breath and while descending, the knees tend to give away. The altitude adds to the discomfort. But I carried on through scenery which is unparalleled, available only in the Himalayas. I saw the joyous streams dancing away like a young girl. The snow peaked mountain was a contrast. The golden rays of the sun reflected into my eyes. The light of the effulgence brightened my inner self. I looked at the blue canopy over my head. The surrounding colour blended by the blue, had a hypnotic effect on the lonely pilgrim, struggling to cross an unknown distance. Where was Rudranath? Oh God! I adore Thee. Give me Thy energy, give me Thy eyes to see and to love this mountain You have created. I lowered myself on the narrow path. I was physically tired but the mind sang songs of joy.

It was 12.30 p.m. I had been walking for almost six hours. We sat down to rest a while and eat our meagre lunch. After drinking some water, one of my friends spread himself out peacefully. Later we began to walk from Kunda-Inn till Kedar, a distance of 30 miles. From Kunda-Inn to Gupta Kashi, it was only two miles but it was a steep climb. Rukmini's mother arranged a dandi (a man carrier) for her daughter. But she refused to climb on to the back of a coolie to proceed on a pilgrimage. She was young and full of life. She told her mother, "I can race up to the top of this climb. You needn't worry, Mama". But she wasn't really able to and fell back. Niloy and Rukmini brought up the rear.

Niloy asked her through his laboured breath, "You are so young and beautiful. Why did you risk such a hazardous journey?"

Rukmini shrugged and said, "I don't know. Mother decided to come. I tagged along." She smiled and added, "Is the pilgrimage for the young ones a taboo? How old are you by the way?"

Niloy picked up a stone and threw it. He again spoke uncertainly, " The quest of religion generally forces a man to face the travails of this hilly journey. Have you noticed the old lady? She may be eighty, yet she is forcing herself at each step to climb to an unknown height. But you do not fall in any such category."

"Why did you come?" Rukmini almost rebuked him.

He looked at her for a while, nodded his head and said, "Good question. I don't know myself. May be, I love the hills, more than anything else." Then with a rueful smile he added, "I wouldn't have met you otherwise."

Rukmini quickly glanced at him and sighed, " I wish we hadn't met at all."

Niloy couldn't speak. It was Rukmini who broke the silence, she said, "Why don't you say something dear. Are you annoyed with me?"

"Why did you say a thing like that?" he asked. "I think that is too harsh on me."

Rukmini shook her head sadly. Niloy could see tears in those

70

lovely eyes. He picked up her hand and asked softly, "What is it my dear? Did I hurt you? Come, let's go and catch up with the rest. Your mother will be worried,"

She didn't move. She whispered, "Wait a little, I must tell you everything."

Wiping her tears with the back of her hard, she spoke with firmness, "You must know the truth. My mother is not an ordinary woman. She has been singing and dancing to entertain customers all her life and I, I do not know who my father is."

Niloy was as if struck by lightning but before he could react, Rukmini left him and ran upto her mother. When Rukmini reached the inn, she was panting. Her mother took her in her arms and asked "What happened, darling, aren't you well?"

"It's all right, Mama. Just a little tired."

The view of Rudranath exploded in front of our eyes. The biting cold forced us to realise that we had climbed to a height of 3680 mtrs from 2745 mtrs. My God, we prepared to face such severe wintry weather. We left our bags in a pilgrims' rest house known as Dharamsala close to the temple and went to the cave temple to pay our homage. I was a little apprehensive. But my apprehension evaporated the moment I saw the Sivalinga and the handsome face carved on top. I haven't seen such a handsome face of Lord Shiva anywhere in India. The face does not evoke fear, it doesn't show a trace of the anger that goes with the name of Rudranath. I folded my hands and prayed. I know You not, my Lord, please forgive me.

We returned to the inn. As the sun hid behind the stony wall, the cold became intolerable. We ate our dinner early and retired for the night. Our scanty bedding could not fight the cold at that height, and forced me to stay awake. I thought of Rudranath. He had killed the demon Andhak at this place. Andhak, Kashyap and Diti (daughter of Daksha Raj), were poised to destroy all creation. The Gods ran up to Mahadeva and prayed and he agreed to destroy this demon.

Narada was asked to raise the destructive power of Mahadeva which could be achieved only if he was annoyed. Narada was in a fix. At last, he decided to make a garland out of the rare and beautiful Mandar flower and went to the great Andhak. Andhak immediately became interested, seeing such rare beauty. He wanted to gather these flowers. Narada cunningly informed him to go to the Rudra mountain in search of the desired flower. Andhak was unaware of the trap. As he stepped on to the mountain, the anger of Mahadeva arose, because he didn't like his privacy to be trespassed. The anger rose like a fire and burnt the proud demon.

I fell asleep only to be awakened at night by a powerful enemy, the cold. I tried to bring a little warmth to my body by curling up tightly, and dozed off for a while. As soon as the Eastern sky lit up, I offered my obeisance to Rudranath and hurried down the slope to reach a comfortable height.

Again, I remembered some interesting banter during my previous visit. I said, "Dadu, last night I saw a frightening sight."

A chorus asked, "What was it, what was it?"

Dadu also became curious and asked, "What is it dear?"

I stammered, "I think, I saw a procession."

"A procession?" again my co pilgrims asked in unison, "How funny?"

"Yes a procession. A procession of lice from Dadu's long hair and beard."

"Ha! Ha! Hee, Hee," everybody rolled on the ground in laughter. One of them managed to ask, "And then what?"

"They were trying to get lodged on my head."

The laughter continued unabated.

Dadu became serious and said, "Please hold your horses, gentlemen. I also dreamt something similar."

The laughter stopped, each one of us looked at him questioningly.

He continued, "It was most unfortunate. The well cared for lice got back to their familiar place when they found a desert unfit for habitation. They failed to discover even an oasis. The poor things had to go hungry all night."

I understood the taunt. I knew he was hinting at my bald head. It was my turn to be embarrassed. I protested. I said, "Why did you compare it with a desert. After all, it is not as barren."

"I know, I know," he carried on smilingly. "Fertility of the head is a must to grow the matter in abundance."

The co-pilgrims began to laugh at my discomfiture.
Thereafter I was careful whenever I got locked in a verbal duel
with Dadu.

We decided to return to Gopeswar via Anusua and Mandal
Chatti. This would be a circuitous route covering a distance of
about (30 or 32 mtrs). We reached Anusua at 1 p.m. after
covering only 11 miles. I saw a small temple in the jungles of
Rom mountain. It didn't look old to me. I was told that an
earthquake had destroyed the old temple with the idol of Sati
Anusya Devi in it. The new temple and the idol had been installed
in recent years. A story from mythology says, "Devi Anusua was
the daughter of Maharshi Kardam, who himself was the son of
Lord Brahma. She was married to sage Atri. Sage Atri and
Anusuya Devi carried out severe penance to get a son for
themselves. The Holy Trinity were pleased and were ready to
give them the desired son as a boon. As a result they were blessed
with three sons, namely, Som, Dattatreya and Durbasa."

In another story we find, "To test her chastity, Brahma,
Vishnu and Maheswara came to their ashram in disguise. When
they found her unflinching faith in God and in her husband,
they were happy to bless her with sons. She then gave birth to
three sons by their divine power. This is the reason, why barren
parents visit this temple often."

About one- and- a- (2.5 kms) from this place we visited the
sacred places where the sage Atri sat for his tapasya. We visited
Amrit Kund, the source of the Amrit Ganga and hurried down

the slope to reach Gopeswar by dusk. From Anusua, Mandal Chati is only three miles away. We covered the distance in good speed but it was not early enough to catch the last bus, as a result of which we had to walk up to Gopeswar. It was dark by then.

We walked to the bus stand in the morning but instead of a bus we got a lift in a truck. The three of us sat next to the truck driver to travel the next 14 miles. It was too early to congratulate ourselves, because we could see steam coming out of the radiator with no sign of any water beimg available in the vicinity. The helper got down and went to fetch water which took an hour and a half. With the much desired liquid to quench the thirst of the equally ancient lorry, the engine coughed a little and began to spew out black fumes before it began to move. And at last we reached Chopta at a height of (2736 mtrs). Very few pilgrims dare visit such an unaccessible place. A few come to Chopta on their way to Tunganath.

We quickly finished our breakfast and set course to climb to a height of (3699 mtrs) from the present 2736 mtrs. A climb of nearly 912 mtrs for a distance of three miles. Of all the sacred places in the Northern Himalayas, Tunganath is the highest which deters pilgrims from visiting the place. The climb was back breaking. The three of us went slowly on the slippery mountain track.

Progress became difficult but we decided to continue. God's will provided us with the much desired energy. One of our friends requested me to tell a few stories about Dadu to lighten the journey.

I conceded.

One day I asked, "Dadu will you tell us the exact reaction of our grandma when you started sporting such a sizeable beard."

"Very serious" he replied solemnly.

"Is that so?" we became interested immediately.

"My God," he continued. "Immediately after marriage she talked about her reservations about the awful tuft of hair under my chin. I didn't give a damn. But as it began to lengthen downwards, the quarrel of the not too newly weds became longer and longer. One night, it became particularly serious. I woke up in the morning and found a tuft of black hair lying on the bedside, which could have been a part of my proud beard. The next night itself, I left home to teach her a lesson. At Calcutta, I began to stay with a friend of mine who gladly accepted me as his burden. I lived happily there for over a month, before my friend once ran back to the house with a newspaper in his hand, which proudly announced my disappearance and mentioned about the repentant wife. I decided to return home. Thereafter, she accepted my long beard and lived happily with it."

Tunganath

76

As I finished the story, the temple top came into view. Tunganath was situated on top of the Chandra Shila mountain. The view of the temple made us quicken our steps but I immersed myself in the backdrop. The breathtaking beauty of the snow-covered peaks made me speechless. Towards East, I saw Nanda Devi, Gandha Madan and Dronachal. In the North, there are Kedarnath, Badri Narayan and Gangotri. Apart from these, there are hundreds of snow peaks but I only knew Choukhamba[11], Bandar Punch[12] and Nanda Ghunti. The mythology clearly speaks about the expanse of the area that belongs to Tunganath. "Length and breadth of which will be equal to about two Yojan, to the south of Mandhata Khetra."

In the book *Kedar Khand* we find Lord Shiva telling his divine consort about the holiness of this place. He says, "My dear lady, this sacred place is full of Mahatamas. Any one who worships me at Tunganath, can get any thing he desires. Any one who pours water on my stone relic with a pure mind, can seek entry to my abode and live there for as many years as the number of droplets of water. Whosoever does parikrama (circumambulation) of the relic, will be relieved of any poverty for one thousand years. The worst sinner is allowed to enter

11 Chaukhamba. One of the most majestic looking peaks of the Himalayas, it has four peaks, the highest being 7,138 metres.

12 Bandar Punch West (6,316 metres). This peak lies to the South-West of Kalanag. In June 1950, JTM Gibson with Tensing Norgay (of Everest fame) attempted it from the south. They were defeated by vertical walls of ice gullies. Once it has been climbed, after avoiding the crevasses and on finally reaching the corniced top, one can get a view of the steep drop to the southern valley, the adjoining ridge of Bandar Punch and the distant Swargarohini peaks

heaven once he has visited Tunganath."

Inside the temple was a self-procreated stone relic of Shiva. At the back, the idols of Shankaracharya and Vyasdeva were installed. And in front there were four Kedars and faces of Parvati made of silver. This completed our visit to the third Kedar. It was miserably cold at this altitude. We hurried down to save ourselves from the cold and the icy wind blowing from the snowy mountains around. We reached Chopta by 12 o'clock.

There are two roads to go to Madmaheswar, one from Ukhimath, and the other from Gupta Kashi. The road from Ukhimath is not easy for the pilgrimage, so we decided to go to Madmaheswar by the Gupta Kashi road. This road has been broadened by the Government. Again we got a lift on a lorry to go to our next destination. At Ukhimath, we changed conveyance and got into a bus for Gupta Kashi.

At Gupta Kashi, we found comfortable accommodation for the night, and decided to begin our journey to Madmaheswar on the following morning. Kedar Nath is only 45 km from this place. People believe that Lord Viswanath resealed himself to the Pandavas and that is why the place is known by that name. Sri Viswanath at this place is also known as Siddheswar. The height of Gupta Kashi is 1474 mtrs. We went to pay our homage to Viswanath and to seek his blessing for our pilgrimage.

I remembered that the Rukmini-Niloy episode took a

definite turn also on the way to Kedar Nath from Gupta-Kashi a long time ago.

I remembered asking him in a light-hearted manner, "What is the progress, brother?"

Niloy became serious. He looked at me, hesitated for a while and then said, "What do, you feel?"

I shrugged, and said, "How do I know the secrets of two young hearts?"

He hesitated again and said, "Are you sure you want to hear."

"If you don't mind."

"What do you think of Rukmini?" he asked simply.

It was my turn to be embarrassed. I stammered, "Why ask me?"

"Just to seek an honest opinion."

I knew he was serious, so I said, "I think she is a good girl."

"Yet..."

Niloy quickly looked into my face and spoke in a whisper, "I heard a note of hesitation. What it is ?"

I was forced to continue. I said, "I know she is good but somehow I feel that she is unhappy."

Niloy understood my sincerity and sighed again. He looked up at the sky and spoke as if from a distance. "I also feel so. But I don't know what it is."

He stopped for a while and again spoke in a distant manner "Now and then I see her happy. She is merry as a young girl

79

should be. She sings heartily. But at times she is pensive. Her mother gets worried whenever she sees her daughter sad. She likes me but they maintain an invisible barrier around themselves. Once I sought her blessing because she is also no doubt a good singer. She only smiled and said, 'Who am I to bless you my child. You seek blessing from Kedar Nath".

The conversation couldn't progress further because Niloy had to get up. I looked at the source of the disruption. It was no doubt Rukmini. My reminiscence was disrupted which brought me quickly from the past to the present. We were called to dinner. Early dinner was a must to start early on the following day.

In the morning, we found Sri Ram Singh as our companion and guide, though a guide is not required on this route. We found out that this was Sri Ram Singh's third visit to Madmaheswar. He is a resident businessman of Gupta Kashi.

We began to walk upto Kalimath at a distance of only three miles. The road condition was excellent. Mr. Singh informed us that the distance to Madmaheswar could be covered in a day though the last part of the journey is a little difficult. It is always better to spend the night at village Rasu and reach Madmaheswar the next day. It didn't take us long to reach Kali Math (1,203 mtrs). From Kali Math the distance to Rasu is only 13 km. We were not in a hurry. Our guide showed us the temples of Mahakalika, Maha-Laxmi, and Maha-Saraswati. The temples are comparatively smaller. Inside the temple of

Mahakalika, we saw a tunnel closed by a rock with a handle. All the offerings are placed in front. When we asked for the reason, Mr. Ram Singh said, "No one really knows what is there in that tunnel. No one is allowed to look inside as it may result in blindness. Each year, during Naba Ratri celebrations on the day of Mahastami, people tie a blindfold over their eyes with cloth and clean the tunnel."

He began to tell us about the sacredness of Kalimath, which is well known as a Sidhpith. "At a distance of three- and- a-half-miles is Koti Maheswari. At Kali math, Mother Chandi killed the demons Shumbha and Nishumbha. Behind the temple of Maha Kalika there is a big stone which is known as the Demon-stone (Daitya-Shila), on which one can find a few red lines scratched. It is believed that the torso of the demon Shumbha fell at this place and turned into stone over a period of time."

Without wasting time, we started for Rasu. The distance was only eight miles. I drew level with Mr. Singh and asked, "There are so many sacred places here including Kedarnath, then why do you visit an obscure place like Madmaheswar repeatedly?"

He replied unhesitatingly, "You may not believe it but this is true." He folded his palms and offered his pranams to that God and continued. "My only son Bansilal became sick at Gupta Kashi. He was everything to me. He was also helping in my business. Gradually his condition became serious. The local doctor was treating him but I could make out that they were giving up hope. I could see only darkness all around. Then suddenly it struck me, the myth about the Himalayas where thousands arrive to seek the blessings of the Gods. Even the Mahatmas go to Kedarnath via Gupta Kashi. Any one of them could cure my son. I closed down my business and sat down on the way hoping to find a Mahatma. In the meantime, I heard the wailing of my wife yet I waited and continued to pray to Kedar Nath. I couldn't get up. I knew my son could die at any moment. I passed the day and night without food. It was evening, I thought I heard a footstep. I couldn't focus my eyes through the darkness, and I was too weak to move. The sound was distinctly of a wooden sandal. I looked up and saw the bearded face of a benign saint. I fell at his feet and sought forgiveness I asked for his blessings for the life of my son. Seeing my tearful eyes, he said in a heavenly voice, 'Blessed are thou my son. Proceed thee to Madmaheswar tomorrow. He will bless you.' He disappeared no sooner had he uttered these words.

"I couldn't wait any longer. Before dawn I began my journey to Madmaheswar. Once I got there, I prostrated myself in front of Him. I prayed to Him and felt better. But I couldn't rest till I returned home. As I approached the house, I didn't hear any crying. I almost ran into my son's room and found him alive, his condition was better. Within a few days he was cured without medicine. This is the reason why I visit this sacred place once a year."

Rasu is at a height of 196 mtrs. With the help of Sri Ram Singh, we found comfortable accommodation for the night. After we unloaded ourselves, Mr. Singh volunteered to show us the temple of Rakeswari. And on the way to Rakeswari, he told us her story.

Out of the 27 wives, Rohini was Chandra's most favourite wife, which infuriated the other 26, who promptly went and complained to their father Daksha Raj about Chandra. Dakhsa became annoyed and cursed Chandra. Chandra then sought forgiveness and carried out penance here which pleased Raja-Dakshya. He absolved him and blessed him with his fulfillment from the first day (Raka) till the full moon following the Amabasya (new moon). From that day on the first day following the new moon Rakeswari is worshipped at this place commemorating the beginning of the moon's journey towards the full moon day.

In the temple next to Rakeswari Devi we saw an idol of Madmaheswar made of eight metals. There were a few round objects next to the idol of Chandra.

On the following morning, Mr. Ram Singh drove us out from a comfortable bed and we had to hit the road early. We quickly covered the four miles to Gaundar (1684 mtrs). We descended from a height of 6,460 feet to 5,540 feet. We didn't stop at Gaundar but continued till Bantauli at a distance of only half a mile. From Bantauli, Madmaheswar is 8.8 km but at a height of 3488 mtrs. I quickly carried out a mental calculation that our rate of ascent would be more than 1000 feet per mile. It was not easy to scale such a height. I was out of breath yet continued to climb. I thanked God that I had scaled the other heights before coming to this place. The sun was up in the clear sky and by the time we completed our laborious climb, the sun God was directly above us. The temple of Madmaheswar was in a beautiful valley. Mr. Singh told us about the temple of old Madmaheswar to the South on a hilltop. We deposited our luggage in an inn and left for the temple. Inside the temple, for the first time I saw a Shivalinga facing south. This relic was also self-created. There are two temples of Parvati and Har-Parvati behind the main Madmaheswar temple. There is a beautiful idol of Lord Shiva whose four hands are holding a vina, the trident and one hand is touching Parvati. Parvati is sitting on his left lap. One of her hands encircles the Lord's neck, the other hand, holds a mirror. I didn't know the mythological story about the place so I requested Mr. Singh, to enlighten us with few mythological banters. He readily agreed and began.

"The four sons of Brahma, Sanak, Sananda, Sanat and Sanatan were ordered to help creation. But they soon became disinterested and went out to gain the supreme knowledge. They went to Brahma, Vishnu and Lord Shiva but were disappointed to see Purusha and Prakriti playing their eternal dubious role not understood by many. They gave up hope of gaining the knowledge they were seeking. As they were returning, they saw a sage sitting in deep meditation, facing South. They didn't know who he was yet they prostrated themselves before this unknown sage. Maheswar (Lord Shiva) was pleased and blessed them with the knowledge they were seeking. Also he taught them about the role played by Purusha and Prakriti and why it seemed to be dubious to the ignorant." Since then Maheswara has been sitting at this place facing South which is quite uncommon.

Mr. Singh continued, "In another story it is said that Madmaheswar was the abode of Lord Shiva when he was in the form of a buffalo, with the legs Tunganath, mouth Rudranath, hair Kalpeswar and the rest Kedarnath which completed the five Kedars as places of pilgrimage."

Mr. Singh turned to me and asked, "Will you be going to Kedarnath from here?

I smiled, "How can I go back without touching His feet?"

The reply pleased him. He said, "I shall tell you about the five Kedars."

I looked at my companions, they were also eager to know, at least their faces said so.

Mr. Singh again narrated a story which none of us knew.

"The Pandavas relinquished their throne and began their final journey to heaven. At the very beginning, they wanted to carry out penance to wash away their sins for killing their relations at Kurukhestra. They sat down for tapasya at Kedar as advised by

Maharsi Vyas. But Kedareswar (Lord Shiva) didn't want to reveal himself to the sinners who had killed their relatives to gain a kingdom. He wanted to leave Kedar but Bhim saw him leaving and stopped him. He prostrated himself at his feet and began to pray incessantly. Ashuthosh saw the repentance, he also saw their purity. He blessed the Pandavas so that they could absolve themselves of their sins. He disappeared and disintegrated into five pieces, and wherever a piece fell, it became a sacred Kedar."

He told us another story from the *Skanda Purana.* "On the advice of Maharsi Vyas, the Pandavas came to Kashi to wash away their sins. Lord Viswanath was unwilling to reveal himself in front of these sinners so he left Kashi and came to Kedar, where he roamed around on the guise of a buffalo along with a herd. The Pandavas followed him to the Himalayas but couldn't locate him in the herd. They decided to trick the Lord. Bhim was asked to stand at a place with his legs apart. The other brothers began to drive the buffaloes through the gap between his legs. They were sure that the Lord in the disguise of a buffalo would refuse to follow the others, that would be below his dignity. Their trick bore fruit. One of the buffaloes quickly tried to enter the earth but was prevented by the powerful Bhim. He held on to its tail. That is why the rear portion of the buffalo turned into a stone at the Kedar while the other four parts dropped in the other four Kedars."

We didn't notice the cold seeping in through the scanty

bedding. As Mr. Singh finished his story, I felt my teeth chattering. I looked at my watch, it was only 9 p.m. The long dark cold night awaited us. I tried to sleep but in vain. No one could sleep. As soon as the Eastern sky lit up, we escaped the height and descended to Gupta Kashi by evening.

We decided to take the 6 o'clock bus in the morning to go to Kedarnath. Mr. Ram Singh came to see us off at the bus stand. He insisted that we must spend a day with him on our way home. He waved at us as the bus began to move. We also returned the courtesy. This kind hearted man had really become a friend in only two days. I have met many such people in this cruel world during my travels whom I cannot forget. A few more people like them could make our world a better place to live in.

The bus route is up to Sonprayag which is 24 km from Gupta Kashi. The last 19 km had to be traversed on foot. We reached *Son prayag* by 7.30 a.m. and started trekking for Gauri Kunda three miles from there. The route was not bad. The road was being built to accommodate the journey by bus till Gauri Kunda (1976 mtrs). At Gauri Kunda there are hot and cold springs. The water is quite warm. We decided to have our bath before proceeding further.

Mythology tells us that Goddess Gauri carried out tapasya here to marry Lord Shiva that is why the place is called Gauri Tirtha. She cleansed herself in the cold spring hence it is named Gauri Kunda. The hot spring sprung due to her sweat.

The ascent began from Gauri Kunda. After covering 6 km of gradual ascent, we reached Ramwada. From 1936 mtrs to 8200 mtrs. We ate our lunch at Ramawada and started walking to cover the final three and-a-half miles ascending another 912 mtrs.

This ascent of Ramawada is as famous as that of Mahagunas on the way to Amarnath. The route may be difficult but the natural beauty is unparalleled. All the travails of the journey can be forgotten if a pilgrim has an eye for the sublime beauty. But I fear that this beauty will soon be trampled by the bulldozers of civilisation. I remembered my hardships, when I walked all the way to Badrinath from Joshimath but I remembered the happiness also. That nostalgia brought me to the doorstep of Badrinath again but my dream was destroyed. Now it will be the turn of Kedar. The sound pollution of the microphones blaring loud music will invade the most sacred place of the Hindus. I felt sad, why did the Lord Himself not stop this encroachment?

I was growing older yet I decided to visit the five Kedars and seven Badris. I loved the Himalayas. I knew the difficulties of a Himalayan journey. But I knew the joy that send a peculiar vibration though the limbs at the end of the journey. I came back repeatedly to feel it.

We climbed ahead slowly. We reached Garuda-Chati at 3344 mtrs. Kedarnath is at a distance of only two- and- a- half km from there.

We rested a while and then began to walk. We saw that heavenly sight as soon as we arrived at Dev Dekani. We saw the golden temple-top with the backdrop of snow covered mountain peaks reflecting the golden sunlight. Such breathtaking scenery makes the pilgrims forget every bit of their troubles of a tiresome journey. They even forget the extreme cold. A little away from the spot, the road made of pebbles begins. The road ends by the bridge on the Mandakini.

I came to Kedar years ago. My fears after visiting Badrinath turned out to be true. The place has become congested. The temple area will be invaded soon.

I had already heard about the mythological stories relating to Kedar. As per the Skanda Purana, Lord Shiva told Parvati that Mahatma Upamanyu achieved Shivlok (the abode of Lord Shiva) by carrying out tapasya at this place. Later, the Pandavas after their penance, were absolved of their sins. Any holy person who says he wants to come here, will have all his descendants and ancestors attain Shivlok.

Kedarnath Temple

Kedarnath is at a height of 3572 mtrs and is situated in a wide valley. To the North of the temple is Mahapanth or Swarga Rohini and Brahma cave. It is believed that the Pandavas began their journey to heaven from this place. Behind the temple there is the

89

Shankaracharya tomb. According to per some scholars, the present temple was built by Shankara. But how? Who made such a grand structure at this height, thousands of miles away from civilisation. Who shaped the stones?

On the East of the temple is the Khir river, on the West the Saraswati and Mandakini, and on the North are the sources of the Mahodadhi and Swarga Dwari Ganga. These five rivers together are known as Pancha Ganga. Apart from these, on the Southern corner, on top a hill, are Bhairavshila and the temple of Bhairabnath. To the west of the temple there are two small lakes Basukital and Chorabarital. The second lake is also known as Gandhi Sarovar because the ashes of

श्री केदारनाथ की मंदिर हिमालय

Kedarnath Temple

MahatmaGandhi were immersed in the lake. This lake is the source of the Mandakini.

During my first trip to this place I planned to visit Gandhi Sarobar, only a mile away. As there was no regular route, we decided to engage a guide. The route was really difficult. We had to cross hurdle after hurdle. But somehow we managed to reach the bank of the lake adjacent to the snow-clad mountain. It was the month of May but the lake was still half covered with snow. Like any other place in the Himalayas, this is also a place which a traveller cannot ignore or forget easily.

We had to come back. After crossing a few hurdles, I noticed the gleaming temple top of Kedarnath. I became confident and ignored the guide thereafter. Gradually, the path became difficult and I had to cross fast flowing streams. I jumped across them and began to feel proud because I was well ahead of my co pilgrims. I reached the bank of another dangerous stream. To cross it, I jumped on a stone midstream and as I tired to cross to the other bank, I slipped into the fast flowing, icy water. Within a second I almost froze and was washed away downstream. Luckily, the guide and my friends reached in time at a place down the stream to retrieve my inert body. They shook me to my senses and helped me walk back in that miserable condition. When I reached the inn, a lady asked me whether I had taken a holy dip.

My teeth chattered, I nodded and said, "Yes, you may go and have a dip also. The place is called Gandhi Sarovar."

I needed a quick change out of my wet clothes. As I opened my valise, I discovered to my utter horror that I didn't have enough to fight the cold. My luggage had been left behind at Rampur. However, I changed into something dry. The doctor helped me with the rest.

On the North of the temple are Amrit Kunda and idol of Nilkanth Mahadeva. On the North-East, there is Isaneswar Mahadeva in Isan Kund or Sufal Kund. On the East there is Hansa Kund and on the south the name of the kunda is Ret. Udak-Kund is in the front of the temple.

It is believed that a pilgrim must touch the water of all five kunds or natural small lakes. Anyone who drinks the water of Udak Kunda will not be reborn. An interesting thing about Ret Kund is that if any one shouts standing on the bank of the kund, it creates bubbles on the surface of the water.

In the morning, I went to the temple to perform my worship of the Lord with flowers, specially the Brahma Kamal that I brought all the way from Hemkund. There was no crowd in the shrine, so I had the Lord to myself. Tears came to my eyes when I thought about his favours and how he had helped me through this difficult journey.

The door of the temple is on the south they casted that long ? In the front, Nadeswar the bull awaits him. On the side of the main door, is the idol of Ganesh.

In the front portion of the temple, there are idols of Kunti and the five Pandavas. On the left is Nar Narayana and in the centrs there is Nandi. To the south of the second door there are idols of Parvati and Lakshmi Devi. Inside the shrine there is the magnificent stone relic of Mahadeva the God of the Universe. This is the most famous among the twelve effulgent relics of India.

My journey was over. After spending three nights, I began my return trip to the plains. I had been living among the Gods and now I would have to go and face the human beings.

Niloy, Niloy. Yes on this return trip he told me the last part of the story. Before we picked up our haversacks and stepped out, Dadu suggested we should say good bye to Rukmini and her mother . Niloy surprised us. Without a word, he stepped out of the inn muttering, "Let them follow." We looked at each other and followed him wondering what could be the reason. On the way downhill, I caught up with Niloy and asked, "Isn't it funny?" He looked at me and replied, "What?"

"As if you don't know," I spoke with suppressed resentment, "You could have at least said good bye to them. I thought you were more than friendly with that innocent girl."

He felt my resentment and spoke in a voice which seemed to me had travelled from a long distance. He said, "I wanted to tell you yesterday itself, but I couldn't."

It was my turn to be taken aback. I was curious, "What happened yesterday."

"Rukmini's mother called me."

Niloy smiled at me. He placed a hand on my arm and said, "Don't get upset. It is not so bad."

I kept quiet. Niloy continued, "She called me aside and said

93

come with me dear, I want to speak to you."

He continued, "I can't swear that I was not a little panicky. Why did she want to talk to me I followed her to a quiet spot and sat on a stone in front of her.

"She spoke almost in an inaudible tone, 'I wanted to talk to you about my daughter.'

"My heart skipped a beat. Probably she sensed that and again spoke in a reassuring tone, 'Don't get panicky dear. I wanted to tell you something about Rukmini.'

"I waited apprehensively. She cast a glance at the temple and began, 'Rukmini is not my daughter. Circumstances forced me to adopt her. I don't remember how many years ago. I went to Calcutta to entertain the rich and fell in love with Bengal which prevented me from returning to Lucknow. I think it was a dark night, around 10 o'clock, when I heard a knock on the door. I was surprised. Who could that be? In my profession you couldn't trust people. The knocking became urgent. Hesitatingly, I asked the maidservant to open the door. As she opened the door, two people entered the room. One of them wanted to talk to me in private. I quickly retorted and said, You may say what you want in front of the maidservant if at all?

"She continued, 'It was my turn to be dumbfounded. One of them said that they have a two- year-old girl with them; her parents wanted to sell her for want of money, because they were unable to feed her, along with five other children.'

"She paused for a moment. I almost screamed at them, Get

94

out or else I will call the police, Then."

"The man had again pleaded, She said, Please keep the little one. You may able to feed her otherwise the poor thing will die.'

"In the meantime, a woman had entered the room with a child in her lap. She was weeping.

"The man again pleaded, saying, "The mother has come herself, don't you see, my dear lady."

"She said, "Yes I can see but what is the proof?"

"She continued, The lady quickly produced a photograph of a couple along with the child. I didn't know what went wrong. I felt a peculiar sensation in my body. A motherly love began to haunt me. I wanted to be a mother. I wanted a child to call me by that sweet name. Without any further hesitation I paid them five hundred rupees and bought her.

'The next day I came to know that I had been tricked. A gang of child lifters had stolen the little one and sold her to me, at least that is what the newspaper said. Impulsively I wanted to go to the police but on second thoughts, I took a train to Lucknow and left Calcutta for good.

'Rukmini grew up as my daughter. My house was full with her. She began her music lessons and soon became a virtuoso. She has grown up into a beautiful young maiden as you see. I wanted her to marry into a good family. But my profession became the biggest obstacle.

'Once one of my admirers cast his evil glance at this innocent flower. He began to frequent my house on various excuses and began to shower gifts on me and Rukmini. He praised Rukmini for her gifted voice unsuspectingly. We also became free with him.One evening I had to go out but left the maidservant with Rukmini. The evil man arrived. He sent out the maidservant on some pretext. As she closed the door behind her, he fell upon Rukmini to assault her physically. The young girl resisted like a lioness. Fortunately, the maidservant returned before he could destroy the child. He escaped but left behind a trauma for my sweet daughter. She forgot to smile, and became delirious. I consulted a psychiatrist and a number of other doctors. They advised me to take her away from Lucknow to a quiet place. That is why I decided to undertake this journey. And with God's grace I found her smiling again when she met you on our way to Badri Narayan.

'I was elated and didn't prevent her from meeting you. I only wanted to see her happy, Niloy looked thoughful and added,

"As she spoke, she held my hand and whispered, 'Promise me, you will look after her."

Niloy said he freed his hands from her grasp and whispered back,"I promise." The old lady began to weep. But they were tears of happiness.

A voice from the darkness called out "Niloy, where are you?"

Niloy said he looked at me and asked, "Please tell me. Have I committed a mistake?"

I couldn't reply. I didn't know what the future held.

Yamunotri
Gangotri
Gomukh

YAMUNOTRI

I visited Panch Kedar and Sapta Badri and viewed the beauty of the Valley of Flowers. I saw the Brahama Kamal at Hemkund but my journey to the Uttarakhand would be incomplete till I could visit and pay homage to Yamunotri[1] and Gangotri. Someone asked, what the hurry was. But I knew that one has to be in perfect physical and mental strength to visit these places. I decided to do it all by myself but it was Ajit who, finally, decided to accompany me. I planned an itinerary and chalked out the details, but the pilgrimage could not take place. So I was little apprehensive about the ways of God. but left the matter in his hands.

The bus dropped us at Dharasu. From here the route branches off to Uttar Kashi[2] and Yamunotri. From Dharasu the distance to Yamunotri is 120 kilometres. Presently the bus

---

1 *The shrine of Yamunotri, situated at an elevation of about 3,235 metres. is one of the four Dhams and is an essential pilgrimage for Hindus. Situated in the direction opposite to Gangotri, the road bifurcates from a place called Dharasu, somewhere between Rishikesh – Uttarkashi and goes upto Yamunotri. The shrine can also be visited via Mussoorie and Barkot.*

Altitude: 3,235 metres. Climate: Summer: Cool during the day and cold at night. Winter: Snow-bound. Touching sub-zero.

Clothing: Summer: Light woollens Winter: Very heavy woollens.

2 *Uttar Kashi: 99 kilometres from Gangotri, Uttar Kashi is an important pilgrimage centre, equated with Varanasi or Kashi in divinity. It is located in a wide stretch of a valley. Situated at a distance of 145kilometres from Rishikesh, and at an elevation of 1,158 m. on the bank of the river Bhagirathi, this picturesque town is also the district headquarter. From the religious point of view as well, it is considered important because the temple of Lord Vishwanath is located here, wherein there is a massive iron trident. A description this temple is given in "Kedar Khand" (Skanda-Purana). The other important temples situated here are Ekadash Rudra, Bhairav and Gyaneshwar. The temple of goddess Kuteti Devi is situated on the top of a hill about 1.5 kilometres away.*

The Nehru Institute of Mountaineering is also located on a hill above the town, five kilometres away. Close by at Ujeli are a number of ashrams and temples. Every year, on the occasion of "Magh Mela" (January 14), people from far and near visit Uttarkashi to take a holy dip in the Bhagirathi along with the idol of their local deities.

route has been extended upto Hanuman Choti, from where the walking distance is only 17 kilometres. Normally the pilgrims complete Kedar and Badri in one trip and combine Gangotri and Yamunotri in another. It was impossible to visit all the holy places at one go those days. We were a party of seven. Myself, Ajit, an old couple from UP, their middle-aged son, and twenty-year old granddaughter Sita, and Swami Atmanand. We decide to carry out our pilgrim's progress the following morning and spend the night at Dharali at a distance of 15 kilometres. Once we finished our dinner, we went and sat with Swamiji. A little later, the old couple and their granddaughter also came and sat with us. He could speak in fluent Hindi and we had to resort to that, although I was not very familiar with this North Indian language.

Swamiji asked, "You look very young. Why are you so eager to go on such pilgrimages?"

I replied, "I came from Calcutta to visit the abodes of God. I have always dreamt of seeing the Himalayas. The mighty mountains beckon me. Whenever I feel tired of my daily routine, I take refuge in this cool comfort. Whenever I come here, I feel that I am with the God."

He was pleased, smiled and saw the intensity of my desire. He said, "I pray to God that your ultimate desire is fulfilled. The inner truth may smile on you." But added, "At a place like this, you must make it a point to feel the religious current and the frequency to get maximum benefit."

I wanted to ask him "Who," but kept quiet.

On the following morning we packed up our scanty belongings and set course for Dharali. Swamiji left us behind. He wanted to be on his own. We walked slowly. The rear was brought up by the old couple – the man may have been about 80 years old and the lady in her middle seventies. Why are they here and undertaking this journey? I decided to ask their son Shiupujan.

He said, " My parents were adamant. They even wanted to die en route. They wanted to visit Yamunotri and Gangotri . We are three brothers. None of us could argue with them. As such, I decided to accompany them."

"But why the girl?" I decided to keep the question to myself.

But Shiupujan filled in the blanks. He said, "Look at this fool." He pointed towards Sita. "She should have been married by now and had children of her own. Instead, she wants to be with the Gods. She refuses to get married." He made a gesture of resignation. "I don't understand," he added with a sigh.

We took leave of Shiupujan and his parents and went ahead with quick steps to cover the distance as quickly as possible. I was thinking about Sita. A good-looking girl with all the charm of a young maiden. Walking or dancing with a happy gait. But at times she was not with us. She lived in a world of her own. I wondered if there was a broken love affair in the background, specially since I heard Shiupujan muttering, "I hope she can fall in love with someone."

We reached Sana Chati. Swamiji was already there to receive us. And some time later, Sita and the gang joined us. We finished our food as quickly as possible and went to enjoy the company of Swamiji.

He asked. "It is difficult to walk on this hilly track?"

But the Himalayan climate helps you to recuperate very quickly and makes you forget the misery of the day and be ready for the next day."

"You are right. He nodded and said, The Himalayas do not attract anyone to give them trouble. They give you a hundred times more joy than the difficulty that you undergo." I remembered this advice every time I came to the Himalayas. And in the later part of my life, I loved to come here and take away the truth of beauty. Sana was like another virgin beauty of these hills. The forest all around, the fast flowing river frothing at its crests. I looked into the clear blue fast flowing river and spent another night there.

Twenty-one kilometres more to go. The distance was not much but the ascent was very steep, mainly towards the end as you approach the shrine. We were at 2,000 metres and had to climb further to 3,250 metres. We were asked to halt at Janki Chati, 15 kilometres away.

We were walking slowly. We did not come across many pilgrims on our way up. But we heard the resounding notes of the thanks at the of completion of the pilgrimage, "Yamuna mai ki jai."

I looked back and saw that Sita was not following us. I went up to her and asked, "Is there any problem?"

She said uncertainly, " No, but..."

I urged her to move forward lest we get caught in the rains. She sighed and began to follow us.

I thought of asking Sita "Why are you here? Why have you taken such a journey?" but restrained myself. I had no right to invade her privacy.

But it was Sita who surprised me. "No sir, you have not done anything wrong. I can't lie at a place like this. But yes, I have a reason and it is very dear to me. I may reveal it someday, if I so feel. But not now."

I kept quiet. We began to move. We decided against stopping at Rana Chati and kept walking towards Hanuman Chati. It was a gradual ascent. Some pilgrims were on horseback. We reached Hanuman Chati at a height of 2,134 metres. Ajit was already there, resting. As he saw us approaching, he jumped up and began to walk. It was difficult for the old couple to walk, so they had to be put on horseback.

We left Narayan Chati behind. And came across Full Choti (2,453 metres) at a distance of 7 kilometres form Hanuman Choti. The climb was continuous, there was no reprieve. Every step forward was troublesome. We ate a meagre lunch on the way and reached Janaki Chati (2,575 metres) by 3 pm. We made ourselves comfortable in a Dharmashala there. Sita asked Swamiji with all earnestness in her voice, " Swamiji, tomorrow we will reach Yamunotri. Why don't you tell us something about it." She looked uncertainly towards me and continued, "I don't know a thing about this place."

Swamiji smiled at her honesty and sincerity. He said, "Yamuna was born to Surya and Sanga, the daughter of Viswakarma. Yama is the brother of Yamuna. You find this mythological briefing in the Haribamsha Purana. Sri Shankaracharya worshipped Yamuna with his famous hymns. And you must have heard that the Pandavas while travelling thorough the Himalayas, came to this place. In the Mahabharata, it says that anyone who comes here and pays homage, would definitely find inner peace."

He added, "Like in the Mahabharat, the Ramayana also mentions the Yamuna and her blessings."

"I think you should go to bed now," he said with all finality. "You must pay your homage to the goddess and go down as far as possible on the following day."

We felt rejuvenated and began to walk. This was the most difficult part of the journey. The ascent was too steep. And though the distance was not much, we took three hours to cover it. We crossed a small bridge and reached the shrine. I looked up directly into the snowy height of the Bandar Punch peak at a height of 6,700 metres. The Yamuna was flowing down the silvery snow line. There were two hot water springs near the temple. The water in the smaller spring was too hot to pour over one's hand. One could cook rice and dal if placed inside the water, secured in a cloth. The larger spring was not too hot. We sat next to it, bathed, and went into the

Yamunotri

temple. We could spend only two hours in the temple before we began our return downhill.

GANGOTRI and GAUMUKH

It was in the year 1960 that I first visited Gangotri, when the fun of travelling was there and we had to walk all the way from Uttar Kashi to Gangotri.

We left Yamunotri and boarded a bus along with the other pilgrims. From Dharasu to Gangotri is a distance of 124 kilometres. From Dharasu Uttar Kashi is only 28 kilometres but from Hrisikesh it is 143 kilometres.

As the bus coughed its way to Uttar Kashi many people began to vomit. The twists and turns around the Himalayan bends turned the stomachs of many of the passengers. There was nothing to be done, they would have to get a hold of themselves. I looked out to take my mind off the disgusting scene. Somehow we reached Uttar Kashi and landed at the last bus stand for our onward journey. I envy the pilgrims of today for they can ride the bus right up to the temple of Gangotri. The bus route gradually got extended to Dharali in 1964, then in 1972, it went upto Lanka. People had to cross over a narrow bridge to Bhairab Ghati and catch another bus to Gangotri. Travelling is much easier now and this has increased the inflow of tourists and pilgrims. But this comparative ease has made the route less charming than before specially since between Uttar Kashi and Gangotri, there are some famous places hidden in mythology. Unless the pilgrims are well informed, they miss the opportunity to visit them.

We made the night halt at the Kali Kamli Dharamshala and decided to start for Gangotri the next morning. Being inquisitive by nature, I wanted to get acquainted with this place rather than roaming around aimlessly. We pleaded with Swamiji to tell us the story about the place.

Being gentle by nature, he saw my point and began. He said. " This place is only 1,090 metres above sea level. Just like Varanasi, Uttar Kashi is also been surrounded by the Ganga, Varuna and Assi rivers. If you happen to go a few miles to the East you will find a stream meeting the Bhagirathi. That is the Varuna, and after crossing Uttar Kashi, you will find the stream called the Assi. And this is the reason why the place is named Uttar Kashi. Here also you will find the temple of Viswanath and Annapurna. In addition, you should find time to visit the temples of eleven Rudras, the Kali temple and the temple of

Sri Parashuram. You should visit the Viswanath temple on this holy Monday."

We departed as ordered by this holy soul and returned after 8 p.m. to our rooms.

I said, "Ajit, it is too early to sleep. Why don't you sing a few devotional songs?"

Sita was jubilant. She also said, "Yes, yes, that would be great."

Ajit began to sing to the Lord. We felt refreshed.

On the following day we decided to do the usual circumambulation of Uttar Kashi. And in the morning, we first paid our homage to Lord Viswanath. Then we left for Ujeli on the outskirts of the town. Ujeli is home to many ascetics who have been living there for a long time. We saw a middle-aged Sanyasi who was about to complete his daily worship of the Lord, and decided to sit next to him for a while, provided he did not object. He didn't. As we sat with him, he asked about our well-being and about our homes. It was very kind of him. He recited a few Bhagawat Gita slokas and left us to think about and interpret them. He indeed had a very sweet voice. Next we visited the ashram of Swami Saradananda. He was a highly respected swami of the place, who besides being in the field of religion, also runs a Sanskrit school. I found him very busy and asked him how he managed to concentrate with such a busy daily schedule.

He replied, "My dear fellow, this work is my worship. I

need not sit down and meditate in your conventional manner."

I didn't understand. I knew little about the ways and means of the community of recluses.

He was busy and we had to part company. Then we stumbled on a very old Sanyasi. He looked at us and indicated to us to sit down in front of him. We prostrated ourselves in front of him and asked, " How do we find the path of God?"

He looked away for a while and then replied, "Your internal thirst for Him will show you the way. You need not go anywhere else for it."

As Sita lifted her head after paying her respects, a mild tone intervened, "My dear, go to Gangotri. Your thirst will be quenched permanently. Don't worry too much."

We were left dumbstruck. Quietly we walked back to our Dharamshala.

Sita suddenly asked, " Dada, it seems to me that you study a lot."

"Why do you ask?" I said.

" Just like that." Sita replied quickly.

I said, "I don't know what you mean? But I try to read as much as I can."

She was jubilant and stated, "I thought as much. Then why don't you tell me the story about the Ganga and Bhagirath?

I looked at her uncertainly and asked, "Are you sure? It will take some time."

She enthusiastically nodded her head and said, "I won't mind."

That is how I began. "Sagar was a very powerful king of the Surya dynasty and 12ᵗʰ seniormost in the ladder of ascendancy. Sagar arranged for a Yagna in which a horse is made to go round the country to challenge the kings and monarchs to stop it from going through their territory if they had the right kind of force or accept subservience to King Sagar. The king of the devas, Indra, became very worried. He thought that if Sagar completed this special sacrificial worship, he would unseat him from the heaven. He decided to steal the horse and hide it in the ashram of Sage Kapila. The accompanying troops became very concerned. But finally they could locate the animal in the ashram of Sage Kapil and this made them very angry. The 60,000 children of Sagar didn't know the facts and took it for granted that this must have been the work of this sage. As they released the animal, they heaped abuses on him, though he was in deep meditation. The noise disrupted his meditation. And he gave this belligerent lot such a look that it burnt all 60,000 into ashes. The king didn't know about the incident. He was worried about the undue delay of the children and the horse. He dispatched his grandson Anshuman to search for them. Anshuman initially couldn't find them but finally he stumbled on them in Sage Kapil's ashram and came to know the reason of their deaths from the king of the mythological birds Garuda, who described for him the incident in detail.

He also told him that only if Ganga were to arrive on earth and touch the ashes of these unfortunates, they will find their way to heaven.

"Anshuman returned with the horse. The worship being complete, King Sagar decided to carry out tapasya for Ganga to descend to the earth from heaven. But he was too old to take on such a difficult task. He passed away. Anshuman thought that it was his duty to liberate the souls of his seniors. He took on the worship of Ganga for a very long time but he also failed to pacify her and force her to descend to the earth. His son Dilip also tried but he too failed. Then came the great King Bhagirath, the son of King Dilip. He heard everything and decided to dedicate his young life to the cause. He began a strict penance at Gangotri. The prince could not be recognised. He became very thin. He could hardly breathe even for one more day. Ganga became worried. She finally came to this king of kings and showed herself.

"The king said, 'My mother, if you are satisfied then come with me to my ancestors. They are waiting for your touch. Or else you may take this body. I offer myself at your feet.'

"The Goddess Ganga could not take away the body of a devotee, just like that. She was the mother of all. She became worried and said, 'Yes, my son, I accede to your wishes. But who will hold my force when I descend on earth. The entire earth will get inundated with such force. It is only Lord Maheswar who can arrest my power to an extent.' Bhagirath began his tapasya to please Lord Mahadeva who promptly relented and Ganga began to flow through his hair, but Bhagirath was surprised when he didn't find the flowing water behind him. Mahadeva arrested Ganga in his hair. He, the Omnipotent, understood the pride of Ganga who thought that she could flood everything and there was no force which could arrest her. He wanted to break her pride. Bhagirath understood this and began to pray to Him to release Ganga from His hair. And finally He agreed and listened to the request from a true devotee. He understood his love. Ganga began to flow freely through His hair. Bhagirath showed her the way and brought her to the ashram of Sage Kapil. The 60,000 ancestors blessed him and their souls departed to their heavenly abodes. It was a difficult journey for Bhagirath. Let us talk about it later. Now let us catch up with some sleep." I ended my story.

Sita was satisfied and she went to Swamiji and told him about the mythology behind the source of the Ganga.

But he asked her, " Do you also want to about the source of the Ganga, dear?"

It was her turn to be puzzled. She looked at him uncertainly and said " I don't think I know about that and I forgot to ask."

"Do not bother, my child. I shall tell you the incident."

She seemed to be relieved and happily sat down to listen to this marvellous tale from the Puranas.

Swamiji began. "Once Maharshi Narada went out to travel

through the worlds and came across a beautiful garden and saw there a few handsome boys and girls. But when he came closer he was horrified to see their features. They were all being severely injured and definitely suffering. Maharishi Narada took pity on them and asked them about their pathetic state.

"They told him, 'We are six ragas and thirty six raginis, on which is based the Indian classical music. And no other than Devarshi Narada is the cause for this trouble.' Obviously they didn't know the identity of the person they were talking to.

"Narada was aghast. He asked, 'Why is this gentleman is to be blamed?'

"One of them blurted out, 'He thinks that he is a great singer. But he does not know that he cannot sing even one raga correctly and that is why we have this problem.'

"Narada almost was in tears. He was stupefied and uttered 'I am that poor soul, who caused you this misery.' He wanted to know how he could help them without revealing his identity.

"They told him, 'There is only one individual in heaven and earth who can sing and get us out of our misery.'

"Devarshi Narada was intrigued and asked, 'Who could that be?'

"They said almost in unison, 'Lord Shiva. He can only establish the purity of the ragas and no one else.'

"Narada was in tears by now. He thought about his ego. He wanted to run away. But he had promised and he could not get away from it now. He told them, 'I am going to Mahadeva for his blessings.'

"He left for Kailash, the abode of Lord Shiva, prostrated before him and asked for his blessings for those poor souls.

"The Lord agreed to sing but he wanted to know about the audience. No music is complete without good listeners.

"Maharisi to Narada was in fix. He understood that neither could he sing nor could he understand the music of the Lord. He was shaken very badly. He whimpered and asked, 'Who could those be my lord?'

"The Lord told him to ask Lord Brahma and Lord Vishnu. 'These are only two who can understand my music.'

"Both Brahma and Vishnu arrived to attend that concert."

"The great music began with all its purity. Nothing like that ever been heard before. Nothing was comparable to such notes. But the celestial Lords got completely immersed in this music. The sound and its effect caused a tiny flow of water from the feet of Lord Vishnu. Lord Brahma saw it, picked it up and kept in his possession. And that is why we say that Ganga flows out of Brahma's water pot."

We began our journey by 6 am. We walked upto Maneri without any hitch. At a distance of 30 kilometres from Maneri, the source of the river Assi, is the famous Doriotal. We kept on going. The gradual ascent and descent didn't bother us and we reached the well populated Bhatoari. This place is also known as Bhaskar Prayag. Here we find a rivulet meeting the Bhagirathi and here also we find the Alokeswar Shiva Linga, the most famous among the 84 Linga of India. Sri Bhaskar received his salvation at this place by the grace of Lord Shiva and placed the Shiv Linga here. During the evening rituals, we joined the temple priest to pray along with him.

On the following day, we walked for 15 kilometres to reach Gangnani for the night halt. On one side of Gangnani, there is the cold river, the Bhagirathi, and on the other side, there are two hot springs, Vyas Kunj and Vasisht Kunj. Some people call these Rishi Kund.

We continued our walk towards Gangotri and came across the first fearful ascent of Sukhi from Lohari Nag, at a distance of only 6 kilometres. This is almost a straight climb, a mountaineer's challenge. The rivers Bhagirathi and Sone Ganga meet and flow from here. But we did not have the time to admire them since we were worried about our progress upwards. It was back breaking. And no sooner had we scaled the height, we had to descend and brake our way to prevent a sharp fall. I injured my poor knee and limped to a distance of 5 kilometres to Jhala. But we didn't stop at Jhala, we continued to Shyam Prayag at distance of one kilometre, from there to Gupta Prayag 2 ½ kilometrs from Shyam Prayag, and a kilometer later, we stopped at Harsil or Hari Prayag. The Shyam Ganga meets the Bhagirathi here. Harsil is a lovely small valley with greenery all around. I nursed my injured knee but I couldn't stay back. That would be disastrous. I limped ahead the next day along with my co-pilgrims towards Dharali.

Somehow I reached Dharali and was told that the Dudh Ganga meets the Bhagirathi here and at the confluence there is an ancient Shiva temple. From Dharali, one can walk upto the source of the Dudh Ganga at the foothills of the Srikant mountain (6,133 metres). It is said that at the foot of this Srikant mountain also Bhagirath meditated for a long time. At a distance of 6 kilometres is a place known as Jangla from where the next fearful mountaineering expedition starts for foot soldiers like us. This is popularly known as the ascent of Bhairav Ghati. But I didn't find it too difficult to scale the height despite my limp and slowly we made it to Lanka. From Lanka we had to scale a height which was not too difficult to climb and finally we reached Bhairab Ghati and our much needed night halt. We decided to make it to Gangotri the next day only a distance of 10 kilometres. Bhairab Ghati is well known because this is the place of the confluence of the Yanhavi Ganga and Bhagirathi. There is a very old Shiva temple surrounded by whispering chir and pine trees. We forgot our troubles. I wanted to sit next to the river and meditate about eternity. From Bhairab Gahti to Gangotri was a comparatively easy journey for us, walking on almost on level ground. We crossed a small bridge over the Ganga and reached Gangotri. We were surprised to be welcomed by Swami Brahma Vidyananda Tirtha. We were allotted five rooms, and a separate room for Swamiji. We were excited to have made it to such a difficult place without any mishap. Enthusiasm overtook fatigue and, we went to pay homage to Shankaracharya, Radhakrishna, Dattatreya, Viswanath and Goddess Durga. Once we completed these, we went to have a bath and pay homage to Mother Ganga.

There is a bathing place close to the temple. It was well into the month of June but it was cold. The water was icy. I felt it with my hand, wondering how I could bathe in it. Finally I decided to jump into the fast flowing river and got out quickly. The afternoon sun took a long time to bring back some sort of warmth to my body.

Gangotri Temple

Bhagirath Sila or the stone on which King Bhagirath had carried out his tapasya is just on the right side of the way to the temple.

It is said that the temple was built by Acharya Shankaracharya. The main deity is Mother Ganga. In the lower part there are the idols of Lakshmi, Annapurna, Saraswati, Bhagirath, Yanhavi and Yamuna. On one side is an idol of Shankaracharya. No one is allowed to go inside the temple where the deities are kept. The temple is kept open from four in the morning till 1 o'clock when the temple door is closed for two hours. Again it is opened at 3 p.m. and kept open till 9 p.m.. One can stay in Kali Kamli Dharamshala or the recently built tourist lodge.

We finished our dinner and went to spend some time with Swamiji.

He said, "It is God's grace that you could come so far without much of a problem. It would be better for you to spend at least three nights in such a holy place before you undertake any further journey."

This suited me fine because my legs could have given up. I wanted to travel upto Gaumukh but I didn't know whether I could.

I asked Swamiji about the holiness of the Ganga.

He closed his eyes and began to recite the eternal hymns. We sat mesmerised gazing at that benign face. We understood the strength of those words coming out of the mouth of someone who had practised Brahamacharya for a long time. He finished his recitation and looked away from us as if in deep meditation. We didn't want to disturb the tranquility and returned quietly to our rooms, thinking about these ascetics of India. Where do you place them in this materialistic world? How do they live, and what for? I wish I knew.

We left him and were on our way to meet some ascetics who had left the humdrum of our known life and had been living here for many years. At first, we visited Swami Hamsananda Tirtha, who does not talk to anyone. If you ask him a question, he replies in writing. I was told that he spends the winter here and at times he also stays at Gaumukh. I didn't know how long he had been meditating here. Some of the pilgrims were already there, conversing with him in his usual way. We didn't wait there and went to our next stop to "Ganga Nivas". Swami Sivananda was living there. He is one of the few sanyasis who live in Gangotri during the winter. I believe that he was an engineer but left home to come here and meditate. We prostrated ourselves before him and sat down.

He looked at us. A serene voice questioned us. We were hesitant to open our mouths in front of such a personality. I think he understood and nodded his head affectionately.

Hesitatingly, I asked him, "Sir, may I ask you something?"

He promptly replied, mostly to reassure me, " Why not."

"Sir", I said, "It surprises me that so much of sin is being absorbed by the Ganga yet her water does not get polluted."

He replied, "You are right. Let me tell you a story. When Ganga was forced to flow on earth, she asked Lord Vishnu, 'You are sending me down to clean the sinners of the earth. But what will happen to me. I was very happy here at your feet.' The God of all Lords replied, 'I am giving you the boon that you will never get polluted even when millions have been cleaned of their sins by you if only one sage takes a bath in you. You will be forever clean, you will be forever the cleanser of sins on earth.

You will be called Patit pabani (he who cleans the sins)."

Now Sita asked, "Why this is called as Gangotris?[3]

He replied affectionately, "Because Ganga came down at this place. And presently it has gone back to Gaumukhs".

We paid our respects and departed to meet another very old hermit who also does not talk to anyone and has been living at Gangotri for more than 30 years. As we reached the hermitage, he looked at us and closed his eyes as if in deep meditation. We decided to return without disturbing him. It was almost evening, time to attend the evening prayers with lights. Then we retired to our rooms. On the following day after breakfast, three of us set course to visit another well known hermit named Narahari Maharaj. He welcomed us with a smile. As soon as we sat down, he told us with a smile that all the doubts will be dispelled as soon as you ask for it in your meditation, so don't worry.

I replied, "That is the problem your holiness. I just cannot concentrate. As soon as I close my eyes the mind runs away to a place beyond my control."

He looked at me with affection in his eyes, and replied,

3 This sacred shrine, situated at an altitude of 3,200 metres, is the source of the river Bhagirathi. It is surrounded by the mountain peaks of Shivling, Satopanth and Bhagirathi sisters. Accessible by a motorable road, it is one of the most pious Hindu pilgrimage destinations.

Altitude	:	3,200 metres
Climate	:	Summer : Cool during the day and cold at night.
		Winter : Snow-bound. Touching sub-zero.
Clothing	:	Summer : Light woollens
		Winter : Very heavy woollens.

"What you need is patience and practice. And if you are sincere in your desire, you can get it, no doubt." Finally he told us to try and try again. There is no other solution. We decided to leave after paying our respects.

On our way back we decided to visit another old hermit named Ramananda who had been doing his tapasya completely naked.

Sita asked me, "Dada, are there no women hermits here?"

I looked at her uncertainly and said "Why do you ask?"

"I will tell you laters," she replied evasively.

"I think so."

"Will you be kind enough to lead me to that place", she almost pleaded.

I said, "Why should I mind. If you are ready to walk some distance we can go to that hermitage. I think her name is Krishna Bharati."

She immediately retorted, "Dada I will be extremely grateful if you will take me to see her tomorrow."

Next morning Ajit told me, "The two of you should visit Mataji. I am not too well and want to preserve my energy for the journey to Gaumukh."

We decided to make it to the ashram by ourselves. Sita asked me, "Do you know anything about this Mataji, Dada?"

"Very little. I have heard that she is from a very well to do family and is very well educated. It is very strange that she has renounced the world."

After walking a few kilometres, we located the ashram. Mataji was there to welcome us and no sooner did she see Sita, she hugged her as if the estranged one had just returned from exile.

I didn't understand this overflow of affection because we had just met her. Sita began to cry. She could not control herself.

Mataji consoled her, "My darling, hold on to yourself. Everything will be all right." She told me to sit and went inside with Sita and was there for at least an hour. When they opened the door I saw Sita was a transformed personality. Her face was radiant with joy.

I asked Mataji, "If you don't mind, may I ask a few questions?"

She smiled at me and said, "Go ahead", without any hesitation.

"You have been here for a long time. Have you received salvation?" The moment I asked, I knew that it was foolish question.

She again smiled and said, "I don't know about salvation. But I am in a particular type of bliss, very difficult to explain."

I was becoming bolder and asked again, "You live all by yourself, aren't you afraid of anything?"

"No," came the prompt reply. "The Lord is my saviour." I looked at Sita obliquely and found that she didn't have any reaction to our conversation. She was only looking at Mataji and praying. It seemed her mind was overflowing with joy.

On our way back, Sita said to me, "You wanted to know why I have undertaken this journey?"

I said, "Yes," but I waited. I knew there was some extraordinary explanation.

Sita said, "I don't think there will be another time. I can only say that this pilgrimage of mine is only due to this Matajis".

I looked at her in surprise, and asked, "You knew her before?"

"No I didn't," came the prompt reply.

"But..."

"I saw her."

Now it was my turn to be surprised. "You saw her? How and where?"

"In my dreams. She used to surface in my dreams day after day and used to call me. I didn't know where I would find her. I saw this ashram also in my dreams. Now after such a long wait I have found her and thanks to you."

I had come across many a strange occurrence in my life and lots of them during my journeys through the Himalayas. And I knew it was all true. The girl had found her destination.

We were in time for lunch. After we had eaten, Swamiji told us, "Come with me, I shall show you Lord Shiva's, hair through which the Ganges came to the earth."

121

We were the most willing followers to a place where the waterfall was really like the millions of strands of Lord Shiva hair. Water was falling down 122 mtrs, creating a beautiful rainbow. It was hypnotic.

Swamiji was also kind enough to take us to another hermit named Swami Brahmananda Maharaj. I liked him. He was very kind to us and gently asked, "You have come all the way from the plains. Would go away without visiting Gaumukh?"

I replied, "Maharaj, I wanted to but these two legs of mine are refusing. I have to go back all this distance anyway."

He looked at me for a long time and said, "Go there, my son. Do not worry about anything. The Lord will look after you."

I was startled to hear this order. I looked at him and wondered.

He smiled again, and said, "Don't worry."

I felt the energy from these words and said, "All right Sire, I shall go. I may not get this chance again."

On the following morning Shiupujan left Gangotri along with Sita and their parents and we began our preparations to trek up to Gaumukh.

I kept my finger crossed. The trek to Gaumukh would not be easy because I understood my condition pretty well. With a doubt in my mind, I went to Swamiji for some guidance.

He said, "Don't worry. The guide Dilip Singh is not there

but that won't create any problem. Swami Twatabodhananda along with two other gentlemen is proceeding to Gaumukh. You can go along with them." Saying this he gave me something that looked like herbal medicine to me. I was supposed to swallow it with water. In the evening, Twatabodahnandaji came and Swami Brahamananda introduced us. The kind-hearted hermit agreed to be our guide to our final destination. We were told to buy some dry rations and were told to take two more blankets.

In the morning, the five of us began to walk after having our morning meal. The other two gentlemen were from Bombay. One of them appeared to be in his mid-forties and the other could have been in his sixties. Our destination on that day was Chirbasa at a distance of 20 kilometres. We planned to halt at night at that place and visit Gaumukh the next day. The herbal medicine given by the hermit improved my condition but I still had pain in my knees. I couldn't walk at their pace and began to fall back. Watching my poor state of health, the Swamiji came to help me. He began to walk at my pace, holding my hand. My first journey to Gaumukh was difficult and the path was on dangerous ground. Presently, the path is on much more even, flat ground. The route that we followed has been abandoned.

We were walking on the side of the Southern hill slope of the Bhagirathi. The indication of the path had been given by small, unrecognisable rocks. Swamiji was full of hope and kept my morale high. He kept telling me, "Don't worry, I shall see that you visit Gaumukh and return." I don't want to describe any more of my troubles because that would be rather boring to read. I only prayed for my safety and desired to reach Chirbasa. Whenever I asked about the distance, the wise answer came promptly, "Just there. Carry on, walk and walk." Finally the road led us to Chirbasa (3,606 metres). We accommodated ourselves in an abandoned room without doors and windows. We could see from that place the three peaks of the Bhagirathi at 6,974, 6,512, and 6454 metres respectively.

Nowadays, pilgrims walk another 5 kilometres to Bhojbasa and rest at the ashram of Lalbaba or at the Government rest house. From there, the distance to Gaumukh is only about 4 kilometres. Bhojbasa is at a height of 3,792 metres.

We had to eat the half cooked rice and dal and tried to make ourselves comfortable in that windowless room. We lit a fire but that created more problems. The smoke almost drove us out of the

Bhojbasa

Gaumukh Cave

shelter. I could not sleep even a wink throughout the night. However, in the morning, by seven we were ready to walk to Gaumukh, 10 kilometres away. These last 10 kilometres were not difficult for us. We could walk comfortably on the even ground. And finally, we climbed to a height of 4,197 metres and there was Gaumukh just ahead of us welcoming us into that icy cave. The cave appeared to me to be at a height of about 122 metres, with a width of about 30 metres. These dimensions change due to snowfall and ice formation.

This was the end point of the Gangotri glacier. The glacier itself is 29 kilometres in length and 5 kilometres in width. We could see the other mountain peaks at a distance. Ajit pointed out Shivlinga (6,543 metres). Apart from this the Gangotri glacier is surrounded by the other mountain peaks like the

125

Kalindi, Nilamabar, Kirtisthambha, Swetbaran, Rakta baran. Vasuki Parvat, Sudarshan, Satpanth, Brigupanth, Meruparbat, etc.

By walking only 9 kilometres on the Gangotri glacier, one could reach Tapovan. During my third visit to this place, I made this journey.

It was very cold yet we got ready to take a dip in that icy water. Ajit refused because he was feverish. But the hermit told him, "Don't worry, my son. No one has ever fallen sick by having a dip here at Gaumukh. Rather, they are cured." Ajit heard that from that saintly man and plunged into the icy cold water, and after a while he confided in me that he was feeling better. Walking became a problem as we had to reach Gangotri the same day. We halted at mid-day to eat.

Gangotri Glacier

But the two of us did not have anything with us so we had to remain hungry. Swamiji was leading me back gently through this path. On the other bank we saw a few people standing on the rock; they seemed uncertain about their position. Swamiji told us to wait and went to find out about them. As we feared they were lost and did not know where to go. They couldn't have gone to Gangotri. It was difficult to find your way those days without a guide. Just short of Gangotri, we stopped at the ashram of Falhari Baba. He welcomed us with some fruits and a glass of juice. We felt relieved after this hungry walk.

After reaching Gangotri, we again went to Brahamananda Maharaj and fell at his feet. I said with tears in my eyes, "O! Holy one, you made me go on this difficult journey. It was only due to your power that I could climb this impossible height. I could not have made it on my own." He hugged me and said, "It was HIS desire. Who am I?"

The elderly Bombayite said that he was a heart patient and was told to not to undertake this journey by his physicians. "But here I have completed the trek to Gaumukh also. I didn't listen to my well wishers and took this trip judging all probabilities. But I can say proudly that I am feeling better."

Swamiji smiled and said, "All His will, my dear."

And Ajit added, "I am feeling better despite my plunge into that icy cold water."

Kalindi
Khal

Kalindi Khal, standing 5930 metres above sea level, is situated in the Uttar Kashi District of Uttar Khand. It is well known for its scenic beauty. For many years I had wanted to scale the peak but my dream materialised only in July 1987.

All expedition and trekking beyond the Kalindi Khal are controlled by the Ministry of Defence and prior approval for undertaking any expedition is absolutely essential. Moreover, since the Kalindi Khal area is declared a protected area, the approval and clearance from the concerned Authorities is also a must. But we did not face any hurdle in securing the necessary permits and approval as our expedition was sponsored by the UP Vikas Nigam.

Our team comprised of 20 members including six porters. The Liaison Officer of the U.P. Vikas Nigam appraised us of the expedition thoroughly.

In the morning after breakfast and with a packed lunch, we started our trekking for Bhujwara which is 14 kilometres from Gangotri. The trekking route was not at all difficult to negotiate, and in the afternoon we reached the Tourist Lodge of Bhujwara comfortably. At last the eagerly awaited day arrived for the long expected expedition, the dream of a life time, but also dangerous to undertake. On 19th July,1987, we assembled at the Tourist Bungalow of Gangotri 3131 metres.

Prior to 1987, I had visited Gaumukh twice and stayed at Lal Baba's Ashram as at that time there were no other place where one could spend the night.

Lal Behari Das, known popularly as Lal Baba in this area, finds great satisfaction in feeding and caring for the pilgrims. In return, he expects neither thanks nor money. He had taken up this service at the command of his Guru, Vishnu Das, who told him that if he served the pilgrims with food and shelter, he would achieve salvation. Lal Baba is, therefore, busy all the time doing this very service, sparsely clad in a 'Kaupin', a 'namavali', rubber slippers and wearing a wrist watch. This is the way he serves the Lord.

For acclimatisation, we were advised to visit Tapovan via Gaumukh the next day. The route to Tapovan required negotiating the Gangotri Glacier which is one of the largest glaciers in the world, measuring 32 kilometre and sprawling over 2000 sq.km. The track was through snow and moraine which made walking very difficult. Big cracks and deep holes were observed in the glacier and we had to take care of these as we moved forward. After negotiating the glacier, we had to climb a steep ascent, at the end of which lay the Tapovan Valley.

The valley is simply magnificent, full of bright and colourful flowers and covered with soft green grass walking on which is a pleasure. The valley is hedged on all sides by many snow clad peaks, the closest being Shivling (6543 mtrs) and a few others like Shwetwayan, Tahilu Babak (5852 mtrs), Sudarshan (6507 mtrs), Bhagirathi I (6856 mtrs), II (6,521 mtrs) and III (6454 mtrs), Kharchra Kund (6563 mtrs) and Meru Shikar (6436 mtrs). There is a stream flowing down the valley and also a big lake. The beauty of the snowy peaks is so intoxicating that one forgets everything of this mundane world and remains immersed in the celestial beauty.

Meru Bamak Glacier, locally knows as "Aakash Ganga", is situated here. The waterfall comes down from the top of a peak and joins Gaumukh (3882 feet) which makes it look as if the river Ganga is descending straight from heaven. The water adds to the snout on the other side where water from Raktavaran Glacier (5016 mtrs) joins Gaumukh. We could see the two snouts separated by some distance from each other. But there were many proofs that the location of the snout of the Gangotri was at Gangotri itself where Bhagirath brought down the Ganga. The Bhagirath Sila on the bank of the Ganga at Gangotri could be the spot where Ganga was seen in the beginning. The glacier could be going up to the Raktavaran Glacier, resulting in the Ganga too receiving water only from Raktavaran Glacier and not from Gangotri Glacier; 50% of the Ganga water is fed by the Raktavaran.

We paid our respects to Saik Bala of Tapovan and he entertained us with a cup of hot tea. After resting there for a while, we began the return journey to our camp at Gaumukh. We could cover the distance in two hours. While crossing the snout of the Gangotri, known as Gaumukh, we just touched the ice cold water with our fingers, but dared not take a holy dip. At that very moment, a huge block of ice crashed into the water from the snout with a loud noise, and started floating on the water. It looked wonderful. In no time, the big chunk broke into small pieces which remained floating, creating a beautiful scene.

We returned to Bhojwasa from Tapovan and, after a night's rest, resumed our march the next morning, 22nd July, for Nandanvan, our next camp, which is 10 kilometres from Bhojwara.

The track lay over moraine covered ground with plenty of loose stones. Walking was difficult as well as slow. After about an hour-and-a-half, we reached the junction of the Raktavaran and Gangotri Glaciers. At this point we had to cross an icy stream.

As we proceeded further up Kedar Dome (6815 mtrs), Kedarnath (6922 mtrs) and Virgu Panth (6992 mtrs) became clearly visible. After crossing the Raktavaran Glacier, we changed

A dangerous but beautiful snowfall

course towards the Choturangi Glacier. The junction of Raktavaran, Choturangi and Gangotri Glaciers was fascinating.

Choturangi means four colours. The glacier deserves the name for the richness of the colour it exhibits. The pure whiteness of the glacier is covered with stones of various colours, red, blue and black, creating a beautiful pattern. The whiteness of the snow is covered under the colours of the stones. At this point, we decided to have a little rest and enjoyed the beauty all around before resuming the march.

The track onwards lay through the heart of the glacier. After climbing a very steep slope, we reached Nandanvan. In all it took us five hours to come to this point from Bhojwara.

Nandanvan is a charming valley like Tapovan, but much bigger in size. The side of the valley along the Choturangi is the longer one and on the other end lies the Gangotri Glacier. In this valley, we came across some animal and birds. We could see some snow deer (borar, as they call it locally) grazing freely in the valley, but when they saw us, they ran away. There were deer of bigger size also, but we did not come across any of them although their hoof marks were present. Besides the borar there were a large number of birds, locally known as "peoli kak". They resembled crows but were much smaller in size; their legs and bills were yellow in colour like those of the maina. They were not the least frightened by our presence and came very close to our tents in search of food.

Our tents were pitched by the side of the stream where

grass was in abundance and stones were scattered all round. From here, the Kedar Nath, Bhagirathi (I,II & III), Kedar Dome, Vrigu Panth peaks were visible so clearly that the distance appeared to be very little. The Shivling top is pointed and milky white, giving an appearance of a throne, on which the Lord of the Universe is seated to rule over His empire. The beauty of Nandan Valley, with the surrounding peaks and the colourful appearance due to the glass and stones, is unparalleled in its charm.

After a night's rest, we did a little trekking towards Vasukital for further acclimatisation and then returned to our camp.

The morning of 24th July was a clear one. The temperature touched 48 F. Our march was resumed at 9 o' clock towards Vasukital, at a distance of seven kilometres. We started walking by the side of the Choturangi with Bhagirathi II on the right. It looked as if a hero was standing erect and was touching the sky. The Choturangi Glacier (5320 mtrs) looked beautiful with stones of different colours set on the white snowy background on one side and barren hills stood on the other. The glacier looked dirty because of the stones from the hill that had fallen on it. We

Chandra Parvat from Suralaya

could see Mana Peak (6688 mtrs) and Chandra Peak (6642 mtrs). As we moved forward, we saw an avalanche falling from Chandra Peak.

The way we had to negotiate was very steep and at times narrow, marking our journey risky. The toughest part of the journey was going across a dangerous glacier where no track existed.

After crossing the glacier safely we changed course towards the right and entered Vasuki Tal, a magnificent lake with celestial charm, which made us forget all the fatigue and anxiety we had suffered in reaching this place. The beauty of the lake is indescribable with the peaks of Vasuki Parvat (6700 mtrs), Bhagirathi Shoulder, Mana Parvat (6493 mtrs) casting their shadows on the lake. We camped at Vasuki Tal for the night.

On our way Suralaya from Vasukital

Next morning, the journey from Vasuki Tal began. The track was full of moraine and loose stones scattered around. With much difficulty, the area was crossed and thereafter we reached the Shwetavaran Glacier. The glacier was full of snow tables which are big white ice slabs resting on similar pillars, giving an impression as if an expert marble mason with great craftsmanship has carved out of all these. We travelled for another hour to reach Suralaya Banik (5,456 metres) which is known as Kala Pathar.

At the Feet of the Kalindi Nath

The morning at Chotarangi camp happened to be very clear. The Bhagirathi Shoulder, Mana and Chandra Peaks could be seen very clearly. After the morning chores, everything was ready at about 9.30 am and the journey was resumed for Suralaya Bamak to Sweta Glacier (5,500 metres). We went down to the heart of Choturangi where we came across another glacier whose name was not known, possibly a portion of Suryalaya which joined Choturangi at this point. The junction had to be crossed and it was really a tough job due to the steep slopes, moraine, loose stones and hard slippery ice. After walking for about four hours, we reached the end of the Choturangi Glacier. Thus, we reached the junction of the three glaciers, Choturangi, Kalindi and Mana. At this point, we came to a roaring stream and stopped there bewildered. It was impossible to cross the stream. After some discussion among themselves, one of the porters somehow crossed the dangerous stream with one end of a rope tied round his waist and the other end tied to a big stone. Then he beckoned us to cross the stream by holding the rope. Anyone who let go of the rope would have been washed away by the current. We had to change our clothes quickly and then commenced walking through the middle of the two glaciers, Kalindi and Mana or Chandra. Mana and Chandra Parbat could be seen clearly on our left. Snow everywhere slowed down our progress and finally we decided to pitch our tents in the snow of the Sweta Glacier (5,500 metres) i.e., at the base of the Kalindi Pass. The night temperature dropped to 10° F.

Chandra Parvat at the background

There was snowfall throughout the night and in the early hours of the morning as I came out of the tent, I could not

Entering Kalindi Glacier

locate a single item lying outside. On the 27th morning after breakfast, the journey was resumed at 10.30 a.m. We walked for about an hour over the ice, and then entered the heart of the Kalindi Glacier. The journey was simply a steep climb. Our feet would sink in the

On top Suryalaya Glacier after a snow storm

snow to any depth from 6 to 12 inches and even at times, up to the knees. It was snow all round and we appeared to be

At Kalindi Glacier

floating in a white majestic ocean. Sometimes the snow was soft, and at others, it was hard, making it difficult to walk. As we approached the top, some members had breathing trouble due to the lack of oxygen. The dazzling white snow could cause extreme injury to the eyes and to protect our eyes we had to use goggles. Our companion, Sri Harbans Singh was very particular and made sure that each one of us used goggles, including the porters. He would even get angry with any defaulting individual. At first, I felt that Harbans Singh was creating a fuss over nothing but when I realised that it could cost us our eyesight, I obeyed him gladly. The beauty of that place cannot be described. It is preserved for only the few of us who were present at that moment.

After half an hour's rest on the top we were ready to climb down. We were told that there was no way except to glide down the slope, which is risky and at the same time, dangerous. Because while doing so, if the direction is changed, an accident is unavoidable and that is exactly what happened to me. I could not keep pace with the high speed and was on the verge of a serious accident. Somehow I checked my speed and seeing my danger, a porter quickly came and rescued me. As a result my right knee was injured and it became very difficult to walk further.

On the other side of the Kalindi Khal, at a height of 5624 metres, we resumed our journey for Rajparav (4,910 metres) and two young men were engaged to help me in walking. From the flat snow table, the peaks would jut out, barren with only sand and stones. In the white snowy background, these appeared to be darker. The peaks had many ridges wherein the snow would deposit and the black and white combination would create a very pleasing pattern. The whole layout appeared to be so charming that I could not help getting immersed in the indescribable beauty in spite of my pain. As we walked away from this, there was a little regret in the heart at this separation. A second chance to visit this celestial place semed a remote possibility. However, what I had seen could last me for the rest of my life. Once again, I was overwhelmed by the mercy of the Lord in helping me through this life and death adventure and it was due to His Grace that I escaped an accident which could have been serious. On reaching Rajparav, we rested for the night.

Next day, we resumed our trekking for Arwa Tal. The track we followed lay between the mountain slopes which were snow clad. Melting ice flowed down the slopes forming a stream which ran on further. Tired of walking over stones and moraine, we looked forward to finding some road or even sandy soil by the side of the river. But the expectation was in vain. Freezing cold water streams, glaciers, moraine, and steep slopes up and down, throughout the day, were the only things we came across again and again.

Walking for about an hour brought us to a big lake, Arwa Tal (3,918 metres). This lake was in the middle and a river was flowing by its side where the lake water descended to join in. It looked very beautiful.

We reached Ghastali bridge, over the Saraswati river just after the Arwa and Saraswati crossing, say 500 yards down. On the other side of the river, we could see some huts. Soon we crossed the river and on reaching the huts we were offered hot refreshing tea, which after hours of the bone racking journey, was very enjoyable. They were soldiers who belonged to the Indo-Tibetan Boarder Police Force (ITBP). At first it was decided to have a night's rest at Ghastali, but the party members decided against it. As I was not in a position to accompany them due to excessive pain in the knee, I was left behind in the ITBP camp with my two escorts and advised to start for Badrinath the next morning.

After a night's stay with the hospitable ITBP people, the next morning we were in a hurry to start early in the hope of reaching Badrinath (3114 mtrs) in time to meet the party. A night's rest had reduced my pain to a great extent and I walked almost normally and reached Hanuman bridge on the river Saraswati, about one kilometre, short of Mana village. The river Saraswati flows down between two hills and the descent is an abrupt drop of almost 300 mtrs. At this point of fall, two rocks have joined together in the form of a bridge and the river water flows underneath. Descending to the legend, when Hanuman was carrying the Gandhamadan Parvat, a small rock fell off at this point and this formed the bridge. After crossing the bridge, we reached Mana village and thereafter Badrinath.

Pindari Glacier

Pindari
Glacier

Ever since I began trekking in the Himalayas, I have been in love with them. Whenever I faced a crisis, I ran away to the Himalayas for succour. Walking over the snow and through dense forests for days together works like a magic balm and a cool motherly touch, which wipes out all worries. In such pilgrimages, I have faced many difficult and dangerous situations, but by the grace of God, I have been able to triumph over all of them. This has also proved to be a blessing, in the sense that my dependence on Him has increased.

When I was selected as one of the camp leaders of the Youth Hostels Associations Himalayan trekking programme which was planned for roaming around the Himalayas for a few days, I was very pleased. My companion this time was Manoranjan. The two of us formed the party for the march to Pindari and we reached Almora on our way to the Pindari Glacier. At Almora, we spent the day in contacting the District Magistrate Sri Surjit Kumar Das, for reservations of Dak Bungalows. He was kind enough to write a letter to the Executive Engineer P.W.D. stationed at Bageswar asking him to make our arrangements en route.

Journey Commences at Bageswar

On 30 April, we left Almora in the morning by a UP Roadways bus and within four hours reached Bageswar. It was noon then and straight from the bus stop we went in search of one Sri Kunwar Ram, a clerk in the Tehsil office. Unfortunately, the day being a public holiday on account of Buddha Purnima, Shri Kunwar Ram was not available in his office. Since meeting Kunwar Ram was important, we could not wait for the next day; instead, we went in search of him and ultimately we were able to locate him at his house. He was kind enough to come down to his office and help us in getting accommodation near the bus stop in a hotel called Rajdoot. It was a newly constructed hotel building with a decent appearance, but like all other cities located at high altitudes the place was plagued by power and water shortages. We booked a room with a double bed and had to eat outside the hotel.

After our meal, we went out to see Kunwar Ram's quarters, a newly constructed two-roomed building. From there, Kunwar Ram escorted us to the Tehsildar's residence since his office was also closed. The Tehsildar wrote out a note for the Kanoongo for rendering all assistance to us and also sent messages to all the Patwaris to look after us. From there we went over to the Executive Engineer P.W.D at his residence, who wrote out letters immediately to all the concerned chowkidars to accommode us in the Dak Bungalows on the way to Pindari. The Executive Engineer explained to us that under the new policy, reservation of bungalows was not done datewise and also rooms were not reserved exclusively for any party. All visitors were to be accommodated by mutual cooperation. Therefore, the instructions were in the form of eligibility to stay in bungalows. We found that all along we were the only party staying in the bungalows, except at a place where a party of 35 had already been occupying the rooms before our arrival. In spite of that they offered to share the place with us but since it was already over-crowded we decided to pitch our tents and spend the night outside, rather than jostle with the others in a small space. We also observed that to cope with the rush of visitors, the P.W.D. authorities were constructing extra buildings comprising two suites each.

Bageswar to Loharket

After spending the night at the Bageswar bungalow, we started for Loharket. The first part of the journey from Bageswar to Bharari via Kapkot was by regular bus service. The distance to Kapkot was 25 kilometres from Bageswar, 2 kilometres from Kapkot Bharari. The Dak Bungalow was located at Kapkot and there were a few small hotels at Bharari. After reaching Bharari by about 9.00 am, we set about arranging for porters. In 1980 we could engage two of them at Rs. 14/- per day with food. We had planned to stay at Bharari for the night, but since we had reached the place quite early, we decided to proceed further without wasting a day there. The road was not bad and the P.W.D. were laying a motorable road to be commissioned in a short time. With the road coming up, Loharket is accessible by bus from Bageswar now.

Before starting from Bharari, we had a nice meal with fish curry to muster up enough strength for covering a distance of

17 kilometres. The road ran along the side of the Sarayu river and we were able to walk comfortably, and at about 4.00 p.m. we were at Sheling, a small village at the foot of Loharket. It took us another hour to reach the Loharket P.W.D. Dak Bungalow situated on top of the hill. It was already 5 o' clock in the evening when we reached the bungalow. Walking all the day in the hot sun we were exhausted. At Sheling, we happened to meet Kharaga Ram (Kunwar Ram's brother) who was going to participate in his brother-in-law's marriage feast. He escorted us to Loharket bungalow and looked after the arrangements for our stay there. He took care to speak to the Patwari and other officials and asked them to look after us. He also went round to the villagers and informed them about us. From the bungalow, we could see the wheat fields, cultivated on terraces all around and these looked wonderful. The villagers were busy in harvesting the fields. For harvesting, they were using two sticks to extract the wheat grain rather than adopting the normal method of cutting the crop. We had never seen this method in use before. I also observed that most of the villagers were well off, with the exception of a few. After Kharaga Ram's information, some of the villagers came to the Dak Bungalow to see us and to pay their respects. Some of them also offered us milk according to the tradition of the area.

Loharket to Dhakuri

The night at Lahorkhet Dak Bungalow was comfortably spent

and in the morning I was very fresh. Getting ready at 5.30 a.m., we resumed our journey to cover the 11 kilometres to Dhakuri. The road was very steep and appeared to have endless ups and downs. There were no trees along the road to provide any shade for us. As we climbed higher, the golden wheat fields below appeared magnificent. After struggling for some six hours on the road in the hot sun, we reached the Dhakuri P.W.D. Bungalow. To our surprise, we found the peon of the Patwari had already informed the chowkidar and the room was ready. He was good enough to have a fire going in the hearth and also put water on it to cook khichuri. Although our porters took a little time to reach the bungalow, a little while later, our food was ready, and we enjoyed the khichuri. To relax, we took our camp chairs out and sat down on the lawns and enjoyed the snow clad peaks and the cool breeze. The peon suggested that we could reach Khati that very evening. Although we were prepared to accept the suggestion, our porters were unwilling to move any further; so we had to drop the idea and had to rest there for the night.

The peon who helped us at Dhakuri, had met us earlier at Loharket also. He had a bandage on one of his legs. We asked him about the bandage. He didn't answer directly but us that one of the members of the Japanese team to Pindari to study the glacier in January 1980 had met with a fatal accident and had died there. The body was still there and it was expected to be removed by a helicopter from Delhi any day. The peon had the difficult task of keeping watch over the dead body and also keeping the S.D.M. Bageswar informed. He was responsible for this and it was a pretty difficult task. Perhaps the peon had sustained an injury while doing this duty and hence the bandage.

Dhakuri to Khati

On the morning of 3rd May 1980, we got ready by 5.30 a.m. as usual and started moving ahead. The road was nice through a dense forest of rhododendron trees laden with flowers. The red, purple, yellow and white flowers were simply magnificent. It was a feast for the eyes. Added to this, the cool morning breeze helped us to walk faster and in two-and-a half hours we covered a distance of about 8 kilometres distance and reached Khati, situated at 7,500 feet. Half way from Dhakuri to Khati was a gradual slope and the rest of the road was through wheat fields. We could see some terrace gardens also. There were many villages here. And a river flowed by the side of the hills.

We continued our journey without stopping at Khati. One of our porters, Dharam Singh, was not a good man, and on some pretext or other, was creating problems for us. Soon after reaching Khati, he was determined to cook his food and to stay there for the night. I was not agreeable to this and put pressure on him to move on, but to no avail. Finally, I threatened him with termination of our contract. At that moment, a local boy arrived and we asked if he would go with us . He was readily agreeable and I thought that was my chance to do away with Dharam Singh's services. But Dharam Singh was also clever and seeing my stern attitude, started walking fast without any further excuses.

Beyond Khati

After walking for about an hour, we reached a stream. We sat down be side it and lunched on roti with achar saved from the morning tiffin. The porters also had their store of 3 to 4 rotis each.

With the rotis and a little rest, we resumed walking by the side of the river Pindari. The walk was very comfortable with plenty of shady trees available. The murmuring river appeared to be goading us to go forward. After walking about 6 kilometres more, we reached a level place by the side of the river with a plenty of grass. We met a poor old man living at the place in a hut, engaged in grazing buffaloes. He offered us milk and in return we paid him two rupees. He was extremely happy at this gesture. I am quite sure he hadn't expected anything in return for his generosity.

After crossing the river we found that the forest was much more dense. We had not seen such a dense forest earlier. There was an abundance of bamboo, which the villager used to make basket's. The sun was hot but walking in the shade was very pleasant. We saw a number of waterfalls cascading from the mountains which seemed to be touching the sky. The scene ry was so remarkable quite we sat down for that a while to enjoy it.

Dwali Bungalow

Covering 11 kilometres from Khati in four hours, we reached the Dwali Bungalow, situated at the junction of the Pindari and Kafni rivers. The Kafni Glacier was not far away from the junction but due to lack of a proper road connection it is unapproachable. The murmuring of the two rivers was audible from the bungalow. The place was very calm and absolutely quiet, undisturbed by any living creature. On our way, we happened to meet a group of 18 members of the N.C.C. from Kanpur, who were returning after a visit to the glacier. With the season on, it was expected that many more groups would proceed to the place, probably disturbing the silence.

The Dak Bungalow Chowkidar, Khusal Singh, was a jolly old fellow. During the conversation, while our food was being cooked, he had a dig at Bengalis who prepare watery khichuri and then fight over the issue of who has consumed more. Also that Bengalis soak 'chura' in hot water and eat it in the morning. We enjoyed the conversation with Khusal Singh since these are common Bengali habits. In the meantime, the porters had completed their jobs and we finished our night meal with roti and potato curry. After a good night's rest. we resumed our journey the next morning from the Dwali Dak Bungalow. Soon we crossed 10,000 feet. The road was not bad with gradual ups and downs which were not very difficult to negotiate. We walked over snow several times. As we gained height, we observed that the rhododendron trees which had been standing upright proudly, were now lying flat on the ground as if making Shastanga Pranams to Mother Nanda Devi or some other God with the offering of their flowers. Seeing the trees in this state, we also derived inspiration to move forward and onward.

As we moved further up beyond the snow line, the vegetation became sparse. The size of the trees became smaller and due to the snow, the trees, instead of standing erect were down on the ground.

Camp Phurkia

After walking for two- and-a-half hours during which we covered five kilometres, we reached Phurkia situated at 10,700 feet. We decided to stay at Phurkia for the day and enjoy the sun and the snowy peaks.

After our arrival at Phurkia, a Japanese mountaineering team, consisting of 6 or 7 members of the Pamor Dwar Expedition, who were camping there, moved out. The whole team consisted of young men and boys. With their departure, the Dak Bungalow was entirely at our disposal. It was Sunday, and the construction workers did not turn up. The Chowkidar too had gone with the Japanese team, so we were the 'monarchs of all we surveyed.' At noon, the bright sun was covered with clouds and by the evening there was a light shower and also snowfall at Pindari. The Dak Bungalow was all right except for the bathroom. Which was in a condition deplorable. Extremly dirty and absolutely unfit for use. We had to go out in the open to attend to Nature's calls.

Assaulting 'Zero' Point

With nightfall, we were on the last leg of our journey. We were to reach the 'Zero' point at 3648 mtrs, at a distance of 7 kilometres from Phurkia. The Bungalow Chowkidar was to they has mored out accompany the Japanese team with some load and offered to lead us for some distance. We got ready at 4.30 a.m. while it was still dark; and resumed walking in the inadequate moonlight.

After half an hour, we found that the road was completely covered with snow which had frozen hard. We were not able to get a foothold on the snow and as a result were slipping down at every step. I fell down and narrowly escaped rolling down the hill. We had no rope with us, so we could be roped to bind of all us together to prevent any single individual from falling down, nor an ice axe to cut a foothold for our feet. We were managing with the help of a stick only. The chowkidar was supporting me from the back. In spite of all precautions, I fell down again. Fortunately the two coolies caught hold of my arms and helped me to stand up. Thereafter, Manoranjan and the porters also slipped; but the worst was for the chowkidar who went down 8 mtrs. But for a large rock which prevented him from tumbling further, he would have been in the Pindari river. The entire slope of the hill from the top down to the river was covered with snow and we were trying to walk in the middle of the snowy slope. It was not only but very dangerous too difficult.

It is said that difficulties do not come alone. At a moment when we were between the devil and the deep sea, the chowkidar also deserted us to keep his assignment with the Japanese team whose tents were visible on the other side of the river. We were left helpless in a very difficult situation and felt terribly depressed. In front we saw a snow covered area of about two furlongs or more; but perceiving the dangers and the difficulties involved, we dared not attempt crossing it. We looked at it helplessly and even thought of giving up the idea of crossing the snow in front to reach the 'Zero' point. However, divine succur came in the form of encouragement from our porter Chander Singh. He suggested that we go down first and then attempt the upward climb from a new position. We agreed, but going down some distance towards the river we found it was very steep and we were not able to keep ourselves steady. Thus, for the next two hours, we constantly vacillated hither and thither trying to establish a foothold for forging ahead but failed in every attempt. Ultimately, we reached a point from where further movement to any side was not possible. To our horror we noticed that the snow was melting, and boulders big and small, started rolling down. The road was sandy and to attempt crossing the gorge was very risky. Our porter Chander somehow crossed the gorge and was all the time encouraging us to go forward. We stood still for a few minutes, unable to take a decision and at last with the help of Chander we crossed that dangerous and risky sandy gorge, staking our very lives. On reaching the other side of the gorge, we were in a position to walk upwards.

At last we came to the snow line, and mustering up all our courage we started crossing it. By this time, the sun had came up and the hard surface of snow became soft due to the heat. The night's snow had frozen hard and it was not possible to walk on it but with the surface becoming soft due to the sun's heat, we could get a foothold and walk steadily. The change in the situation delighted us, and what had seemed impossible a few moments earlier became possible. We were able to walk steadily and 'Zero' point was within our reach.

We reached the temple of Nanda Devi and Shiva Shakti. This was a small stone building with a slate roof. The images inside were beautiful. We offered a few chocolates and also some money and prayed for our safety. We also noticed a small room attached to the temple. The room was big enough for two to three persons to spend a night in case of necessity. However, room was under three feet of snow and it could be used only if cleared. We left behind our extra luggage and food to walk up to 'zero' point.

'Zero' Point Conquered

Very soon we were on the 'Zero' point. What a sight! What a scene! We were simply overwhelmed. It was snow and snow all around. In front there was the Pindari snout which stood like a huge ice cream cone surrounded by snow-clad mountains. We looked down at the fields below; they were also covered in snow. We were as if in a kingdom where only white, the sign of purity, prevailed. We were charmed and our hearts were full of joy. We had forgotten all the risks and dangers we had faced earlier in reaching the place.

While entering the glacier we saw to our left, on the other side of the Pindari river, Nanda Ghunti, Baljuri, Pawari Dwar, Nanda Khat, Pindari glacier snout and Bangattia and many other unknown peaks. To enjoy this heavenly beauty, we sat down at that spot and took many photographs. By 10 o'clock the sky became cloudy and we prepared for our return.

Return Journey

We reached the small temple where we had left our belongings while going up. We enjoyed our store of hard roti with achar and after that continued our return journey. On the way it started snowing and we had to run to avoid the snowstorm. Somehow we reached the Phurika bungalow, for shelter in good time. At the bungalow, we met a party from Nainital. After resting for some time, we continued the journey to reach

Dwali by 3.00 p.m. By this time, we were very tired and hungry also. Reaching the Dwali Bungalow we found that a team of 35 members belonging to the Central School, New Delhi, were occupying the rooms of the bungalow, leaving no space for us. Luckily, we had our tents and we pitched them for the night. The boys offered us rice and curry and since we were very hungry, we accepted gladly. Later our porters cooked khichuri at night, but I was in no mood to eat. We calculated the time from early morning when we had started from the Phurika Bungalow for 'Zero' point and thereafter coming down to Dwali. In eight hours, we had covered about 23 kilometres. No wonder that we were so tired. And I found I developed fever at night, with shivering. I spent the night in great discomfort.

Down to Khal Juni

On the morning of 6th May the school party got ready at 3.00 a.m. and left the place at 4.00 a.m. for Pindari. A little later, at 5.00 a.m., we started on our return journey. It took us three hours to cover the 11 kilometre distance, and we reached Khati. While we relaxed, the porters got busy in preparing the only dish that they knew. And having finished our brunch we resumed our march at noon so that we could reaching Khal Juni village as soon as possible. The sun was pretty hot, and walking was becoming difficult. We had had no respite for the last 3-4 days. Even a short distance of going up or down was becoming impossible for us. We walked very slowly and after an hour reached a hilltop at a height of 1520 metres. At this point, we heard that we were to cross another hill to go down to Khal Juni village. We were half dead by now. It appeared very difficult and we had no strength left to move forward. At this point, we hired a boy for Rs. 10 to lead us onward. We started following a cattle path through the forest, under the shade of the trees. Surprisingly, we observed that the hill had an abundance of trees and we discovered that the village Panchayat was very strict about not allowing any cutting down of the trees. It was remarkable as such sentiments seem to be absent elsewhere in the country.

We followed our guide through an unending road. It was a great struggle to climb the hill. We rested for a while and then started walking down through some non- existing tracks but fortunately under the shady trees. The ground was full of dry leaves and to walk over them was an onerous task. On our way, we came across a Bhutia hut where a few dogs were keeping watch. One of them started chasing us. In spite of our best efforts we could not dissuade him from running after us, particularly after me, a Sadhu dressed in saffron clothes. He continued chasing us, scaring the daylights out of us. After a long chase, he gave up, considering us a poor match for his might, but we heaved a sigh of relief.

After a while we could see the village and almost started running towards it. God was kind enough to bring us near the village when every ounce of our strength had been exhausted. We approached the village headman who received us very cordially. To recover our strength, he immediately arranged for tea and milk and showed us our shelter for the night which was reasonably comfortable. A clean small room to sleep and an attached room to cook our food. The main livelihood of the villagers was cultivation and both men and women worked to raise the crops. Due to scanty rains, the crop was poor. The area had no hospital anywhere nearby and ailing folks couldn't get any medical help. While they came to meet me, their only request was for medicine. I gave them whatever was available with me. That made them happy. I was also happy to be able to serve them.

A Visit to Sahasra Dhara

Next day, 7th May, we thought of visiting Sahasra Dhara, the origin of the Saraju river. We set out early in the morning, accompanied by our guide, Diwan Singh, hired for Rs.10 since our previous guide, Dharam Singh, was tired and stayed back to prepare the meals. The road was mostly through the villages by the side of wheat fields. While walking through the village we could see more of it. It was a regular small township with paved roads and lanes. People were living together in a collective

Sahasra Dhara

161

manner. There were a few kuchha huts also inhabited by harijans who appeared to be comparatively poorer. They earned their livelihood by making bamboo mats and baskets and also by cultivating the land. The village as a whole appeared to be prosperous. Within an hour we crossed over to Jhuni village which was bigger than Khal Jhuni. There was a school here in which children from both villages could study.

After walking for about two hours, we reached the Saraju river. The way was down and down, through thick woods, but there was danger from wild bears. We reached the waterfront where we found a waterfall cascading from the top of the hill as if it was falling straight from the sky. Although we had seen many falls on our way to Pindari, this spot was the origin of the Saraju river, said to be from a large number of springs, perhaps a thousand in number. That is why the place is called Sahasra Dhara. It is considered very holy by the villagers. We could have gone further to Satamuli, the source of the river, but since we were tired, we didn't press for it, nor was the guide willing to take us there. We saw a nice Shiva Temple there and two young sadhus engaged in meditation in a small room close to the temple. We finished our tiffin of dry roti and then achar and walked back to the village.

We were entertained by the headman of Juni village on our return. He took us to his house and offered us tea and milk, and also gave a cup full of pure ghee extracted from cow's milk. We consumed a little ghee and saved the rest of it. In the morning, our porter Dhara asked for some ghee for preparing dal from the small quantity I had saved. Reluctantly I parted with some. The ghee of the region is very famous for its quality. I liked its taste. The headman saw our preference for the ghee and gave us a little more. I was overwhelmed with emotion. Such concidences have happened so many times. I desired the ghee, the Lord saw the desire and fulfilled it immediately. I didn't ask anyone, but I got it anyway.

After enjoying our mid-day meal of hot rice and dal flavoured with the famous ghee of Juni village, we took leave of the villagers and moved on. The villagers came to bid us farewell. Our attachment had grown only in one night and we were moved by their feelings. We passed the Durga Temple on the top of the hill. The villagers walked with us and sincerely asked us to come and live with them again. They would make place for us in the temple. I could only nod and wipe away my tears.

It was noon when we resumed our journey. The sun was hot. It had no pity on us. Luckily the path was downhill. We reached a village called Supi and halted for a few minutes at a roadside tea shop for a little water and tea.

We had walked for hardly 20 minutes, when the sky became dark and there was thunder. It started raining and soon turned into a hailstorm. We were caught in a helpless state since we could see no shelter anywhere nearby. We began to run hopelessly and suddenly we noticed a big projecting rock. There was enough space under it for us to take shelter. Somehow, we managed to save ourselves from the heavy rain, which continued for about 15 minutes. As the sky cleared, I came out of our hiding place and looked around; we were surprised that there were no other shelter anywhere nearby other than this rock. We thought again about God's Grace in abundance. The rain had descended on us suddenly but that was the very spot to give us shelter under that only rock. Others might be surprised by such coincidences, but I was not . I had received His blessings many times in my journeys through the Himalayas.

Night at Shelling Village

Continuing to walk further, we reached a motorable road. This road connecting Bharari and Loharkhet was under construction. It was five in the evening when we reached Shelling village. We had been walking for about eleven hours and had covered a distance of 28 kilometres. all of us except, Dharam Singh who had not accompanied us in the morning to visit the source of Saraju river. He had that extra energy and wanted to press on further for another 17 kilometres to Bharari. I looked at him in disgust and threw myself on the bed for the night's rest. Our old friend, Kharag Singh was living in a village close to Shelling and we requested the shopkeeper to send word to him. He came and was very happy to see us. We reached Bageswar after three days.

Pancha Challi

Chiplakot Darma Valley, Pancha Chulli Base

It all happened in the month of September. I had a lurking desire to visit the Hindu pilgrimage shrine at Chiplakot at a height of 4742 mtrs. It is one of the many far away places of Hindu mythology and only the seekers of religion go in search of them. to quench their desire to be a part of that serenity and receive the blessings of the Gods. It was by chance that I met Mr. Dharmendra Kumar, the ADM of Pithoragarh, who kindly consented to take me along on this treacherous journey. He was doing his duty but for me it was nothing but divine intervention. The Lord desired me to see Him. Permission from the District Magistrate proved no difficulty at all as the ADM himself was my guide.. Otherwise clearance from the CID would have needed to visit such a place of strategic importance.

On the following day, I commenced on the journey with this official at about 3.00 p.m. in his official jeep. The party consisted of four people: the ADM, myself, and two of his supporting stuff. After all, an IAS officer has to be looked after. We halted at Kanalichina,30 kilometres from Pithoragarh, where the ADM met some of the BDOs, completed his official sojourn and commenced the journey to Okhla. From Okhla, you may either go to Dharachula or to Thai. We took the road to Dharachula, which wound through the field and terrace cultivation. It was very pleasing to see the greenery of the paddy and mandua fields. The chalai flowers were in bloom. As I looked back from the jeep, it seemed to me as if a number of

Persian carpets of varied hues has been thrown around. The beauty of chalai in this part is that when it is green it is eaten as a vegetable, and once harvested, it produces "Ramdana" or as the locals call it, Khai. The Ramdana laddo of North India needs no separate mention. They are light to eat and delicious. The jeep wound its way through the green fields and thick forests, and along the deep gorges, through which ran the swift rivers. We crossed many dancing hill springs. It was a driver's peril, but I was blissful and a sense of contentment was spreading through my limbs. My personal advice to those who only want to escape the summer heat of the plains is, never come to the hills during the summer if you want to enjoy the divine beauty. I speak from complete conviction from my over 30 years of experience in the Himalayas. Winter will greet you with its white coat, but summer is brown and hostile. You may have the comfort of cool air-conditioning but that's about all. You must never miss the post rainy season sunset in the hills.

We reached Dharachula in the darkness. This is a small township 900 mtrs above the sea level on the bank of the river Kali. Across the river is Nepal. Cross the tiny bridge and the Nepalese beauties will greet you with open arms. But do not depend too much on that otherwise you will lose out on your primary objective. The Nepalese villagers foray across the river to India for their daily rations or some livelihood. The village looked beautiful to me. On the foothills of the mountain, the slope rolls into the river, through the green fields. You may click the beauty in your mental retina.

The PWD Bungalow, built near the river, was our resting place for the night. The visit was probably preplanned because many from the local populace came to greet the ADM who had been the Sub-Divisional Magistrate of this place a few years earlier. And he must have been a good officer, because he was popular. The BDO of the place came to see him. He didn't have much of a choice in any case. The ADM writes his confidential report. The BDO confirmed the arrangements for the onward journey on the following morning. I was an unnecessary appendix to this journey, but the BDO had no choice.but to accept me. He dared not question his boss about me. Next in line was the Sub Divisional Magistrate who treated us to a good dinner.

A golden rule to be remembered while journeying though the Himalayas is: never be late to start. Forget your lazy pace at home. You may slow down during the evening but never ever be late to commence your journey. On the following morning, I got up early but senior Government officials cannot be hurried, they have their own pace. I went to buy some eatables but not much was available. The apples tasted sour to me. Salted biscuits had not been heard of. The journey commenced at about 10.00 a.m. after some light refreshment. Alaged, at a distance of 20 kilometres from Dharachula and at a height of 1368 mtrs, was the destination. The motor vehicle covered the distance easily and left us at a point from where we had to climb on foot through a treacherous route full of thorns and paddy fields to Jumma village. Sri Puran Singh, the Gram Pradhan, was there to receive us. He served us tea and roasted maize as snacks. It tasted good to me. In any case, I was hungry. It looked to me that Sri Puran Singh was rich and was well respected by the villagers. We had a good lunch and at 5 p.m. we decided to climb further into the hills to reach the other side of the village. We reached the village temple adjacent to a big playground, difficult to find at such a height anywhere in the hills. On enquiry, I was told that the height of the place was 1976 mtrs above sea level. As sun went down behind the tall trees, the villagers gathered in the small temple, which did not not boast of any deity. But devotional music came from the heart of these simple people. I looked into the lonely room of the temple and found something was covered with a cloth. I was told the cloth is removed only during Durga Astami day and the Goddess Durga is worshipped. The floor could not provide us with much comfort but we decided to lie down on a hard bed and spent the night in the temple itself. We drifted into an uncomfortable sleep but the brightness of the morning with its breathtaking beauty mesmerised us. Looking up as far as the eyes could see, there were the snow-clad mountains of Nepal. The Nam Phu and Arguajung peaks were beckoning us from that distance.

We ate at about 10 a.m. and began to walk. The party

consisted of Sri Dharmendra, the BDO of Dharachula, his peon, Sri Puran Singh, one schoolteacher, four porters and myself. There was no well-defined route, we had to trek through a bushy path and there was a gradual ascent. The route gradually passed through a dense forest of deodar and other trees rich in timber quality. We could see the far away villages. I wondered how these villagers survive. What could be their means of living? How did they get medical help to such a hostile place? We walked, we ascended and descended number of times, we walked along the plain path and that is how we covered a period of three hours. No habitation could be found. The last place of civilisation was Jumma. There was rich grassy land, but except for two desperate families, we couldn't find any other living being. We sat close to one of the families and began to make tea. I didn't have a taste for the tea. I wanted to drink a little water, and asked for same. The family members pointed towards a shallow pit filled with rain water. It looked to me a social drinking place. The drifting shepherds drink the water, the buffaloes have their regular bath in the same water and the tea was also prepared from that water. I suppressed my desire to drink the water and preferred to remain thirsty and wait for the next opportunity. The locals have faith in the purity of the rain water but I had yet to get used to it.

We rested for a while and resumed our walk. The guide showed us the path and we were good followers. Under his able command, we moved forward over knee deep, grassy uneven ground. I saw a "monal", the rare Himalayan bird that looked like a peacock to me without a tail. And then we stumbled into the rarest of beauty. I had never even imagined that there could be another **Valley of Flowers** in the whole world. I was proved wrong. The expanse of the valley full of flowers was beyond any description. A kaleidoscope of colours touched the horizon. I could find neither the beginning nor the end. I was not ready to believe that there only seven basic colours. I have visited the famous Valley of Flowers in Bhuyinder valley near Joshimath but this was no less. There were numerous varieties of trees and flowers. Rhododendron and Ratpa of light blue colour grew there. These do not grow beyond a height of 3800 mtrs. We were in an ocean of colours. I thanked God and Sri Dharmendra for showing me such beauty. Thank God, tourists have not found the place yet. Otherwise its beauty would have been lost. The Valley of Flowers has lost much of its charm due to the invasion of civilisation. This Valley of Flowers comes into full bloom after the rains and withers away soon enough. If one has to enjoy this beauty, one has to come fully kitted because no life saving comforts are available here. One should not forget to bring water lest one wants to be satisfied by drinking from the rainpits I have described earlier. I hope the ITDC does not take this place up as its next project. Let it remain a trekker's paradise.

I saw an Antirrhinum kind of flower in full bloom. The seeds of these flowers looked like Balsam flower seeds and tasted very nice to me. The locals call it "Kaju." I respect their kaju which could be found above the height of 3800 mtrs or above, no resemblance of the kaju that we know. Probably the simple folks here do not know what the real kaju is or else they would have given it some other name. However, I ate the seeds, and walked on, avoiding the poisonous plants. But I had a feeling that these are medicinal plants that we do not know about yet. Ayurveda lost its charm a long time ago. Aconite flowers were in plenty. We walked through a big field full of grass locally called "Gaju" . Out of nowhere we came across a cave surrounded by flowers of various kinds. I could see some yellow flowers like Calendula but much smaller in size. The cave could accommodate at least twenty people. Rain water from the hilltops flow through the cave and gets deposited in a depression. But it could contain just about two buckets full of water. This was the only water that we could use for washing, drinking, etc. I can recall that the name of the place was Gumpha or Garamphu, at a height of 3192 mtrs above sea level. No doubt, a romantic place surrounded by flowers, if you could only avoid hypoxia. We managed to clear a little place to spread our beds for the night. The ground was damp due to the constant water flow from both sides of our beds. I tried to sleep on an island, shivering throughout the night. The bed made out of dry leaves was no comfort at all. The stone roof on top was almost touching my nose. I could smell the mud. I looked at the fire created by the porters with dry leaves. Finally the warmth of the fire led me to leave my makeshift bed and sit near its warmth and comfort. The night dawned into a beautiful morning. We began by having our tea. There was dew on the grass and on the flower plants. Shoes and clothes didn't take any time get wet. We were walking through a wooded area, the sun refused to shine on us through such barriers. We were walking above the height of 3000 mtrs. I felt cold. We walked for about two hours through the flowers and Ratpa (Rhododendron) forest. And once we broke out of the forest, it was only Gaju and Gaju as far as we could see. It was not easy to negotiate through this Gaju and on an up and down path. This route led us to a glacial moraine path. It was difficult to walk but somehow we managed to chug along slowly. By noontime, we reached a small stream and halted to cook our lunch. Mr.Dharmendra was looking ill. He had not slept well at night and now he couldn't take it any more. He had a splitting headache and felt feverish. He had no strength left in him to proceed any further. He pleaded with us to go without him. But I refused. I decided that the journey would either proceed with Dharmendra or end right there. I thought this could either be high altitude sickness or the poisonous plants may have affected him. Somehow he managed to move along with us, helped by the fellow travellers. The progress was very slow through the grassy land. By evening we reached the top of a hill. The sight was exhilarating. We could see Jaljivi and the Gouri river and many other places. Even Almora could be seen at a distance. Walking became slightly more comfortable through the smaller grassy but plain field. The great Pancha Chulli peaks could be seen not very far from the place we stood at. The clear sky kept our morale high. The mountain tops could be at heights greater than 4256 mtrs. Finally, we reached the Chiplakot area, a green valley adorned by velvety flowers, beautiful beyond description.

We discovered another small cave to spread our beds for the night, but only four or five people could be accommodated. All around was a dry glacier /moraine. We left the BDO and his boss in the cave and ran to touch the water of Chiplakot Lake, only a mile further up. We climbed a hilltop and slid down through grassy patches to the lake. It was small, perhaps about 91 mtrs × 60 mtrs in dimension and about 3 mtrs deep. The bottom could be seen very clearly. We saw many types of coins in the water that must have been offered by earlier pilgrims. There was no temple. But the Lord was worshipped in the belief that Lord Shiva was hiding here in the water. He would come out if he was pleased. As such, the pilgrim offered flowers, fruits and coins for atonement. There was huge stone inside the lake and that was the object for worship. We did our circumbulation and worshipped Him along with the villagers. We learnt that the villagers come on this pilgrimage once in three years. They would come together, worship together and leave, looking after each other. They never visit this place a second time during the same year. They said that they would remain on the bank of the lake for only a day and would not return to see it again the next day – such was the custom. Sins are washed by only one visit, and one must never return. I had to forego my wishes for a return visit. I picked up a coin with the image of Goddess Durga on it. Immediately a villager warned me. "Don't do it. You will get into trouble.' I quickly left the piece where it belonged. "The things offered to God, belong to Him. You do not have any right over it. Do not invite the wrath of his Holiness." Such was the belief of these simple folks. I remembered a pundit from Dharachula. He had asked the ADM about the purpose of his visit. The ADM answered that from the official position he came to inspect the lakes which could be turned into fishery. The pundit shook his head in disbelief. He said, "No one goes to the lakes with any other intentions than to worship the God. He won't let you go anywhere close to them." The senior Government official refused to believe such nonsense. And it just happened that despite being perfectly healthy, he had to stay away from Chiplakot Lake. He could not inspect his future fishery. He had already visited Lipu Lake at 5168 mtrs but only at 4560 mtrs he fell ill. Why did he get high altitude sickness here? Did the aconite strike him? But we had also gone through those aconite fields. Then why did we not get the same aconite punishment? I believe that the Lord kept him away. The villagers do not like any adverse remark about their God. Religion is their mode of life. It was late and we could not visit the other two lakes.

We returned to the small cave. The dimensions were very small. We selected a broader portion and the others crawled to a much narrower side and spread themselves out for the night. The large opening of the cave was initially covered by some sticks but these got blown away in no time. The cold night wind kept us awake. No one will understand sheer misery unless he has spent an autumn night at a height of 4560 mtrs without many woollens.

We could not eat because there were no cooking medium. We did not carry a kerosene stove. Dry wood or leaves were not available at that height. We depended on the arrangements by the villagers and did not have any knowledge about the environment at all. They could provide us only with some sweets, which was insufficient. Hunger, exhaustion, cold and uneven ground kept me awake for the second consecutive night. I only prayed to God I would not fall sick. I was amazed at the others. They slept throughout the night and I kept the night watch.

The cave was surrounded by moraine. It must have been inside a glacier once upon a time. Once the ice melted and the glacier line moved up, it left the debris for us. Another cold night finally broke into a lovely dawn. The sun rose in the eastern sky reminding us of the famous Gyatri mantra "Om Bhur Bhuba sha," etc. But we were not up to it to chanting the hymn. We had to descend quickly and find some food for ourselves. We hurriedly retraced our steps. I looked into my meagre belongings and was surprised to find some broken biscuits. Then the sun came out from the behind Pancha Chulli, gold in colour, making Pancha Chulli glow.

We began to walk slowly through a frosty path. Dharmendra was yet pick up strength. He needed assistance. Once we reached the stream, we cooked our food but Dharmendra could not. We picked up our tired bodies and limbs and began to walk again. We reached a Gumpha and decided to stop over for the night, but when it was discovered that we did not have anything to eat, we decided to walk. Dharmendra had to be carried by two people – he could not proceed even a step further without assistance. He had to be literally dragged. And, finally, a strong porter decided to carry him on his back. Night was creeping in. We halted at a place to get some warmth by burning some bamboo sticks. Again we commenced our journey, using the burning bamboo sticks as torches. These also got burnt out. Torches could not be used because the cells had all been discharged. The villagers picked up speed leaving me behind. They knew the way well but I could not keep up with them. Neither could I find the path in that darkness. I proceeded blindly in the general direction hoping desperately that I wouldn't fall into a deep gorge or any such trouble. A little later, I found my companions resting. They picked up the trail and began to walk. I fell and broke my walking stick, but thank God it was not my hand. We walked continuously for about 18 hours from morning till midnight, and covered a distance of about 40 kilometres in the hills. Exhaustion and tiredness was in every limb of ours. Luckily, we were accommodated in the school building and also provided with the utmost luxury of cots and beds. And also there was water nearby. We washed ourselves in the middle of the night and a miracle happened at that moment. Mr. Dharmendra became absolutely fit. He became normal with no difficulty whatsoever. Like all of us, he was hungry also. Sri Puran Singh provided us with some milk, followed by atta and potato. We cooked a hearty meal of potato curry and paratha in the early morning hours. I spread myself on that de luxe bed and kept thinking. The villagers at Dharachula had cautioned us that Chiplakot is holy, perhaps holier than even Kedarnath, don't demean it. Don't show any kind of disrespect. The wrath of the God can be very severe. Sri Dharmedra refused to believe about the admonitions of the panditji and I saw what happened to him with my own eyes. Even today, I haven't been able to figure out why he suffered and how he recoverd.

We were not a in hurry in the morning. With the success of the journey, happiness was seeping through my bones. Weariness was all forgotten. We ate our breakfast. The host was the Gram Pradhan himself. And after lunch, at 11 am or so we decide to leave for Tawaghat at a distance of 20 kilometres from Jumma village. The jeep arrived at about noon and we handed over ourselves to the driver.

Pancha Chulli

Following the successful visit to Chiplakot (1672 mtrs), I decided to see Pancha Chulli. But I was told about the difficulty of the trek. The route did not provide anything for a trekker. Food and shelter were difficult to come by. Discerning my keenness, Puran Singh arranged a porter for me. Sri Dharmendra extended my permit upto Dukku village of Darma Valley and gave me his blankets also. He gave me a permit to purchase atta and rice.

Tawaghat is at the junction of the Kali and Dhauli rivers at a height of 1124 mtrs. It is a small place, with one or two tea stalls to cater for the very minimum requirements of the scanty population. There is a PWD bungalow and many military barracks. The caretaker was instructed to provide me with shelter for the night and also didn't forget to inform the local police about my journey and safekeeping. I was grateful. The police officer promptly sent wireless messages about a lonely insane human wanting to trek through some hazardous route. The river Kali originates from a glacier near Mansarovar and flows along the border of Nepal and India. It dances through the hills to Tanakpur. The Banabasa bridge could be seen over the river which links Nepal with India. The other river, Dhauli, originates from a glacier near Pancha Chulli ahead of Darma Valley. Earlier, the pilgrims for Kailash used to go via this place. One can find the trekking route from Tawaghat to Lipu Lake, which is the last border post of India under complete military protection, and that is why civilians are not allowed beyond Tawaghat without a permit.

Sri Dharmendra left by 3 pm. I thanked him for all the arrangements. My porter Sri Jayabhan Ram went out to grind the wheat in a pan chakki which turns the wheels by hydel power. I was left all by myself to enjoy the beauty and meditate. The high mountains all around, misty coolness in the air and the verdant Deodars had a soporific effect on me. I looked afar. There was terrace cultivation of crops like paddy, manda, etc on the side of the hill ascending upto the village Khela . Khela at a height of 1400 feet about 3 kilometres from where I was staying is a resting place for pilgrims going to Kailash and Mansarovar.

My reverie was broken by the arrival of Jayabhan with fresh atta. We went to buy a few other things but there were nothing much to be found. We had to be content with some red chilies. Jayabhan began to cook. I am not very critical as long as I can get something hot to eat. An Army marches on its stomach and so do I on a hilly trek.

We got up very early and the moment the day broke, we started on our way, on 8th September. It was not cold but definitely cool enough to wear woollens. The sky was clear and we walked along the river Dhouli and began a steady and steep climb. The sun came up from the behind the hills. The land below looked so graceful. We walked for about two hours and arrived at a small village. A small tea stall could be found next to the river. We decided to have our breakfast with the parathas prepared by Jayabhan on the previous night. We didn't relish the tea but could not substitute it with milk because it was just not available. We picked up our luggage and walked for another hour to reach another small village. Here we rested a while, and carried on with our journey on foot. Around a bend, someone said, "Namaste" the famous Indian greeting, which surprised me greatly. I looked at him in surprise and returned the greeting. He asked to my utter astonishment, "Are you from Calcutta?" I nodded. He wanted to be helpful, and he gave me a few hand written notes for some villagers in the next village who had been traditional hosts to the pilgrims of Kailash. He assured me that they would look after me, as I was planning to visit Pancha Chulli, the famous five peaks. We said adieu to this unexpected host and began to walk and arrived at New Vhobla village (1672 mtrs). We cooked in a tea stall. The stall keeper was kind enough to allow us to cook here for a very small sum. We didn't know what was in store for us the next day, so we cooked enough to last us at least till midday. Apples were growning in abundance at this place. We stocked some of the good variety for our onward journey. We left our extra luggage with the postmaster and decided to walk on the following morning. As planned, we got up very early and started for our destination. Due to military movements the road was in fairly good condition. It was narrow but stone paved and was not difficult to walk on. We reached Sela village at a height of 2432 mtrs where we rested to eat our dry rations and apples. The road began to ascend steeply, There were waterfalls on both the sides of the road, but beauty didn't prevent us from gasping for breath. Just prior to sunset, we reached Nangling (2900 mtrs) and took shelter with a shopkeeper. One of our letter from the roadside stranger was for this shopkeeper, who was glad to have us there for the night. I was hungry and cold. Jayabhan began to cook. Many ITBP and CID people came and began to question us. They tried to trap me in their mild interrogation. But when they were satisfied, supported by the permit signed by the ADM, they left me alone. We slept after a good meal. But by about midnight, the drumming rain on the rooftop woke us up and water began to seep inside. We tried to sleep.

Nagling is a big village. There is a school, a post office and a PWD rest house. The villagers are fairly well to do and many of them have decent houses. Some of them even have modern buildings. Rooftops are made of slate slabs and are low slung, probably to save the houses from the heavy snowfall during the winter. They grow potatoes, ogal, etc. but buy wheat from Dharachula. I found some ration shops in the village and a few military barracks.

From Nangling the village Duktu (3192 mtrs) was not very far. The route was also not too bad. We started in the morning and walked along the river. Many streams had to be crossed. The villagers have made bridges with logs. Waterfalls could be found in abundance. We reached Duktu by about 10 am. No sooner had we entered the village, we came across the PWD rest house. There were a few shops and the village was well populated. I had to go to the High Altitude Sheep Breeding Centre because the DLO of Pithoragarh had asked me to contact him. He was glad to receive us. And happily served us with hot khichuri and butter at a height of 3800 mtrs. Then we began the last lap the Pancha Chulli. We reached the glacier and looked at the majestic sight. The proud five peaks rose to a height of 6840 mtrs above sea level. They were all white with snow. I do not know whether Draupadi cooked for the Pandavas on them or not but it was worth the trouble to come all this way to see them at such close quarters. Each peak was separated by quite a distance but looked so close to me when I saw them from a distance. I stayed there for as long as I could endure the cold with my thin clothing. The clouds came in broke my line of sight and I decided to return to the safety of the rest house. Some of the villagers made a beeline to see such a funny stranger who braved this treacherous journey to see the mountain peaks which were a part of their daily lives. They trek everyday to the foot of those mighty peaks to graze their sheep. One of them invited me to his house. I went reluctantly with him, but he was very hospitable. The low roofed house were two-storyed. The lower part contained a store and a pen for the sheep. The upper part was the living area. They kept a fire burning throughout the day and night. Water was also boiling. I had to accept their invitation to have tea and snacks cooked in some greasy substance with a foul smell. I swallowed some of it out of respect for the host. But I would preferred not to. I saw a small but a neat Shiva temple as I returned to the rest house.

At night, the first winter snow began to fall. The morning was cloudy and windy. How can a man from the plains negotiate such treacherous weather with only a half sleeve sweater? But it was 11th September and we could not wait any longer. We began our return trip. I had to decide on the return journey despite a strong desire to stay for on one more day. The clouds and cold forced me to turn my back on these gorgeous peaks. We were walking in a drizzle. Generally, at this altitude it doesrn't rain heavily, it only drizzles. We came back to Nangling and had our breakfast. Nangling grows "phura" and "ogal" and this "ogal" is made into atta. This atta is used to break the fast during some religious functions. The seeds look like wheat seeds but are black in colour, with three corners jutting out. We came to Sela and found a place to rest in a small gang hut of the PWD by the side of a river. The place seemed like in a black hole. The sun does not shine in this place for more than 3 to 4 hours a day. The sky looked like a small fish bowl. I never had seen such a restricted view of the sky during my entire journey through the Himalayas. Bereft of any sunshine it became very cold. We got up in the morning and began to walk cautiously, using our torches. We returned to Dar, purchased some apples and collected our rations and other baggage from the postmaster and came to Chobla village for the night halt. It was just before sunset that an ITBP officer walked into the gang hut and asked if he could also stay there. We managed together. I heard from him for the first time the report about the Indo New Zealand ladies party disaster at Trisuli in the month of May 1974. I also heard for the first time about Milam Glacier from him. On the following morning we bid good-bye to this ITBP officer and returned to the Tawaghat PWD bungalow. After lunch as we were about to take rest, some police officers walked into the rest house and began the typical coercion method of eviction. I held on to my ground and told them about my prior reservation with the kind permission from the ADM. I think that settled the issue. They didn't want to make it an issue with their higher authority. One of them agreed to sleep in my room. I only hoped that he didn't snore. I was tired and desperately wanted to grab some sleep.

The police officer kept his promise and didn't snore. I got up in the morning refreshed, crossed the river Dhouli and began to climb to Narayan Ashram. Sri Narayan Swami established it on top of hill (2584 mtrs) about 50 years ago,. But it lies in dispute among his worthy disciples. The conflict among them became so bad that the Government decided to take over the management. However, the ashram people had been told about our arrival. They received us with grace and served us with good food. It was again the unseen hand of the ADM that did the trick. They understood my closeness to him. Here I found a big library and a lot of accommodation. Apples are grown in plenty now under the Governmental care. After eating our food we came down to Jyoti village and spent the night there. The distance from Tawaghat to Narayan Ashram is only 10 miles but the people take almost the whole day to reach here. We covered a total of 13 miles by mid-day. That was good progress. We were accommodated on the verandah of a newly constructed building. And returned to Tawaghat in the morning at about 8 am. The bus was to be there only at a distance of four miles but as we reached the boarding point we found in our horror that it had already left. There was no ADM to save us from our misery. We had to walk all day to cover a distance of 31 kilometres and finally boarded a bus for Pithoragarh.

Damodar
Kund

We, the two members of Youth Hostel, decided to visit Damodar Kund in Nepal via Muktinath and, as per schedule, one brilliant morning in June, we set out on this difficult trek. The sky was clear and Dholagiri was visible. The morning sun was pleasant and appeared to be nearer than usual. After half an hour, we reached the vicinity of a village called Chankar. The village was a little out of the way so we just walked past it. After walking for one hour, the landscape changed into a wonderful scene. Snow peaks were all round us. High peaks and low peaks, bereft of trees and barren, appeared like ocean waves. We had never seen such wonderful scenery. Hills without a single tree and covered with small grass like juniper bushes, mile after mile, did not look bad. There were also other small bushes with flowers of different colours, creating scenic beauty.

After walking for four hours we reached a trijunction. The road leading to the left went to Mastang and from there it was six days of walking. As we turned back, we could see Muktinath Temple very clearly. We prayed for Muktinath's blessings and took leave of Him. It is said that since Damodar Kund is Muktinath's own place, without His approval and permission nobody can reach Damodar Kund. We were fortunate to receive his blessings; as such, we were sure to succeed.

Our path lay surrounded by hills on all sides. The significant thing about them was that they were absolutely barren and resembled temples standing side by side carved out by expert engineers and masons. At many places, the resemblance was so close to the caves of Ajanta and Ellora and the temples of Konark and Khajuraho that one was wonderstruck at this work of Nature. The formation of hills in the area, according to the geologist was of recent origin and they were still soft. Since the hill sides had no forests or trees, the sides were inundated by rain and snow, creating such beautiful structures. Stones were so rare in the area that people building houses in Rani Pauwa area were seen using mud bricks. We also found that at times, to hold down our tents, we searched for stones in vain.

Our journey onward continued in very difficult terrain. By about 10 o'clock, we reached a shallow stream and used the water to cook rice and potato curry for our meal. The porter cum guide who accompanied us, in order to lessen his burden, buried some rice and potato under the soil, which could be taken out on our return journey. The saying "Man proposes and God disposes" is very true. Since we finally did not return by that route, the buried food remained there. What mother earth had given for sustaining us went back to her.

After eating, we resumed our journey. But the climb was very steep, the sun was scorching and the wind was extremely strong and the combined effect made our journey very difficult. At the end of 12 hours walk we reached the Situng Khola river bed to camp for the night. All the way we had moved slowly due to the extremely difficult road conditions. The worst was coming to the river bed from the top. The path was just like a straight line full of sandy stones and it was very difficult to get a foothold. Every step appeared to be the last. Fatigue and unending difficulties wore us down. Ultimately, we reached the river bed and crossed the shallow river by taking off our shoes. But our troubles for the day were not over yet. There was no level ground suitable for camping. With difficulty, we levelled a small patch and pitched our tents. The porter did not know how to cook 'khichuri,' therefore, I had to give him instructions on this art.

Next morning, we began our journey with refreshed mind and body. In the Himalayan climate, fatigue disappears in no time if one takes some rest. The previous day the journey was mostly downhill; the process was reversed now and it was just going up and up. The climb was unending and every step appeared to be more difficult than the previous one. When in misery, people think of God. I too started thinking of Him with tears in my eyes and prayed to Him to bestow on me the unwavering faith and belief that Ganesha had. The story goes that Mother Durga held a golden necklace in her hand and showing the same to two of her sons, Ganesha and Kartika, told them, "Who ever goes around the world first, will get it". Kartika dashed out on his peacock to go around the world. But Ganesh did nothing of the sort and getting up from his seat just went round Mother Durga once. He had the firm belief that the Mother was the entire universe by herself and it was more than enough to go round her. Mother Durga bestowed the necklace on Ganesha.

In spite of the difficulties, our journey continued on the very steep climb. On the Indian side of the Himalayas we had observed that the journey was a mix of going up and down, with level ground in between. On the other hand, on the Nepal side, when it was going up it continued for six-seven hours at a stretch and while going down also, it was a long march. That made us extremely exhausted and we could not walk fast. The porter with us was walking very fast and we failed to keep pace with him.

We had been walking for four hours, inching forward slowly. The scorching sun was overhead and snow-capped white peaks covered almost three-fourths of the horizon in a magnificent manner which was a novel experience for me. On an earlier excursion from Sandakphu we had seen these peaks, Nilgiri, Dhaulagiri I,II and III but they were at a distance. We were seeing these very peaks again but at a closer range. We were lost in enjoying the heavenly beauty of the creator – how beautiful He would be who could create such beauty par excellence. How fortunate we are that He has chosen us to enjoy His wonderful creation! We went down on our knees and with tears paid reverence to the all Powerful, Omnipotent and Omniscient Being. We enjoyed the celestial wine through our eyes and got simply charmed by it.

At the end of four hours walking, we reached the side of a small stream. Till this point it was only climbing up and up, without meeting any level ground. We decided to rest and allowed the porter to cook the food. As long as we were walking, we were not able to enjoy the serene beauty around. While we were resting, we looked round and what a sight! The horizon was completely surrounded by snow-covered peaks. It appeared as if we were seated in the middle on a patch of green grass with almost all the named peaks of Nepal, including Damodar, clad with snow, forming an amphitheatre. The sight of these made us so happy that the bone-breaking journey was all forgotten. What splendour! How magnificent must be the glory of the creator who could give us such things to enjoy. We felt very fortunate to be able to witness such celestial beauty, the glorious creation.

As we were enjoying the glory of the creator we also saw some animals. We observed some remains of an animal – bones and hair – in the grass. We were told that in that area there was an animal that was both carnivorous as well as herbivorous. We failed to identify the animal. Besides that, we sighted some hares also and were keen to catch one but were not successful.

The journey after some rest was downhill to reach Tanjia village which we could see from the top of the hill. The way down was very narrow, full of sand and stone pebbles; as such, getting a foothold and keeping ones balance was extremely difficult. At every step, we ran the risk of tumbling down, to land a few thousand feet below. We were terribly scared. The struggle continued for a full five hours and ultimately we reached the Tanje Khola river bed. The bed was dry and full of stones of different sizes and we had to walk over them. The place was well known for the availability of the Damodar Salgram and all of us were keenly searching the place to get a Salgram. It looked like a fossil of the shell of a water 'Shamuk'. Evolution scientists have claimed that the Himalayan region was once a great ocean and the land swelled up due to some catastrophe to form the mountains. The theory gains credibility on seeing the structure of the Himalayan ranges situated in Nepal.

We had to cross two streams. which we did barefoot. It took us almost 12 hours to reach village Tanjia and we spent the night on the verandah of a house. The construction of the house was a little peculiar. The ground floor was used for the cattle and the upper floor comprised the living quarters. Adjoining the house, the toilet was constructed in such a way that human excreta and animal dung all got dumped there. In the course of time it formed into manure for cultivation. The villagers were poor but simple with very few needs. Rice, wheat and barley were the crops cultivated and they made their clothes from sheep hair.

The third day's journey started at 5.00 a.m. Dhaulagiri was just in front of us and the light of the morning sun made the scene beautiful. We crossed a stretch of level ground in half an hour and thereafter again started scaling up. The level ground was good for cultivation but since the area was absolutely devoid of water, nothing could be grown. The condition of the road was similar to what we had covered earlier — narrow, sandy, full of pebbles and very steep.

We came close to a village called Cherang and from that point we saw 'Nakli Damodar' like a cow's face. The pilgrims who could not reach the real Damodar Kund visited the base of that hill and for that reason it was called "Nakli Damodar". All around us hills stretched like a garland . Ultimately, we reached the bank of the Neti Khola river. The water was very cold and we thought of cooking our food but could not find any firewood; consequently, the porter cooked half boiled rice and enjoyed it. We had to be satisfied with the roti and potato curry left over from the previous day. Our rations were getting severely depleted. Whatever we had procured from Muktinath was all we had. We could not replenish our food from any other source since nothing was available.

After finishing our meal, we resumed walking by crossing over to the other side of the river. The path snaked up almost vertically and it was extremely difficult to walk. The road was full of sand and stones and there was a strong wind. A little further up there was no path at all and we had to use a pickaxe to cut out footholds in the dead wall.

We faced another almost impossible climb that seemed beyond our endurance. All of us got terribly nervous and were unable to decide about what to do. Added to that, we were not sure which road we needed to follow and as such, all we could do was to blame ourselves for undertaking such an adventure so foolishly.

With great difficulty, we crossed over to a high level ground with a slight gradient. Reaching the ground, we saw that there was no water anywhere in the vicinity and all that we were carrying with us had almost been exhausted. Therefore cooking could not be undertaken. But why should the stomach co-operate! Soon it started making its presence felt. But we were quite helpless to satiate it. The sky was absolutely blue and the horizon was dotted with an unending chain of mountains. There were a few small fragrant plants also known as tulsi. We also secured some Damodar Shila. It was almost 4.30 p.m. and we decided to camp there itself for the night since the place was somewhat level and we had no further strength left to go on. But the wind was terribly strong and stones were not available to hold our tents. Pitching our tents was quite a problem. In addition, the place was absolutely without a trace of water in the vicinity. So no cooking could be done. Luckily we had a handful of popcorn still left, which we shared. Although it was tasty, we found it quite difficult to eat. But then how to quench the thirst? In the absence of any food and water, we spent the night hungry and thirsty.

For two full hours in the morning we struggled with hunger and thirst carried over from the previous night and reached a place from where it was all downhill and at the end of which we expected to find some water. We searched our belongings for any remaining food and discovered some 'chura'. This was distributed like prasad, a pinch to each; with that insignificant pinch of chura we seemed to recover a little to carry on with our journey down the hill on a sandy and very uncomfortable road. We saw the grass like 'gaju' growing in the area and also evidences of 'chamari gai' living in the area.

After some rest and food, we continued further walking over the frozen river or at times by its side, towards the top of the hill. With great difficulty we got to the top. Suddenly I started feeling uncomfortable and had difficulty in breathing. It appeared we were at a height of 5776 mtrs and, therefore, the lack of oxygen was causing the inconvenience. However, an aspirin tablet helped. In the meanwhile, the porter had gone ahead. I looked at my watch, it was already four in the evening. According to the calculations, we had to travel two more hours to reach a water point and camping ground. But the way down was difficult beyond description. With caution, and prayers on our lips, walking for almost thirteen-and -a- half hours, we reached the water front with our tongues hanging out due to exhaustion. We set up our camp there to rest for the night. The night before we had to fast since there was no water. The next day again. We fasted because though water was available, fuel was not. Fortunately, we carried a small oil stove which saved our lives that night. The porter soaked fried and boiled wheat in water and prepared something called 'chamma' and we managed our dinner with the same. The stuff was new to me and was very hard to digest. We suffered stomach aches and subsequently loose motions in the morning.

We started preparations for the forward march. We were on the last stretch of the journey to Damodar Kund. The plan was to use the last camp as the base camp and come back to the same point after visiting the kund.

We started walking. The path continued to go up sleeply. After two and a half hours difficult climb, during which even the last ounce of strength was utilised, we reached the top of the hill. And on reaching that point, when we found that we had to climb further, we felt like praying to Damodar that we had enough of it and did not need any more. He could with pleasure remain immersed in samadhi in His snowy kund and spare us to live on.

We continued on our desperate trail, staking our very lives. At last, we reached a point from where the kund was visible. It appeared so close, especially the 'Nakli Damodar'. Some of the peaks situated in Tibet and China were also visible from that point. The scene was beautiful and we felt every moment the glory of Lord's creation. But the amount of torture we had to undergo to reach the place did not allow us to really enjoy it.

After six hours of a very hard walk, we succeeded in reaching the Damodar Kund. The last six hours' walk was a little better than the previous day's. The road was through green gaju grass fields with small juniper bushes. We could observe some hares and the holes of other animals, a change from the earlier terrain. The kund – a small pond – was situated at the foot of Damodar Peak. In one corner of the kund was a small temple consisting of some stones heaped at one place. We sat down there, at the feet of the Lord, with folded hands.

Once we had completed the visit to the first kund, we set forth for the second kund. This was much bigger in size and was completely frozen. Water was coming out from the sides. There was a small temple with a collection of simple stones which had been offered by a group of devotees who had visited the place earlier. We happened to meet them while they were returning. They were 65 in number and consisted of men and women. After paying our respects to the Lord at the second kund, we returned to the site where our porter was engaged in cooking. After enjoying 'khichuri' and 'papar fry', we prepared to return to our base camp. With great difficulty, we reached the base camp.

From our camping place at the river-bed, we started climbing up and took about two hours to come up to get to the top. For the next two hours also things did not change, at the end of which we again touched the river-bed. We cooked our food and after eating, resumed walking. It was an unending up and down journey. At last, we reached the top of the river bed which was like a huge football ground. The ground had no trace of grass or trees, nothing except sand and stones. We decided to rest a while and then resumed walking on the stony soil on which it was a problem to keep one's balance. With great difficulty we reached the river bed and decided on a place to rest. The place was used by shepherds as a night-shelter for their goats. It was full of stinking goat-dung and absolutely unsuitable. But as there was no other better place nearby, we pitched our tent there.

Resting in our tents we felt greatly relieved since we had walked almost twelve-and-a-half hours that day. Unfortunately, we had nothing to cook except half a kilogram of rice. The porter cooked the same and added plenty of water with chillies and salt. This we shared to fill our empty stomachs. The river was known as Natikhola and originated from Damodar Kund. And a little further from our camping site, it joined the Kali Gandaki river.

The night was comfortable since we already had come down to a lower height; there was no anxiety and we knew that the way further down was less difficult. Quite relaxed, we got up in the morning. In the morning sunlight, when we saw the nature of the hill behind our tent, our blood froze in our veins. The hill was just a huge heap of mud and could have collapsed on our tents any moment. It was surely the mercy of God that saved us.

The journey the next morning was resumed at the usual time. We crossed the river by walking through the ice-cold water and then climbed the hill on the other side. After labouring for about five hours, we reached a village called Tanjia.

After a good many days we were back again amidst a village crowd. All of them flocked around us and asked us for just one thing – medicines. We obliged them with whatever we had. We took our meal in the village and said good-bye to our porter who belonged to the village and thereafter continued our journey. The way was all up and down and terrible in the freezing cold. All this made it difficult for us. Finally, we reached the camping ground and selected a place for setting up our camp. It turned out to be the resting place for goats and chamari gai. Within a short time of our putting up the tents, a large number of goats with loads from Pokhra came and virtually dislodged us by occupying the place. We had to go up the slopes but the wind and uneven ground made us very uncomfortable. It took us three more days to return to Pokhra.

Muktinath Temple

Muktinath

From Kathmandu, the bus took us to Pokhra. The road was by the side of the Gandaki river and was quite smooth. On the way, the bus stopped at the town for lunch. My friend Jyotirmoy and I, and our better halves got down.

After lunch, the bus started again and the road continued by the side of the Gandaki river. On both the sides of the road we could see green fields of maize, paddy, sugarcane, etc. The sight was very pleasing and made our bus journey rather enjoyable.

By about 2.30 in the afternoon we arrived at Pokhra, checked into a hotel and started sorting out our luggage. Since the permissible limit per passenger was 15 kg, the extra luggage was packed neatly and deposited with the hotel manager to be collected on our return journey. With a little time at our disposal in the evening, we visited Kahendrapul, the main bazaar of Pokhra with the idea of purchasing some postage. Unfortunately, this was not available. We did get some bread and butter, but avoided purchasing anything more to avoid being overloaded for the flight.

On the morning of 24th May, we reached the airport much before 6.00 a.m., the scheduled reporting time. The staff of the airport had just casually mentioned that the previous day depending on the weather conditions, they undertook two flights in place of the usual one. Accordingly, the first flight had departed before the scheduled time. In expectation of a second flight, we hurried to the airport.

As soon as we reached the airport, we were informed that due to bad weather at Jamsom the flight had been cancelled. The news was very disappointing for all of us. The Jamsom airstrip lay between the Nilgiri and Dhalagiri mountains. The weather was frequently bad there and high winds prevailed which made it difficult for the aircraft to land.

Next day, we were lucky enough to get four vacant seats in a small plane. The flight took off smoothly and within 20 minutes we landed at our destination. It was terribly cold and windy. We approached a hotel for shelter for the night and decided to begin our trekking for Muktinath the next morning.

Early morning, we started trekking, leaving our extra luggage in the custody of proprietor of the hotel. From Jamsom Muktinath was about 6-7 hours walk and could be covered in a day's time. The road followed the Kali Gandaki river. The normal course of the road lay on the other side of the river but the road had a number of ups and downs. Therefore, we preferred walking on the flat dry river bed itself. But the river bed was full of stones and pebbles, making it uneven, and walking difficult.

Near the airfield, we could see some houses and office buildings; some were located even on the other side of the river which we could see from a distance but due to want of time, could not go over to see them. As we were walking by the side of the road, we could see many more shops selling daily commodities of requirement.

We had to cross the river at two places on temporary bridges. Within two hours of our starting from Jamsom we reached a place called Eklabhati where a small tea stall was run by a lady assisted by her young children. They could not have been more than 6 to 7 years old. We decided to rest there and ordered some tea.

We reached Jorhat and I decided to go ahead of the party and reach Muktinath quickly in order to find a suitable shelter. I reached Muktinath around 5 p.m, arranged for shelter, but in vain. My co pilgrims which included my wife, failed to arrive. I spent a miserable night. I was relieved to see them on the following morning . The ladies could not move on due to exhaustion, so they decided to spent the night in a hotel in Jorhat. And here I had waited for them and also paid for the rooms for them.

On way to Muktinath

Immediately after a modest breakfast, we went to the temple of Muktinath. The structure of the temple resembled a pagoda and had a stone 'parikrama' (a path to walk around the temple). The deity of the temple is a golden coloured full sized Vishnu in a sitting posture. There were two small rooms next to the temple. The purpose of these rooms was not clear. I thought that they were for the devotees to sit and offer their prayers. Another thing that surprised us was the photographs of many persons including the King and the Queen of Nepal hanging in front of the temple door. I was a bit perplexed by this. It may be that they have dedicated themselves at the feet of Lord through their photographs or their relatives while visiting the place on their behalf might have left the photographs there. However, since we did not find out the reason, it remained a mystery.

We went inside for a 'darshan' once the devotees ahead had finished their prayers and offerings to the Lord. As we entered the temple, a full size golden coloured Vishnu idol in a sitting posture with a smiling face greeted us. The sight of Lord Muktinath's serene and bright face made us forget all our troubles, and our difficulties were washed away in a moment. The mind became absolutely still and a celestial joy permeated through and through. I sat there motionless, for how long I could not recollect. Getting back to the normal senses, I found myself immersed in a sea of eternal bliss only. No words were coming out and tears were rolling down. I continued to pray at the feet of the Lord for a long time and gained lasting peace and comfort.

After receiving the blessings of Lord Muktinath, we took leave of Him. Vishnumurti was seated on a platform and there were smaller images of Lord Buddha, Shiva, Garuda, Shiva-Parvati, etc encircling Vishnumurti. Saraswati and Lakshmi stood on the right and left of Vishnu respectively holding their raised arms over the head of the deity. Vishnu was adorned with a beautiful pearl on his forehead.

The temple was very simple, with no pomp and show. The doors of the temple were open for everybody without any distinction and people could offer prayers and puja according to their own liking. The priest of the temple was a very simple man and did not demand anything from the devotees. There was no shop outside the temple selling the necessary items for the puja. People who wished to, brought these things with them. Otherwise incense sticks, cotton wicks dipped in ghee and such like items were available with the priest at a nominal price. There was a Temple Committee that looked after the temple administration. All the offerings went to the committee fund. The priest received a salary from the committee and never demanded anything from the pilgrims. While we were in the temple, a group of devotees came and asked the priest to perform some puja for them. The priest completed the job with all devotion and told them they could give whatever they liked for the service. I was amazed at his selflessness. We also offered a puja at the feet of Lord Muktinath.

In front of the temple, there was a small, square paved water tank and a courtyard where a stream of water was flowing through many artificial cows' mouths. Behind the temple also there was a stream of water emerging out of many cows' mouth. The Kali river emerged from the spring behind the Temple and joined the lake. It assumed the name Kaligandaki thereafter. Devotees coming for darshan of Lord Muktinath took a bath in one of these springs and then went inside the temple. But on our part, we walked straight with the dust laden feet to the Lord for his darshan first without wasting time.

Close to the temple, there was a small room with the side facing the temple completely open. It was known as the Dharamshala and we saw two hermits staying there and preparing their food. In the vicinity of the temple we found water in abundance and also the Bhutia Pipal tree (Thala Tibet) which could be grown by simply planting a branch of the tree. Surrounded by the trees, the place was cool and exceptionally quiet and appeared like a 'tapovan' conducive for meditation.

We returned to Muktinath hotel which was run by a newly married young Nepali lady. She had lived in Delhi for some time and had picked up Hindi well. The hotel was neat and clean and the charges were reasonable.

On the way to Muktinath area, there is a Buddhist monastery and a Japa Chakra situated on the right side of the road. We stopped to have a look at them. Some Lama men and women were seen engaged in prayers and study. One of the side rooms had a statue of Buddha in a sitting posture on a platform. At our request ,one of the lady attendants lifted the curtains surrounding the platform. Two flames were visible under the seat. They are considered very holy and one always kept covered.

After spending three nights in Muktinath, we returned to Jamsom and were stranded there for three more days due to lack of reservation in any flight. On the fourth day, we were lucky to get four seats on the flight to Pokhra.

Tents at Gunji

Kailash and Mansarovar
– *A Pilgrimage*

Two hundred and forty miles from Almora in UP and 800 miles from Lhasa, the capital of Tibet, stand Mount Kailash and lake Mansarovar, constituting one of the grandest of the Himalayan beauty spots. Holy Kailash, called Kang Rinpoche in Tibetan, of hoary antiquity and celebrity, the spotless design of Nature's art and overpowering beauty has vibrations of a supreme order from the spiritual point of view. Mount Kailash is revered in Sanskrit literature as the abode of the All Blissful Lord Shiva and his divine spouse Parvati, the all enchanting Prakriti (Nature). It is 20 miles off the Holy Mansarovar and the Rakshas Tal on the South, bedecked with graceful swans.

The Holy Mansarovar called Tso Mapham or Tso Mavang in Tibetan, is the holiest, the most fascinating, the most inspiring and the most famous lake in the world. And perhaps the most ancient known to civilization. The circumference of Mansarovar is about 54 miles (86 kilometres) The great sage Pranavanada, who actually undertook 25 circumbulations, describes it as skull like, roughly 16 miles (24 kilometres) in length and about 14 to 15 miles in breadth . Even before the dawn of history, Mansarovar had become a sacred lake and has remained so for four millenna. It is majestically calm and dignified like a huge bluish green emerald or a pure turquoise set between the two mighty and equally majestic silvery mountains, Kailash on the North and Gurla Mandhata in the

South; the lake Rakshas Tal or Ravana Hrada on the West; and Osmne hills on the East. From the spiritual point of view it has an aura of the most supreme order that can soothe even the most wandering mind into sublime serenity, and transport it into ecstasies. It stretches over an extensive cradle of the Tibetan plateau, hanging at a heavenly height of 4544 mtrs above the sea level with a depth of nearly 90 mtrs, covering an area of 200 square miles (320 kilometres). There are eight monasteries on the holy shores, wherein Buddhist monks strive all their live to attain sublimity of the eternal silence of Nirvana." (Exploration in Tibet by Swami Pranavananada (6-8).

While talking about Manas and its climate, the Swami has described the weather as generally cold, dry and windy. The monsoon sets in late and rainfall is scanty but when it rains, it does so in torrents. In summer, all the streams and rivers flow rapidly, specially in the evening due to the melting of the snow. The sun is hot in summer but it becomes very cold as soon as the sky becomes cloudy. During the pilgrim season (July- August), very often the Holy Kailash and the Mandhata peaks are enveloped in clouds playing hide-and-seek with the visitors. The weather changes suddenly. You may be perspiring in the hot sun but moments later you will be shivering when the sun goes behind the clouds.

Twilights are unusually long; there is plenty of light for nearly an hour or even more just before sunrise and after sunset.

Due to the very high altitude and the consequent rarified and dust free air, distant places and objects appear to be closer than, they are really are. Sometimes, even when there are high waves near the shores of Mansarovar, the middle of the lake is as smooth like a mirror, reflecting the mountains or the midnight moon and stars[1]

The sages from time immemorial, have journeyed towards the Himalayas, meditated in that serene atmosphere and seen the Gods and had the realisation of the soul dawn on them. The worldly, tired of their daily routines, trek through the hazardous routes of the Himalayas, to reach these places of meditation so that they can derive solace for some time. The eternal hunger for the soul to be free, to tear away from this bondage of *maya*, always made me run away from this material world to that surcharged atmosphere of the most exquisite holy places. I love to travel. I love to travel through the expanse of the Himalayas. The love for the journey through this silent beauty brought me repeatedly to the feet of Kedarnath, Badrinath, Gangotri, Yamunotri and Gomukh. To learn the truth of mythology I went back to many forgotten temples hidden in the bosom of the Himalayas. I went to pay my homage to those ancient sages who told us the stories of the five Kedars and seven Badrinathas. My thirst for knowledge gave me the strength to travel through tortuous paths, never bothering about the danger. But I had not

---

1 P 61-62 (Exploration in Tibet)

had the chance to visit Kailash and Mansarovar, because by the time I was ready physically and mentally to travel there, the Chinese occupation of Tibet began. The Dalai Lama migrated to India and China went to war with India in 1962. Gradually, Kailash receded from the devout Hindu.

The unsatiated desire to be in the Himalayas makes me touch the feet of these mighty mountains at least twice a year. I go to the holy shrines again and again. I pay my homage to that Omnipotent in different names. I have prayed at Badrinath, and at Amarnath. After each visit, I come back to crowded Calcutta and forget at least for a few days the dreariness of life. My desire to travel to Kailash brought me at the door-step of Mani Mahesh or Chhota Kailash; from there, I treked to Kinnar Kailash. But the route to actual Kailash has been guarded by the Chinese soldiers since the early sixties. A humble pilgrim like me could not concern them in any way. Yet I waited for twenty years for the gate of Kailash to be opened by the 'Chinese. These ruthless atheists never bothered to understand our desire. We, the pilgrims, didn't want to concur or bring any malice to that occupying force. We only wanted to pay our respects to Lord Shiva and Varuna.

Finally, China changed her mind. A visit to Kailash was permitted. I got this electrifying news through the media. My desire to visit Kailash and Mansarovar surfaced strongly, but by then I was twenty years older. Doubts arose. Will my desires ever be fulfilled? How long will I have to wait? Is it too late for me to undertake this hazardous journey?

In 1981 the pilgrimage began at last, after a lapse of two decades. Three batches could visit Kailash and Mansarovar starting on 9th, 17th and 25th September with 17, 18 and 20 pilgrims respectively. I couldn't be a party of these lucky ones because I got this exciting news only on my return from one of my Himalayan journeys, and the last date for filling in the application had already expired. As far as I was concerned, it was a disaster.

In all, there were a total of 57 pilgrims but only 54 could visit Kailash. Three pilgrims had to return due to physical incapacities. A few women pilgrims were among these batches. In the first batch, there was only one woman pilgrim among the 17, whereas there were two and three women respectively in the second and third batches of these pioneers of Kailash travellers. The first woman pilgrim for Kailash was Smt. Nabinlata Joshi. These three batches took a total of 26 days only to touch the feet of Mount Kailash and return. The Chinese authorities permitted only an eight days' stay in Tibetan territory for each batch.

With a broken heart, I started counting the days, hoping that the Chinese would not change their decision and cancel the pilgrimage. My wait bore fruit. The news filtered through the morning newspaper that the Government of India would allow 8 batches of 25 pilgrims for the pilgrimage of Kailash and Mansarovar, and a total of only 200 pilgrims were to be selected.

In the old days, most travellers went to Kailash via Almorah, although there are about 12 confirmed routes for this journey, viz., (a) Almorah— Amkot — Khela — Garliyang — Lipulekh Pass (16850') —Taklakot—238 miles (b) Almorah— Bageswar—Milas— Unta—Dhura Pass (17590')—Jauanti Pass (11500')—Kungri Bingra Pass (18300') - Gianira Mandi— 200 miles -, (d) Joshi-math—Gunla Niti Pass (16600')—Natra Mandi—Shivchilim Mandi—Giednima Mandi—200 miles ; (e) Joshimath—Darujan Niti Pass (16200') —Tonjanla (16050')—Shivchilim Mandi Gianima Mandi—160 miles -, (f) Joshimath—Hotiniti Pass (16390') Tonjanla—Shivchilim Mandi—Gianima Mandi—160 miles (g) Badrinath—Mana Pass (18400')—Thungli Math— Dapa—Mabra— Shivchilim—Gianima Mandi—238 miles ; (h) Simla— Rampur—Sikri Pass (15400')—Chargetils (16400' —Loaehela (18510')—Gartok (15100')— Chargelils (',6200') Tirth-puri—445 miles (i) Simila—Rampur—Sikri Pass— Saringla— Thumglidapa—Shivchilim—Gianima Mandi-473 miles; (j) Qangotri - Nilang - Jelukhage Pass (17490') - Piling Mandi -Thuli Dapa—Shivchilim-Gianima Mandi—243 miles j (k) Srinagar (Kashmir)—Jojila Pass (11478')—Nammik— Kotula (13446')—Seladak-Taglang la (17500')—Demchok-Gartok-Chargot La (16200') -Tirehpuri- 605 miles; (1) Kulu-Ram-pur Busayar—Tuling Dapar—Shivchilim Mandi-400 miles.

On Saturday the 19th June, as per the telegraphed

217

instructions, I reported at the proper place. Other pilgrims were also there. A little later a representative from the Ministry arrived with a list of names. Some pilgrims were absent. In all, 18 out of 25 pilgrims were present. At 10.00 a.m. a luxury bus took us to the Indo-Tibetan Border hospital at Khanpur for our medical check-up. The Ministry had already warned us that permission to travel to Kailash would not be given if a pilgrim was found to be a patient of heart disease or high blood pressure.

We were given the forms for the Chinese visa. After completing the form, we attached two copies of photographs and Rs 60 as visa fee and handed over the same along with the form. We also had to give a non-judicial stamp paper of Rs.10 as an Indemnity Bond duly signed by a First Class Magistrate. We had brought all these along with us as per earlier instructions.

On completion of this session, we started a question/answer forum which lasted about four hours. Finally, after receiving instructions for Monday and Tuesday, we dispersed.

On Monday, we reported at 36, Janpath, Chandralok Bhawan, at the Tourist Information Bureau of the U.P. Government and deposited Rs. 2500/-. This was for the U.P. Government to provide transportation by deluxe bus from Delhi to Champawat (440 km)—Dharchula (171 kilometres)—Tawaghat (16 kilometres). A distance of 527 kilometres had to be covered. From this deposit-money they would provide food and lodging from Tawaghat to Lipulekh plus porter charges for 25 kgs. of luggage. Apart from this, if any individual wanted to engage a horse or a dandi, the charges per day were Rs. 80/- for a horse and Rs. 2,000/- for a dandi respectively.

On Tuesday the rest of the formalities were completed. We got our visa – only 12 day's tour in Tibet was permitted; Rs. 3,080/-was also converted to foreign exchange of and 420 dollars.

On 20th July, we would return to Delhi and accordingly, I made a reservation for Varanasi on 22nd July on the Kashi Viswanath Express.

Chanting the name of Lord Shiva, 26 of us got into the bus to commence our journey to Kailash on 23rd June. Wednesday. In this batch of ours, there were seven women pilgrims.

At 07.20 am, the journey began. We had to cover a distance of 865 kilometres from Delhi to Kailash and the bus covers a distance of only 627 kilometres. The bus started moving through the Delhi morning traffic. The morning was cool and the sun was already up. The happiness of the mind brought me to a state of meditation.

Selection and crossing the hurdle of the medical examination does not mean that the visit to Kailash is a certainty because the year before, 57 pilgrims started the pilgrimage but three had to return. Such incidents are quite common en route to Kedar, Amarnath, Gomukh and Manimahesh.

The memories of my pilgrimage to Manimahesh started

haunting me. We reached the hills with a happy mind and with tremendous mental energy. We reached Bharmor and the next day was fixed to begin the trekking for Manimahesh. A porter was engaged and we bought all the necessities.

All of us decided to prepare khichuri, a concoction of rice and dal with the addition of spices, to satiate various tastes. Our porter Thapa was given the task to prepare this Bengali dish in his Pahari way. We were hungry and we ate our fill. But the hilly variation of the Bengali dish took its toll. . After the usual post dinner-gossip, we went to bed. I started feeling uneasy and got up. Acidity almost started driving me mad. Then started incessant vomiting. I couldn't sleep and became very weak. As a result, our journey was postponed by another day.

But my condition started deteriorating. Anything I ate led to nausea. I became weak and had to be evacuated by my friends. Manimahesh didn't want me to visit the shrine.

A friend of my mine had once started his journey to Kedar along with his family. At Gaurikund his condition became so bad that he had to return from there on his own.

Apart from such problems, natural calamities are also a part of any Himalayan trek. That is why a constant worry nags you until you have completed any pilgrimage in the hills.

In the bus, we were three Bengalis, two from Calcutta and the third individual was from Assam.

Six more batches were to follow us. The third batch on July, the fourth batch on 15th July, the fifth batch on 26th

July, the sixth batch on 6th August, the seventh batch on 17th August and the eighth batch on 28th August. On the return of last batch on 24th September, the year's Kailash pilgrimage would be over.

Now my only worry was whether I would be able to complete the journey. Fatalistic as I am, why should I worry? The entire creation is His will. Who am I? If He desires, I will go. My fate has brought me so far, will that Omnipotent be so cruel and send me back from this pilgrimage for which I have been waiting for years? We human beings can only try, the results are in the hand of the Almighty.

The tranquillity was spreading. Our eyes started enjoying the morning sun and scenic beauty. I remembered, "At the immortal touch of thy hands my little heart loses its limits enjoy and give births to utterance ineffable" (Tagore)

If there is bliss at all then this is it. Going to the abode of Hara-Gauri and Lord Kuber. Lady Luck, must be smiling. Such opportunities do not come again and again.

Another thought came to my mind. It may sound ridiculous. In the Delhi Kalibari dormitory 13 people had been lodged . and when we went for the medical examination, we were 13. Superstition of unlucky 13 was at the back of my mind. However, the result was not disastrous and here I am on my way to Kailash.

In the bus, we were 25 pilgrims along with the Liaison Officer from the Ministry of External Affairs, Shri Jaimini

Bhagwati and the Liaison Officer from the U.P. Government, Shri Tiwari. That made the total 27. We completed our breakfast and lunch on the way.

At 8-30 pm, we reached Champawat.* The distance from Delhi to Champawat is 452 kilometres. Next morning, we started from Champawat and arrived at Pithoragarh by noon. Lunch arrangements had been made. At Pithoragarh, we came across that famous personality, Swami Pranavanandji, He was about 90 years old and still quite active. He came along with us to the P.W.D. Rest House and sat down to have lunch with us.

Swamiji is the only man who has carried out circumambulation of Kailash 32 times. Once for a period of 12 months and again for a period of 16 months, he remained in the Kailash-Mansarovar area continuously and collected invaluable data regarding the weather and geography of this area and prepared a comprehensive report of the same. Swamiji's work was acclaimed by the Government of India as most singular and he was awarded the "Padmashree*. Moreover he was also selected as a member of the Indian National Geography Committee. In 1968, during the International Geography Congress, he represented India. In 1940 he was elected a Fellow of the Royal Geographical Society. The foreward of his famous book on Kailash-Mansarovar was written by no less than the first Prime Minister of India, Pandit Jawaharlal Nehru.

Swamiji was extremely happy when he met this batch of pilgrims for Kailash. We pestered him with thousands of questions which he answered most willingly. Some of us took a few photographs of Swamiji. He explained to us on a piece of papers, the vantage points for the best views of Kailash. Our stay was short, and hence reluctantly we had to part with of such company.

Our next destination was to be Dharchula. The night halt was to be there. Champawat to Dharchula is a distance of 171 kilometres only.

We were in the hills, having crossed Lohaghat, from where the road bifurcates to Vivekananda Advaita Ashram (the bus route from Delhi has been changed from the year 1987 and instead of Tanakpur and Lohaghat, it goes via Bageswar and Chowkadi, Mayavati). For some distance, the hilly stream Sarju was our companion.

We crossed Kanalichina, Ogla, Askot, Jauljibi.

I started thinking about my fellow pilgrims. 61-year-old Mr. Chopra was the eldest and 27-year-old Miss Madhumohan was the youngest. We had with us Smt. Uma Sanyal from Calcutta, Smt. Supriti Roy from Assam and Mr. Verma from Lucknow. Verma tied a turban and wore a beard like a Sikh and as a result some of us started calling him Sardarji. He refused to shave and cut his hair till he had completed the Kailash pilgrimage. Also along with us was Dr. Laghu, a Reader of physics of the Banaras University. Dr. E. V. Shankar and his 56 year old mother, Mr. and Mrs. Rao, Mrs. Padmini Rajurkar, wife of an Air Force Wing Commander and a social worker, Miss Gupta alias Bhakti Bahin, and Swami Gahananda of the

Ramkrishna Mission.

Shankar and I became friends. He was only 33.years old. His scientific mind had got intermingled with religious faith. He was carrying with him his house deity, Lord Narayan. There should not be any break in the daily worship of Narayan. "He is the creator. He is the Lord of all. If I carry him along with me, He will protect me." This faith drives millions of Hindus on this beautiful path of religion.

It started raining. Through the torrential rain, we reached the P.W.D. rest house at Dharchula for our night halt. There were only two rooms in the guest house. Some tents were also pitched for accommodating us. Shankar and I were allotted tent accommodation.

Before dinner, we were handed over to the medicos for another medical check up.

Some of the pilgrims went across the bridge over the Sarju to Nepal to buy foreign goods.

At Dharchula, one can buy anything required for trekking but the charges seemed a little higher.

Dinner was like the Pithoragarh lunch, consisting of chapatis, rice, dal, vegetables, papad and pickle. At all our camps, potatoes dominated the vegetarian dishes because other types of vegetables are not easily available.

At 3.30 am,. we again heard the raindrops falling which caused the night temperature of the Himalayas to drop.

The morning greeted us with a clear blue sky. Breakfast was completed with tea and parathas. We got into the bus for our next destination, Tawaghat, only 19 kilometres away. We reached Tawaghat within an hour and that brought an end to our bus journey. We had travelled a total distance of 62 kilometres by bus so far.

From Tawaghat commenced our pilgrimage on foot. We had to weigh our luggage. If the luggage remained within the stipulated 25 kgs, then no additional amount had to be paid. But in case it exceeded this limit, the payment had to be borne by the pilgrim. The weight of my luggage came to 34 kg and as a result, I had to tie up with Shri N. J. Dodia of Bombay. Our total luggage weight came to 34+ 15 = 49 kg. So I didn't have to pay anything for the extra 9 kg. of weight.

At 09. 30 am, we started our journey on foot. Tawaghat is at a height of only 914 metres. I didn't feel cold. We had to go to Pangu, at a distance of only 9 kilometres.

Our batch got enlarged with the addition of porters, horses and six policemen of the Uttar Pradesh Government. A wireless operator with a radio set to keep in touch with Delhi, also came with us.

At the commencement of this journey we crossed the Dhauli-Ganga. From the bridge I looked down into the face of that destruction, looked into the face of beauty, with white surf in its bosom running down from the home of the Gods to the plains of earthly beings. It has that promise to destroy sins, it has that promise to reestablish goodness.

It flows unhindered, getting annoyed if obstructed, as if questioning, who can stop me? Am I not the representative of the Omnipotent?

I wanted to enjoy such beauty in isolation but alas the pressure from my fellow pilgrims made me start moving but most reluctantly. We were going uphill, it was tiring, back breaking. If the beginning of our journey was going to be so difficult, I wondered what it would be like later. Climbing and resting alternately, the progress was slow, more difficult due to the wet and slippery road. The night's rain added to this extra. While moving up, I noticed the famous mountain tracks. These routes are short cuts in a hilly terrain but I was not in a position to follow them because of the road's slippery condition. Secondly, I could have been prevented by the police from taking such a course of action. Therefore, breathing heavily, I kept on moving, came up to a height of 1,920 metres and rested for a while in a small tea shop at a place called Thanidar. Only 330 metres left to climb for that day. At 1.30 pm we reached Pangu climbing from a height of 194 metres. to 2,250 metres.

A welcome arch had been built to welcome us by the inhabitants of Pangu. Our lodging was in a school – seven female pilgrims in one room and 19 of us in another. The climb had really made us all tense. We attacked the food that had been prepared for us. Mostly the food had been the same everywhere with slight variation here and there but we got a cup of soup everywhere.

With hunger satiated, my attention returned to the only mode of travel i. e. my legs. In half a bucket of hot water to which I added an adequate amount of salt, I took a footbath. Most of us concentrated on such a exercise. It is really refreshing. And it relieved all my pain. By 2.30 p.m., all the pilgrims had arrived. The doctor checked our blood pressure. We all managed a footbath but scarcity of water prevented us from having a bath.

After leaving Delhi, we had got plain rice only at Pangu (Bengalis to note) but at Champawat, Pithoragarh and Dharchula we got polao instead of plain rice which I didn't touch because the memory of the Manimahesh pilgrimage was still fresh.

Everywhere the food was vegetarian about which we had already been briefed.

Breakfast at Pangu consisted of milk and cornflakes. At all the camps, we got tea, Bourn vita, biscuits and some fried stuff like puri, sabji or alu paratha for breakfast and evening tea.

We started from Pangu at 7 a.m. in the morning for our next destination,Sirkha, at a distance of 8 kilometres. We descended 2 kilometres on a downhill track, and then commenced a steep climb. After crossing a village named Sosa, the climb became slightly gradual and finally descended a little, to reach our destination. Sirkha is a very small village. On arriving at the P. W. D. Bungalow, I checked my watch, it was only 10.00 am The scenic beauty of the place was unique. An evening rainbow added to this natural beauty.

A cup of Bournvita revitalised my diminished energy. Again a footbath refreshed me immensely. Even more refreshing was the bath, in cold water. I enjoyed this bath because I was not sure whether there would be any chance of bathing during the next few days. Sirkha is at a height of 2440 metres. Day temperatures are very comfortable at this time of the year but the nights are rather cold. A blanket is a definite requirement. I was able to get good night's rest. The night dawned on to 27th June. I got up at 5.00 am. because we had to traverse a distance of 16 kilometres to our destination Oipti. I arranged my luggage, handed it over to the porter completed breakfast with two alu ka paratha and tea and got ready for the journey. I also collected a packet consisting 5 puris, vegetable and some pickle. We started exactly at 6.00 am for Oipti, which is at a height of 2,378 metres – 62 metres. less than Sirkha. I thought the journey would be comfortable, but I was wrong, The first one kilometre was a steady descent to a village called Samuri (2,316 metres) consisting of a few huts and shops. After Samuri, we faced the most steep ascent. This was like climbing a staircase, climbing from rock to rock. This is a very difficult type of ascent. The path was beautiful which somewhat redeemed the difficulties of the ascent. There was greenery everywhere. But breathing and physical difficulties overshadowed all else, and I wondered when it would end.

The ascent continued till Rungling Top or Sumaria Dhar (3,048 metres). Gradually, we went deeper into the forest. The serenity was disturbed by human beings. The sun was playing hide and seek through the dense branches. The greenery was a botanist's delight. I didn't know the names of the plants. They were just beautiful. The silence would get disturbed by the murmur of the leaves as if they were singing in unison, welcoming the cool breeze. The cool breeze refreshed us. A wide expanse of the valley below presented a panoramic beauty, the trees looked like small bushes from that height. They seemed alive an expanse of truth, meditating in the fold of this mighty mountain.

It reminded me of the famous book "Aranyak" written by Shri Bibhuti Bhusan Bandopadhyaya. "Nature bequeaths to worshippers the wealth. Immerse yourself in the nature, you will understand her boons, you will receive boons of bliss, of beauty, and tranquillity, your enjoyment will be supreme. Day and night nature will enchant in thousands of ways, she will help to develop a new outlook, she will expand your mind's life and will lead you to realise the Super Being."

The panorama of Nature all around made me realise the truth of these words.

All of a sudden our back-breaking climb came to an end and Rungling Top appeared before me. There is a small temple here, and a place for travellers to rest is a part of this temple.

We rested a while and commenced our journey on foot again

for our destination. Now started the steep descent. In the hills, steep ascent and descent both are equally difficult to negotiate. However, descending is comparatively easier because you do not get out of breath. The feeling remains the same because your perceptions of time and space disappear, only the agony remains. We descended from almost the top of the mountain to the bottom of the side of a hilly stream, the Sinkhola. I finished my lunch here and picked up my way for Jipti.

From the river again there is a climb but mercifully it was gradual. We crossed two small villages, Galla and Binda-Koti, and could spot our camping sight at Jipti. We reached Jipti at 1. 15 pm. I was feeling hungry, the puris in our lunch packet had turned into stone as such I had to abandon them for a good cause and only ate the potatoes for lunch. Hence, the immediate requirement of hunger had to be satisfied by two cups of Bournvita.

The weather of Jipti was also like that of Sirkha. I managed some lukewarm water and had my bath before the others thronged into the camp. We could spot a black cloud formation and finally it broke into a small shower at 3.00 pm and the hill tops all round received their quota of snow.

My tent mate, Shankar, and I got a small tent for ourselves. The night was cold due to the rain and sudden drop in temperature. I couldn't sleep well

Six days ago we had left Delhi. Our next stop was Budhi, at a distance of 17 kilometres, from here and at a height of 2,740 metres. Though the distance is only 17 kilometres the height difference is 326 metres. The difficulties of a hilly terrain cannot be judged correctly by such correlation of distance and height which I understood later during my journey.

I got up early, finished a breakfast of halwa, boiled potatoes and tea. We were given a packed lunch but that day I was careful to pack some additional boiled potatoes and salt along with usual quota of 5 kachauris and pickle. The memory of yesterday's lunch was fresh with me. We left Jipti a little before 3 o' clock. The Kali river became our companion from here. The road was initially tolerable with slight ups and downs, but later became a steep ascent. On our way, I came across a number of waterfalls but the one that we saw on our way to Budhi was dangerous and glamorous. It is called Najung, and comes down gracefully from top of a mopuntain with a great noise. Its beauty stopped me in my tracks and I could only gaze at it in wonder. It was an amazing cascade, an unending flow of silver. The poet Jatindranath Bagchi's famous poem "Jharnadhara" came alive in front of my eyes.

"*She is a dancing bride, pure stream flows merrily like the companion of the mountain. As bright is the mascara and like the falling specks of snow, it rises and it falls, without rest. She is always flowing,*"

My fellow pilgrims forced me to go on. I had to tear myself away from this hypnotic beauty. The group was moving on. Some slowly, some quickly, I maintained a steady pace. Dr. Verma gave me company, maintaining a steady progress. Our companionship flowed into conversation. His Lucknow version of Hindi mixed with Urdu was difficult for me to follow so I had to answer mainly in monosyllables. He was mostly the speaker while I was the listener. Whenever my attention diverted towards my safety and not on Dr. Verma's dialogue, he reacted immediately at my not being attentive. But how could I answer?

The beauty of the landscape was enhanced by the various springs. Some are pure white, some dirty gray, falling, flowing, dancing like a youthful girl. Singing with sweet tones. I cannot make out the language, I can only concentrate on the tune. It seems they are all chanting the name of God, why else there should be such music? Who created them, who composed their tunes? Alas, nobody answered my questions. Such beauty cannot be explained, such beauty cannot be photographed, such beauty cannot be imprisoned on an artist's canvas because it has been created by God himself. Such beauty makes you forget the troubles of the journey. What is happiness? What is bliss? The sorrows of the journey are temporary. But the bliss of the atmosphere remains as a permanent jewel in your mind. Eternal Bliss is God, Shruti mentions:

"All are descendants from this bliss, all are reared by this bliss and all will mix with bliss at the end."

At 2.40 p.m. we reached Budhi. Shankar had arrived there earlier and reserved a tent for the two of us. When we reached Budhi we were greeted with a hot cup of Bournvita. After this, the usual exercise of a pedicure started with salt and hot water. Here we had some company. As soon as we started from Tawaghat hundreds of small flies followed us or rather ganged up against us. They really made our life miserable on the road and started troubling us in the tent as well. Night brought us some relief from these little foes but the Himalayan cold finally caught up with us. The cold got intensified by the torrential rain. We went out of the tent to have our dinner. During dinner, we had an unpleasant incident,that may have been the cause of mild hypoxia.

Hypoxia is caused by a lack of oxygen. At higher altitudes, the oxygen content of the air reduces gradually and the body does not get its full quota of oxygen and as such , various ailments arise such as headache, nausea, loss of appetite, breathlessness, sleeplessness, fatigue and irritation. Though 1 had not been affected so far by hypoxia, I have faced such ailments before.

During dinner, one of the middle aged pilgrims started shouting at the caretaker of the inspection bungalow just because he had to ask twice for rice. It seemed so silly? Could it be an attack of hypoxia? We pleaded with him to restrain himself. Such incidents were not uncommon during our journey. Somehow we managed to satiate our hunger and returned to the tent for a night's rest. The cold became uncomfortable, making us miserable in our blankets. We could not get sufficient warmth to battle this cold. The rain ceased at 9 pm . and that brought some relief.

We woke up in the morning of 29th June. Six days earlier , on 23rd June we had left Delhi. Today's destination, Gunji, is at a height of 3,500 metres and at a distance of 14 kilometres from here.

Our departure got delayed. The morning of 29th June greeted us with an austere breakfast comprising tea and pakoda only. We were also given three potato stuffed bread slices and pickle as our packed lunch. We commenced on foot at 6.30 a.m. The flies became scarce as we went forward and finally they gave up their war against these innocent pilgrims. The sky was a deep blue. Not a speck of cloud could be seen anywhere. But the treacherous mountain weather cannot be trusted. It can change all of a sudden. All around a wall of high mountain surrounded us. We could see the tree line, beyond which no vegetation can survive. Two prominent triangular snow-covered mountain peaks could be seen at a distance. Down below, the Kali river was our companion. It demarcates the border between India and Nepal.

After walking for two kilometres, we crossed the narrow Chhiyalekh Mountain Pass. That denoted that we had to climb from 2,740 metres to 3,350 metres. The mountain cold made its presence felt at this height. Finally, we scaled this ascent, with some difficulty. Again, the road was on the descent. After negotiating this descent, we came on flat ground. The name of this place is Chota Thanga.

At the end of this flat ground there was a gradual ascent.

Not very difficult to negotiate. We reached Garbiang, a large village surrounded by exquisite natural beauty. Here is the junction of the Kali and Tinker rivers. We heard that a portion of Garbiang had been swallowed up by the hungry Kali river, which is source of constant worry for the populace of this place. A number of shops and a post office mark the market place, prominent among the hilly villages in this area.

We drank tea at a tea shop, took a little rest and resumed our journey.. After travelling some distance, we came to the junction station of the Kali and Kuti Ganga. The Kuti Ganga is much more fiercer and wider than the Kali. This river can be crossed by a wooden bridge which we came across, and you can step into Nepal. The roads to Kailash in India and Nepal run parallel to each other. The rest of the journey was easy. We reached Gunji, The tents had been pitched in beautiful surroundings. Gunji is at the junction of Kuti Ghati and Lipu Ghati Valley, surrounded by snow peaked mountains in the green meadows. Terrace agriculture adds to the beauty as this staircase has gone higher up to touch the top. I wondered if God had given away his entire treasure to this land. The gentle touch of this land removes all weariness. The surrounding of Gunji reminded me of a beautiful poem of Tagore,

"*Oh lord, in this eternal world of yours, wherever I go with my heart and soul, no sorrow, death or discord are found anywhere.*"

A little later, the doctor called us to check our blood pressure. We spent a very peaceful night in the tents. The previous night's experience of cold had made me wear my coat parka even while sleeping, so the high altitude cold did not disturb me. But one lady and a gentleman of our team fell sick. One contacted fever and other had nausea and loss of appetite. Our doctor treated them and gave them a physiological boost as well. We also enjoyed a clear day. The evening rain did not arrive as usual. Then the 30th morning dawned. We had to travel only 8 kilometres. The destination, Kalapani, is at a height 130 metres, lower than Gunji, so there was no hurry. Also the cause of our delay was the ceremony of the handing over of the pilgrims by UP Police and their doctor to the Indo-Tibetan Border Police (ITBP) and their physicians. Around 8 a. m. six policemen of the ITBP came to escort us up to the Indian border Lipulekh Pass.

We started at quarter to nine. The road was on the bank of the river Kali. After a little distance, in a sparse pine forest, we were welcomed by the I T B P with hot coffee. We left the forest and started our journey on the rocky terrain. It was not difficult because the wind was cool and there was no ascent or descent. After about two hours we could spot our camp tents at Kalapani. Just before our tents, the ITBP had pitched their tents. On a small plateau there were eight tents for our accommodation and two tents were pitched for cooking and as a dining room. About two kilometres before Kalapani, I spotted a big cave. Dr. Tripathi of the I.T.B.P. told me that the cave is known as Vyas Cave because sage Vyas Deva had worshipped there for a long time.

Just before we stepped into the boundary of Kalapani, we saw a small Kali temple that had a small spring at the bottom. This is the source of the river Kali. There was a small arch at the entrance and it seems that Goddess Kali is at peace with herself in such peaceful surroundings. A room attached to the main temple housing the Goddess has a Shivalinga. The temple is clean and the appearance clearly indicates that this is a place for regular worship.

Perhaps this place was so named because it may have been destroyed by the fury of the water sources all around. A number of streams and hill springs have joined with the Kali river on its way towards the plain and thus given her a fearful shape.

About half a kilometre from this temple is a hot spring. We entered Kalapani. There was a beautiful welcome arch built by the locals to welcome the pilgrims. The place is at a height of 3,770 metres. Though it is at a lower height than Gunji the cold was more intense, mostly due to snow-clad mountains all around. However, the afternoon sun was very pleasant at that time of the year (June).

Kalapani is the last Indian check post. Again we had to fill up some forms and submitted them along with our passports.

Kalapani greeted us with tea and Bournvita in the morning, and rice, chapati, dal and vegetables for lunch. We had tea in the afternoon., and dinner was completed with rice, chapatis, dal vegetables and papad.

The night was cold. I put on two pullovers and a coat parka, and with a blanket was warm enough, but the night was uncomfortable, perhaps due to the height.

Next day, after breakfast, we reported to the doctor for our blood pressure check-up. Dr. Misra advised us adequately and gave us each a list of medicines along with the drugs to be taken for various ailments. We were already carrying a sufficient quantity of medicines. With this new list, we now became a moving dispensary ourselves.

We proceeded towards the tent of the Immigration Officer to collect our passports. Dr. Laghu was keen to meet me because he had noticed that my home address Varanasi and had almost come to my tent in the night to meet me, but considering the lateness of the hour, he restrained himself, Dr. Laghu came from Varanasi and was keen to meet someone from his hometown. He told me that the Inner Line Permit is issued for the Kailash pilgrims from Kalapani.

The previous night, a high ranking ITBP official had informed us that the photographs taken by each one of us till Lipulekh Pass (Indian border) had to be deposited at this place. The films would be sealed and returned to us on our way back. This caused trouble. Some of us had exposed a few frames only out of an entire film, and some did not have a sufficient number of rolls. We pleaded with the official but it was of no use. We had to deposit our half exposed films. We had not been aware of this prohibitive order.

The condition of one of our fellow pilgrims was causing us worry. His loss of appetite and nausea had increased. Dr. Misra attended to him. I was lucky to have only a severe headache.

Before starting from Kalapani, I went and offered my prayers at the Kali temple and finally we departed at about 8 00 am for our destination, Sungchim, at a distance of 9 kilometres. We were told that our camping ground has been selected at' Navitang, one kilometres short of Sangchim, due to the snow at Sangchim. Sangchim's height is 3,962 metres, only 592 metres more than Kalapani.

Our cavalry consisted of 10 pilgrims, but two decided to abandon the horses and walk, because of severe bodyache. After all, a horse ride is not so comfortable.

My legs were used to this hardship by now and this route brought me no serious problem. Even my bodyache had reduced to a large extent, The going was smooth with some rest. I had Dr. Verma for company. The two of us left the normal route and started scaling the distance over hilly tracks through the jungle. The flowers blossomed around us with varieties of colours,. Some were unknown flowers, whose sweet fragrance made the mind ecstatic. Added to this beauty was the hilly company of the Sangchung stream. Dancing, singing and flowing smoothly to meet her destiny. The atmosphere was heavenly.

We had to break our journey to accept the hospitality of the ITBP again just one kilometre short of our destination. They greeted us with a cup of hot coffee. Finally, we reached Naving at 11.00 a.m. There were five tents in a very small plain area on the bank of the Sangchung stream. This area is surrounded by high snow peaked mountains and the cold was biting due to the windy weather. The mountain peaks looked like temples to me. To the North, I could see a small glacier with a stream flowing from the bottom of this glacier. I took shelter in my tent which brought some comfort from the cold.

It was our last night on Indian soil before we proceeded to Kailash. Gradually, the pilgrims trickled into the camp, followed by the coolies. Again, all of us got a cup of hot Bournvita and sat down in the sun to gossip. I started thinking 'will I be able to cross the final hurdle?' But it was a useless thought. I had come so far and now had to proceed. I could not look back now. God would help me. His will is supreme. If He wishes, I shall climb the highest mountain, I shall cross the hardest hurdle. Only have faith, depend on Him. I paid silent obeisance to Him and prayed for my protection. Hand over yourself to Him and only follow. His wishes, you will reach Him, you will be guided properly. Thus, said Lord Sri Ramkrishna. In the Gita, Lord Krishna says, "In His grace you will get perfect peace and perpetual happiness."

Such thoughts cleared my mind. I started feeling happy and cheerful, and prepared myself for the hardest part of the journey. My mind found its way through the hymns of the great poet Rabindra Nath Tagore.

"I was not aware of the moment when I first crossed the threshhold of this life. What was the power that made me open out into this vast mystery like a bud in the forest at midnight. When in the morning I looked upon the light I felt in a moment that I was not stranger in this world, that the inscrutable without name and form had taken me in its arms in the form of my own mother" (Gitanjali).

The sun got obscured and the cold intensified. I retired to my tent to find the much needed warmth. We had been provided with a mattress each. I spread out the mattress and made my bed. However, it is best to have a sleeping bag on such journey. The night dawned into a beautiful day. Breakfast consisted of Bournvita and biscuits. Lunch was given in a packet, consisting of five puris, a few pieces of potatoes and pickle.

At 7.00 a.m. we started for the Indian border, the famous Lipu Pass, only at a distance of 5 kilometres but we had to scale a height of 1372 metres. i. e. from 3,982 metres. to 5334 metres. The thought depressed me somewhat because mostly the route was covered with snow. Only a little distance away the steepest ascent started and we contacted snow. It was the last stage of the journey. My God, this may be the real end. Breathing trouble started due to the height, even our feet gave up and refused to move further. Only 5 kilometres more, but Oh God! A few steps and then somerest was the only way to progress. The road was slippery. I was losing either my foothold in the snow or was getting stuck in it. Dragging my weary feet, I was progressing slowly. Oh God! give me energy. It is killing, Looking above, the snow white peak was ready to embrace me, but getting to the top was the problem. Finally staggering and limping, I climbed up to the top of Lipu Pass.

A temporary halt was called because the first batch of pilgrims had to return to this place before we could proceed further. The Tibetans call this place Chang Labochhe La.

I opened my lunch packet and to my utter distress found that the puris had turned as hard as stone. I had to abandon the idea of eating them and donated them to one of the porters who gladly accepted them. I ate only a few pieces of potatoes. This could not satiate my hunger and only made me to feel more hungry and miserable. I spotted snow melting into a stream at a distance and drank some water but it was of no help.

A quarrel attracted my attention. An elderly pilgrim had become annoyed with another individual on a very petty matter. He had only requested him to give him a clear place to sit, free from snow which the other person did after a little delay. This angered him. He shouted for some time and finally settled down to brood. I remembered hypoxia playing its tricks.

Around noon, the first batch of pilgrims started trickling down. After they had all returned we could start our descent. I started getting restless because if we had to wait for all of them to return it would be night before we could start. Moreover, travelling on melting snow would be dangerous. However, we received permission to proceed the moment few pilgrims from the first batch reached the top. The glare of the snow was becoming unbearable and we put on our sun glasses. I got up to leave but was horrified to see that the descent route was through snow. Wherever you looked it was snow, snow and more snow. Apart from this, it was a steep descent. Dr. Tripathi asked two porters to walk through the snow to make a pathway for us. The two porters became our vanguard and we started following the track made by them. What a dangerous descent. If you lose a foothold, the fall will be straight down to the bottom, a couple of thousand feet below. One could only hope that the fall would be on snow as that may be the saving grace. One by one, we followed each other; all the pilgrims had a stick except me. Every step was slippery. Some could manage after a little descent. Everyone was cautioning each other but the anticlimax came when the cautioner himself slipped and rolled. Immediately getting up from such an unusual descent and calling out "Careful!" Our feet were definitely not under our control, sinking into the snow and slipping. It looked as if all of us were a part of a dance drama, each one carrying out his own part most dexterously. Sometime swaying, sometimes falling, sometimes rolling down. It reminded me of the "Holiday on Ice Ballet" which an American troupe performed in Calcutta a long time also..

Two gentlemen were ahead of me. The first one slipped and rolled, and the other , following him, sympathised and went to help pull him up. I saw both of them rolling in the snow as if performing a duet snow dance. Lovely sight! But my happiness receded immediately because I also slipped, rolled and joined them. One gentleman slipped and rolled to the bottom of the pass to shorten his journey. Luckily, he was safe.

At last, the dance drama ended at the bottom of the Lipu

Pass where the Tibetan porters and horses were waiting for us. The Chinese authorities had arranged 26 horses for all 26 of us. As a result, our foot slogging ended for the time being. We formed a cavalry. The destination of the cavalry was Taklakot at a distance of 20 kilometres. The Tibetan name of Taklakot is Pulanchug. We could not start immediately because the porters had to bring our luggage down from the height. At about 3.00 pm., a huge regiment started for Taklakot. I was the only footslogger. The bodyache that would follow the horse-ride deterred me. The road was flat but I was gradually being left behind the horses. En route, my shoes got soaked while crossing some fast flowing streams. I carried on for about 4 to 5 kilometres. I caught up with the cavalry at a halt for drinking tea. I could not have completed the remaining 16 kilometres on foot. As a result, with extreme reluctance I got up on a horse. And I was told that whether I use the horse or not I will have to pay the Chinese for the horse ride.

We started moving. Day rolled into night. We crossed Pala at 4252 mtrs. It was becoming difficult to remain seated on the horse. My horse had neither reins nor a saddle. Two stirrups hanged on both the sides from a wooden plank (saddle) as foot rests. I would have definitely preferred a journey on foot. On top of it all, my animal was an overtaking expert. It wanted to go ahead of the others. In its stride it pushed, dog legged and finally landed up ahead of the others, without any consideration for the human being it was carrying. This peculiar cavalry finally reached Taklakot (4256 mtrs) at 21.00 hours IST and at 2300 hours as per Chinese time. Taklakot

Taklakot

was asleep at that time of night. But such a large force created enough noise to wake up the inhabitants of that place whose curiosity brought them out to see our procession.

The entire route is on almost flat ground with hardly any ascent but one patch of the descent was not comfortable at all. The entire area is surrounded by the merciless stony walls of the Himalayas. We were above the tree line, as such there was no sign of trees or grass. Certain fast flowing small streams had to be crossed to reach Taklakot. On arrival, we were welcomed by the Chinese authorities. A Chinese lady acted as the interpreter.

At Taklakot the accommodation is provided in a proper building. In front of a big dining hall, we spread ourselves out on easy chairs. Young Chinese girls served us with cold water.

After some time, a Chinese official appeared and informed us about the dos and don'ts in their territory and directed us to go to another adjacent building i. e., to the Customs Office. We were given three Declaration Forms to fill. Information like passport number, foreign exchange, camera and list of other articles was to be given. We filled up the forms and handed over them to the Customs officials. A thorough check was carried out of our belongings and finally we were sent to our rooms with an escort.

The accommodation was quite good. The dining hall building had three rooms consisting of a dining hall, office and store. Around the main building there were eight small buildings of which four were allotted for our lodging and the other four comprised the kitchen, Customs Office, etc.

Completion of all formalities took us to midnight. Finally, we were asked to go for dinner. Everybody hastened towards the dining hall, which had ten odd tables with four or six chairs at each table. I sat down eagerly to eat. But the food was appalling. All boiled vegetables, out of which I could recognise only the cabbage leaves. Other boiled vegetables could not be recognised by us. We were also served with small bread rolls along with tasteless chutney like the colour of a cockroach. No vegetable had any oil or spices, even the sauce-type concoction was bereft of any known taste.

When you are hungry you eat whatever you get. As such, I also managed to eat to satiate my hunger. In the dining hall, there was a showcase neatly stacked up with Chinese liquor.

Some of the thirsty among us spotted this and immediately ventured to buy few bottles to lift up their spirits. I was only a silent observer. I came back to the room at 3.00 am. The rooms were neatly kept. For five persons, it was spacious. Each room had a big cupboard, a six feet tall stand-lamp and a centre table. All the rooms had electricity supplied by a generator. There was a Chinese painting on the wall. I looked at the well-made bed. It was really inviting. Clean bed sheets with clean pillow covers seemed a luxury on such a journey. A nice quilt and also a blanket on top gave a very decent appearance. I quickly changed to go to bed. There was a knock on the door. I opened it, a young Chinese girl appeared with two tumblers of water, one with cold water another with hot water. She also gave each one of us a sweet smelling soap, a towel and one empty tumbler.

Being very tired, I planned to go to bed, but could not sleep. I kept tossing in the bed and there was some uneasy feeling in my stomach. I got up and picked up a bottle of water and ran towards the lavatory. The condition of the lavatories were horrible. Totally dry sanitation. In the half-built building one portion was a urinal and other portion had been divided into four cubicles as lavatories. No privacy. If some one has to occupy the last cubical on the row, he would have to walk in front of the other open cubicles. The embarrassment from the both sides can be well imagined. However, even such condition could not deter me from using the facility repeatedly. The whole night I ran up and down from my room to the lavatory and back. I was sure that hill diarrhoea had caught up with me. Morning came without any relief. I became very weak. There were no bathroom as such. I washed my face outside the room. In the meantime, the breakfast gong was sounded I knew – I would not get an appropriate diet here, so I decided to eat a little food to keep the energy to proceed further on this journey. I was in real agony and worried as well. After such an arduous journey. I did not want to get stuck at Taklakot. I went to the dining hall to eat a little. After a very austere breakfast, I returned to my -room to find that the room has been reorganised neatly by these Chinese girls. It was very pleasing. Two of my co-pilgrims were bed-ridden. This was reported to the authorities. On receiving the information, they immediately called for a Chinese doctor along with the interpreter. The doctor came, made his diagnosis and gave medicines to these ailing pilgrims. Of course, it was not free of cost. The doctor took his fees and the cost of the medicines as well. These medicines looked like our Ayurvedic medicines, made out of herbs, etc. I believe that allopathic treatment that we use for our daily use is not available at all in China. I did not report to the doctor and started taking my own medicine. My diarrhoea kept me busy almost throughout the day, but towards the evening I started feeling slightly better. Before dinner, Shankar came and informed me that due to shortage of accommodation at Kailash and Mansarovar, there will be two batches of 14 and 12 pilgrims respectively. Shankar was to be the leader of the batch of 14, whereas Mr. Bhagawati would be leader of the batch of 12. I decided to be in

Shankar's batch. Our batch was go to Mansarovar first and Mr. Bhagawati's batch would proceed to Kailash first. After three days, we would change places. I gladly accepted this arrangement and we all went for dinner. After dinner, the Chinese authorities arranged a film show in the dining hall as an entertainment programme. I declined the offer and returned to my room to take rest. Next morning, the last lap of our journey was to begin.

Next morning, I got up early to divide my luggage and food into two sections, one for Mansarovar and the other for Kailash. Some part of the extra luggage could be left behind at Taklakot. Three days food stuff was kept for the Manascircumambulation and the rest for the remaining days at Kailash.

After breakfast, 22 of us got into a military truck and four in a jeep. The last lap of our journey started on a rocky uneven road. The distance to Mansarovar and Kailash is 50 and 80 kilometres respectively.

The military truck progressed gallantly over this road, jolting and shattering our bones. It must be used to this journey, but the captives at the back of the truck were certainly not used to it. The truck was covered , so I could not see much of the scenery outside. But it could be seen that the journey was through a most inhospitable mountainous terrain. Not a touch of greenery anywhere. After about four kilometres, a trace of greenery came into view which indicated the presence of a village. Yes, it was a Tibetan village, named Toyo. Ten kilometers, later, we crossed a stream named Ring Gang. The road is almost on a plateau which may be the famous Tibetan plateau. There was not a single living soul to be seen. only barren hills, and snow-covered peaks here and there.

After a little distance, I could see Rakshas Tal[2] or Ravana Hrada and to its South the Mandhata mountains. It is only at a distance of 2 to 5 miles to the west of Mansarovar. The circumference of Rakshas Tal is about 77 miles and its East, West and North coasts are about 18, 22, 28 ½ and 8 ½ miles in length respectively. About 2 ½ miles from the shore, there is a monastery on the North-Western corner, named Chepgery Gompa. There is a story about

Mandhata Parvat

Rakshas Tal and Ganga Chhu, the outlet of the Manas into the Rakshas. Rakshas Tal was the abode of demons; as such, nobody drank the water out of it. Two golden fishes that were in the

2 Exploration in Tibet pp 25-26

Manas, fought against each other and one pursued the other into Rakshas Tal. The course that the golden fishes took is the present course of the Ganga Chhu. When the holy waters of Manas flowed out of it into Rakshas Tal, it became sanctified. From that time people began to drink the water of Rakshas Tal. This outlet is about 40 to 100 feet in breadth, six miles long and 2 to 4 feet in depth. This Rakshas Sarovar is the placewhere Ravana is said to have done penance to propitiate Lord Shiva, the third of the Hindu trinity and the dweller of Kailash. Tibetans call it Langak Tso which means conjugation of five mountains that are supposed to be immersed in this lake.

Our route was on the bank of the lake. The water is clean and a deep blue in colour. But no pilgrim stops here to drink the water or to have a dip. Probably the closeness of Mansarovar may be the explanation.

After travelling about 3 to 4 kilometres, Mansarovar[3] came into view and the truck stopped at the Base Camp. The Manas parikrama party carried the minimum food that would be

---

3 The water of Mansarovar is as sweet as that of any river or any glacial lake. The Holy Manas provides fine caves on her shores near Gossul and Cherkip Gompas for hermits and fine camping grounds and good sites here and there for Tibetans to build monasteries and houses. It is marshy at certain places and rocky or sandy at others. There are some lakelets and lagoons scattered all around the Lake. In winters, shepherds flock to her shores and in summer, they move to the upper parts of the valleys. One peculiarity of the lake is that at times when there are high waves near the shores, the middle is calm and clear like a mirror, reflecting the silvery dome of Kailash if seen from the Southern side of Mandhata giant heads. On full moon nights, with the noon majestically looking down upon the holy lake, the scene is simply indescribable. At sunset, the whole of the Kailash range on the North becomes a fiery region all of a sudden, throwing an observer into a trance. On other occasions, the whole of Mandhata catches fire and terrible flames with rolling columns of smoke rise in the West only to be buried very soon in the depths of abysmal darkness. Pp29 (Exploration inTibet)

required for the
parikrama and the rest
was deposited in the
camp. Then they got on
to the truck. I followed
them as well. We got
back into the truck
because the transport

View of Mansarovar

would go 16 kilometres further to a transit camp, to help, the Manas party to cross a not very deep but strong hilly stream, which is difficult to cross on foot. Again, after travelling to some distance, the truck stopped. I got down. But what a surprise. In front of me was my lifes dream "Lord Kailash".

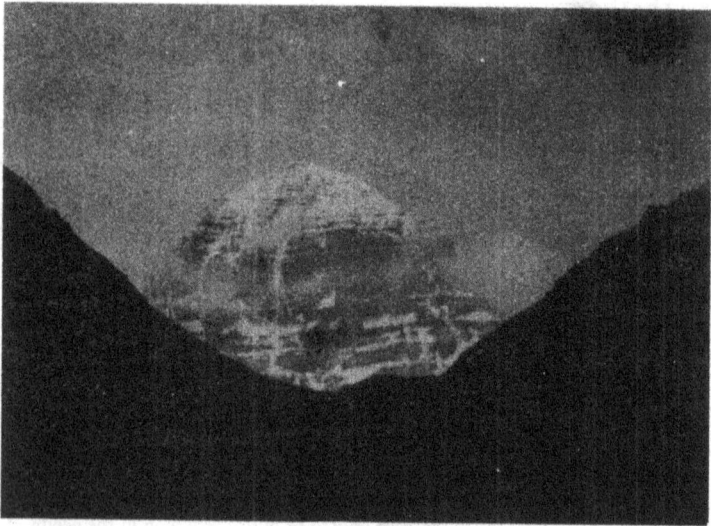

Kailash

252

What grandeur! What beauty! I have been living all my life for this moment. I could die of happiness. My head bowed down to His feet automatically. I was spellbound. I have arrived. I have come to You, oh my Lord, Lord you have done it. You have helped me. With Your love, Your blessings, my life's yearnings have come true. Quickly, I abandoned my idea of Manas parikarama and got down with my luggage i.e. food supply. I could not proceed a step further, leaving my Lord behind. I had came only for this, I had come to see Him. I had come to touch His feet. He has brought me and I am not going anywhere. I want to spend my limited days here and only here. No power can take me away from here. Shankar, asked "Ghoshda, why did you get down?".

I replied, "Brother, I cannot proceed further. Kindly excuse me," I did not tell him the real cause. How could I tell him? What was my mental condition? Such inner feelings cannot be explained to anyone.

Bhakti Baheen also followed me. I asked her "Why did you get down?".

She replied, "I do not know, I saw you getting down and without any thought I also decided to get down".

The truck departed with 14 pilgrims for the Kailash parikrama instead of 12 ,as originally planned. All of a sudden, a thought came to me, why did I do this? Why did I get down? But could not find a satisfactory solution. The sight of Kailash made me forget my surroundings, my plans.

My main intention had been to see Kailash[4], touch His feet. That is why the truck diverted here instead of going to the Manas transit camp first. I saw Him and felt that I have reached my goal. Lord Kailash brought me here to Him. He knew my life's dream. That is why this care, that is why this love.

Later, when I assessed the situation a little coolly, I found that I would be short of food because as originally planned, I had left most of my foodstuff at the base camp of Mansarovar along with my hunter shoes without which the Kailash parikrama (the travel of 32 kilometres around Kailash mountain) is impossible.

I picked up my bag of food and parked myself in the tent. The bed was already there. There was also big stove on which was boiling a big kettle of water and next to the stove was a container full of kerosene. But I found out about the presence of kerosene in that container in a very awkward manner, a funny incident which I will narrate later.

Outside the tent, it was windy and also cold but it was a clear day and as such it was pleasant to sit outside in the sun.

I was staring at Kailash and thinking. Is this really my dream? Is this really Kailash? Finally, my innermost dream has come true. Lord Shiva must have listened to my years of silent prayers.

---

4 The walls of Kailash peak consist of conglomerate rock composed of pebbles cemented together through the course of ages and pressure which is considered to be not later than the Eocene period, which is 55,000,000 years old. The mountains of this region in general and of Purang valley, those separating the two lakes and all those around Kailash in particular, mostly consist of conglomerate.

He has blessed me to fulfill my desire. I remembered a beautiful spiritual song of Tagore.

"Even in my life have I sought Thee with my songs. It was Thee who led me from door to door, and with them have I felt about me, searching and touching my world.

It was my songs that taught me all the lessons I ever learnt. They showed me secret paths, the brought to my sight many a star on the horizon of my heart. The guided me all the day long to the mysteries of pleasure and pain, and, at last, to what palace gate have the brought me in the evening at the end of my journey" (Gitanjali).

I sat down to meditate. I sat down to pray to Lord Shiva and His divine spouse Parvati. I have come to their home. I sang in adoration of Lord Ashutosh.

The peak of Kailash was covered with snow. The height is 6,690 metres (22,028 feet). The mountain, a symbol of Shiva Linga is situated in the South-West part of Tibet. The distance from Lahsa, the capital of Tibet being 1,287 kilometres. Its Tibetan name is Kong Rimpochhe. Sarat Chandra Das, in his book on Tibet has named this as Tisre. In the Mahabharat, Kailash has been called Hemkut, the abode of Lord Shiva and Parvati and the God of Wealth, Lord Kuber.

The Kailash mountain range spreads from Kashmir to Bhutan. The highest peak of this range is Rakapasi (7,788 metres). At the centre of this mountain range, in the area which is surrounded by the Lachu and Jhengchu mountains, is Kailash mountain. In the Northern part of this range is Kailash peak.

We are today at a distance of 865 km from Delhi. The height of this place is 4,550 metres (4544 mtrs). The main mountain peaks of this place are Gurla Mandhata (7707 mtrs). Sureny (6885 mtrs) and Kang Lang (6696 mtrs).

At about 1.00 pm, I started feeling hungry. The condition of my stomach was still not very good so I decided to eat something very light. I took out some flattened rice (chura) the lightest of all food. Anybody with stomach trouble can eat this without any doubt. I wanted to clean my utensil and poured some clean liquid from the container lying beside the stove and it turned out to be kerosene. My work load increased. I cleaned the utensils properly and ate my austere lunch, adding only sugar and tinned milk.

Another party, a little distance away, also started to cook their meal. Their predicament became worse than mine because they poured the Kerosene into their cooking pot thinking it was water. Immediately, the whole thing caught fire. Somehow the fire was extinguished, but now there was no food available, because the rice and dal were immersed in kerosene. They did not have any additional stocks, so they had to wash the rice and dal to cook their meal again. Later, I asked one of them "How was the preparation?"

A curt reply came, "Excellent". I did not pursue the matter any further, because it had to be 'excellent' in the circumstances. The alternative was hunger.

I went and sat outside the tent. The sun was going down

and the cold was intensifying gradually. I looked at Kailash and started thinking again. This is the Kailash about which Sage Lomasa told Yudhisthira in the Mahabharata, "Oh my King this place is visited by many Gods, Yakshas, Rakshasas and Gandharvas". History also tells us that in 269 BC, the King of Kumaon, Nandideva, brought this area under his control. Even during the period of Hu-En-Sang (635 AD), Western Tibet was under the control of the Kumaon Kings. Later, during the decline of this Kingdom, the area went out of their control.

In 1926 AD, the Portugese Jesuit Antonio-De-Andrade established a church at Chabrang, near the source of the Sutlej. The French geographist, D'vil, put Kailash for the first time on the geographical map, and in 1866 AD, the first geographical description was given by Pandit Man Singh. In the 20th Century, scientific research was carried out by Swami Pranavananda about this area.

Kailash became colourful at sunset. After sunset, we assembled in the tent to discuss our plans for the Kailash parikrama (circumambulation) of 32 miles. Of the 14 pilgrims, three declined to go for this trek, which left only 11 of us. I was in trouble due to my spontaneous decision to get down at Kailash without my shoes, as mentioned earlier. My shoes were in my luggage at the base camp of Mansarovar. Everybody around advised me against such a hazardous trek without the hunter shoes. Suddenly, it occurred to me that three pilgrims were not going for parikrama, so why not ask one of them for their shoes?

I asked Dr. Laghu first who was also from Varanasi. Since we hailed from the same place we had become quite close. Dr. Laghu was not going for this parikrama. He gladly agreed to lend me his shoes for the journey. With great expectations I tried on his shoes and was surprised to find that they fitted me better than my own shoes. Again that surprising coincidence; to a believer of God it is the will of God, but to a non-believer it is just a coincidence. As far as I was concerned, it was the will of Kailash that made me get down here instead of sending me to Mansarovar. He had now provided me with the necessary means for performing the parikrama.

The Chinese authorities had engaged a Tibetan gentleman named Mr. Dorji to look after us at Kailash. He was well conversant with Hindi and had studied in India for some time. Dorji fixed up six horses for us, three horses to carry our luggage and the other three to be used by the pilgrims in turn during this journey. Next morning at 6.00 am, the holy circumambulation (parikrama) would begin.

I returned to my tent and covered myself with a heavy quilt, warm enough to enable to sleep even in the open air.

It was a moonlit night. The full moon was only two days away. At 10.00 pm, I came out of my tent to have a look at Kailash in the hypnotising beautiful moonlight. What a transformation. I had seen Kailash in the sunlight, but now it had an altogether different appearance. He was benign. He was not the destroyer of creation. He was the keeper of all beings. His blessings and love are the only things that can be sought by the believers of God. In this holy place, He stands like a vigilant guard watching over the well-being of the human race. I offered my prayers to Him and went inside to sleep. The night passed quickly bringing the dawn to our doorstep. We hurried to get ready, and had our breakfast of coffee and biscuits. We had to cover a distance of 55 kilometres. We were told that there was a transit camp after 15 kilometres. We got ready to go. In all, we were 11, including Miss Madhumohan and Bhakti Baheen. Six Tibetan horsemen and the 67-year-old Mr. Chopra also accompanied us.

We kept Kailash on our right and started moving on the hilly trek of the Kailash region. There was hardly any ascent or descent. We started coming across a few Tibetans on this route of the parikrama. Kailash is an important place for Buddhists also. The saying is that Lord Buddha, after his enlightment, along with five hundred Bodhisattvas, lived on the top of holy Kailash and four footsteps of Lord Buddha can be seen around Kailash. Tibetans also believe that the ringing of bells and chanting of hymns can be heard from the holy peak of Kailash.

Tibetan mythology calls Kailash "Kangri Karchak" and claims that Kailash stands at the centre of the world, as its balance. The surroundings are covered with gold, embedded with priceless jewels. The name of the Lord of this place is Demchok or Lord of Justice. He has been described as wearing a tigerskin and a necklace made of human heads. In one hand, he has a damru (small drum) and in the other he holds a khattam. He is embraced by his divine consort Dogre-Phangmo (Vajra-Varahi). Hundreds and hundreds of Gods surround this mountain with bowed heads seeking blessings.

The Jains also consider Kailash an important place for pilgrimage. They call Kailash Astha-Pada or Padma Hrada. Their first Tirthankar, Adinath Hrishavadeva, attained Nirvana (beatitude) at this holy place. Kailash is a place of pilgrimage for three mighty religions, Hinduism, Buddhism and Jainism. The only other place in the world is Bethlehem which is a pilgrimage place of three great religions i.e. Judaism, Christianity and Islam.

We crossed a few small streams on our way. I was mesmerised by the atmosphere, by the thought of being so close to Kailash. The stones, their colours, the wind, the spring, everything seems to be singing the praises of Lord Shiva. There are many descriptions of Kailash in the various scriptures in India. Some of them flashed through my mind.

Everybody progressed at a good pace except Dr. Verma, 58 year-old Mr. Menon and I. Mr. Menon's health was not suited for this arduous journey. He had accompanied us with the hope of riding a horse for as long as possible, but the three horses left us behind. There was no chance of catching up with them. At that altitude, it became difficult for Mr. Menon to progress. He could walk a few steps and then had to rest. We became worried for him. We started giving him hope and leading him further by saying, "We are almost near the tents" At a little distance, we saw a few yaks and their owners. Dr. Verma went to ask for help from these people but could not achieve anything because language was the biggest barrier. However, we could not stay there; neither could we go back. As a result, our trio started making progress at a snail's pace. Finally, we made contact with our camp. We were at a height of 5,000 metres. It was too cold to remain outside. All of us retired into the tent to rest and prepare ourselves for the journey of 48 kilometres.

One of the pilgrims had brought along some rice. He prepared the rice for all of us and another gentleman provided some pickle. We made a grand dinner out of the rice and pickle. I was happy to eat rice after so many days. The transit camp had thick quilts for all of us and as such we did not have any problem at night. Next morning we got up at 4.00 am as per the instructions from our leader, because the hardest and longest part of the journey lay ahead. On this route, we would have to cross the highest point of our journey, Dolma La or Dolma Pass, at a height of 6, 200 metres.

In the morning, Mr. Menon greeted all of us with coffee and biscuits. Exactly at quarter to five we set off. The day was holy, full moon day (Guru Purnima). If we could not reach the base camp, we would have to spend the night in the cold open air. Mr. Menon was allotted a horse at the outset.

In earlier days, the pilgrims used to get accommodation on this route in the five Buddhist monasteries of Kailash,viz. Nyanri or Chhuku Gompa (West), Dira-phuk Gompa (North), Zuthul-phukGompa (East), Gengta Gompa (South) and Silung Gompa (South). That is why parikama was not so troublesome in those days. But I could not locate any monasteries on the entire route.

The Chinese have probably destroyed them.

On our way, we came across a strong stream. The horses crossed over. Some of the pilgrims went ahead to cross over the snow-bridge, and two pilgrims took off their shoes and got into the stream to cross it barefoot. Only two of us, Mr. Chopra and I were left behind. A horseman took pity on us, and helped us to cross the stream on his back.

We had been travelling on plain ground till now. Gradually the ascent started for crossing the Dolma Pass. Three of us were staggering behind, while three went ahead with the horses. We kept contact with each other, because in such areas, there is every chance of getting lost and taking the wrong route. Such an incident happened with one of us, as I shall narrate later.

After some distance, it seemed to me that a horseman had climbed the top of Dolma Pass and was standing still like a statue. The silhouette against the sky looked grand. At first, I thought that somebody must be meditating in such an exquisite place, but as I drew closer, I found that it was Mr. Menon on horseback. We passed him without asking any questions. After a little while, I looked back and found that he was still there. I became curious and worried, because unless Mr. Menon moved he would be delayed considerably.

There was a blue sky, bright sunshine, and high, snow covered mountain peaks all around as if touching the sky with glory. Against this background there was this still horseman. Totally unacceptable! I looked back again. Oh God, the scene had changed. Mr. Menon was rolling on the ground and the horse was running. I tried to catch hold of the horse but it skillfully evaded me, so I ran towards Mr. Menon to help him. I asked

Dolma Pass

him why he had got off the horse at the very beginning of this ascent. He said ruefully, "I did not leave the horse. It has left me". As long as the horse was with the group it carried on without any problem. But the moment the distance grew between him and the other horses, this horse refused to move. Mr. Mennon tried his best to coerce it to move forward. But without success. When Mr. Menon saw us, he tried to get down from the horse to join us, and it flung him off and ran. Great timing by the animal!

We started moving on the snow. A little later, Mr. Menon stopped. He could not move an inch further. Assessing the situation, I left Dr. Verma with Mr. Menon and hurried towards our main group to ask Mr. Bhagwati to send a horse for Mr. Menon. Without a horse, Mr. Menon would not be able to move or to cross Dolma Pass. I came across one of the pilgrims, Mr. Pai, and told him about the pitiable condition of Mr. Menon. He asked me to follow him and hurried away to inform our leader.

Mr. Pai was blessed with a good physique. He was a worshipper of Lord Mahavira and a regular student of physical culture. But even Mr. Pai had to resort to a horse ride due to physical ailments during this journey. On my way, I met Mr. Chopra and a little later we met a few Tibetans on the circumambulation. Some more pious pilgrims were doing the sashtanga-danda-pradakshina (prostration circuit). It would take at least 15 days for them to complete tèe circuit.

On this route we had less breathing problems because we were now acclimatised and the ascent was gradual, though the altitude was much more. Slowly, at a painstaking pace, we reached the top of Dolma Pass. Here I found a number of small coloured cloth pieces around a huge rock and a few colourful flags planted into the rock. I was curious to know about the four footprints of Buddha, the Enlightened, but there was no one I could ask. The Tibetan could not understand a word of mine.

The descent started from here. I was told that en route we would come across Gouri Kund, where Goddess Parvati had prayed and meditated for Lord Shiva, sitting on a rock. However, I was unable to locate this rock.

I spotted Gouri Kund (lake) on the Eastern side of Kailash Peak. It was by now noon, and as such I could not go down to touch the holy water of this kund. The Tibetans call it Thuki-Zingboo. It is a small beautiful oval-shaped lake, about 3/4 miles long and 1/2 miles wide. For most of the year, it remains snow covered but luckily we were able to see the water. The maximum depth of the lake, as recorded, is 84 feet and it is at a height of 5593 mtrs above sea level. We increased our pace a little and met a horseman, who told us that he was going on a rescue mission for Mr. Menon.

After some more descent we came across a small plateau on the bank of a small stream. Some moss-like growth could be

Kailash Parikrama

seen here and there. Such exotic serenity was hidden away by the surrounding mighty mountains. Everybody went forward, leaving behind the luggage carrying troops and their leader. They asked us to sit a little and rest a while before progressing further. I had a few biscuits which I shared with Mr. Chopra and drank a bellyful of ice-cold water to quench my thirst. Surprisingly, a little later I felt no thirst or hunger. Perhaps

Lord Shiva wanted us to fast on this holy day keeping in mind the tradition of fasting on the full moon and the new moon. I accepted it as His will.

The enthusiasm was contagious. It affected both of us and we started our journey at a brisk pace. We came across a number of streams. We took off our shoes, crossed the ice cold water a number of times but finally we stopped at the bank of a stream which was flowing furiously. It seemed to be dangerous. After trying for about half an hour, the old man, Mr. Chopra, managed to cross at a point towards upstream but I just could not manage it. I was feeling totally helpless. At last, I found a Tibetan and could make him understand my desperate condition. Surprisingly, he understood, came across and lifted me on his back and I crossed the stream effortlessly. I have received such blessings many times. I kept on going. At 4.00 p.m., the sun had gone down below on the Western horizon. I did not know how much further we had to go. Gradually weariness was setting in along with the usual worries. At around dusk, I saw again our luggage carrying horses with our comrades. They invited us to sit with them for a while, to eat a little and rest a while. But we refused this hospitality and kept moving because of the apprehension that at this moment of the day it would be unwise to take rest. This was a wise decision, which we came to know later. If we had accepted to their invitation, we could not have reached the base camp on the same day.

Mr. Chopra left me behind. I tried to keep pace but steadily fell back and tried not to lose him. Gradually, the sun went down, the full moon appeared on the horizon. The place became lonely. I was enjoying such solitude. Though company is always preferable, at this moment my enjoyment was supreme in isolation. Loneliness stirs up the mind. It wants to meditate. I was overwhelmed with the exquisite beauty of Kailash, its peculiar grace and charm. The indescribable beauty was really fascinating. Serenity and grandeur were revealed before one's eyes.

In the full moon night, the atmosphere had become supercharged with mystery. Mahayogi Asutosh, the Holiness of the Holy, the keeper of the world is present here. My head bows to You. The name of Lord Shiva is Shome, because He carries the sign of the moon on his forehead, and today that moon is shining on His face. I felt really blessed by Him to be present here on such an auspicious night. My entire trip was rescheduled by Him to bring me here at this auspicious moment of the night.'

Sivapurana defines five different forms of the Lord. In one form, He is the destroyer, in another, He is effulgent as the sun, in another He is as soft as the moonlight. He is the creator, Kuber and Brahma. Today I am watching that kindness of Him. He is ready to give boons. But are we ready to accept them? He gives Salvation or Nirvana to all, that is why He is called Shankar. He does good to all and that is why He is known as Shiva. He has swallowed the blue poison or all sin and as such He is known as Nilkantha.

Progress generally gets out of phase in such an atmosphere. The path led us to another dangerous stream. It was looking even more inaccessible in the moonlit night. I tried for half an hour to cross this stream but finally gave up. All of a sudden, I spotted two Tibetans crossing the stream. I ran up to them and with my sign language, I persuaded them to help us to cross the stream. Somehow, again they understood my gesticulation. One of them came across and lifted me on his back and crossed the stream with me. Next he went across to lift up Mr. Chopra. Before they could commence this crossing, the stick from Mr. Chopra's hand dropped into the stream. I would have let it go but the Tibetan refused to give up. He jumped into the water, ran a distance along the bank of the stream and finally retrieved the stick for Mr. Chopra. He also brought Mr. Chopra on his back. We tried our best to give him some money but he refused.

This was the second time my Lord had come to my rescue. We only worry, we only think, but every action is being arranged by that Omnipotent God,

It was 8.00 p.m. now, but there was no sign of the base camp. I became weary and worried. I told Mr. Chopra that I feared we had lost our way. He did not pay any heed to my foreboding but carried on. I followed him without saying anything more.

Another hour passed. I had almost lost every bit of my energy. My feet started giving up. Walking like a robot and praying to God to give me little more energy, I started thinking

268

that if I had to die, why not at the feet of Kailash? Who can have such a good fate? If the end has to come, it should be here. At last, my prayers were heard by my Lord. After travelling further for about 45 minutes, I heard the sound of music, the music of the stream close to our base camp. That music was beautiful, it sounded the end of our journey, and a little later, I spotted the white tents of our camp with great relief. Automatically, our pace increased but we came to a dead halt at the stream. We just did not know how to cross it. I started yelling at the top of my voice for Dorji, who finally responded and came to our rescue. He advised us to go slightly downstream and cross over a log. But my shaking legs refused to move any more. I pleaded with Dorji to help me to cross this final hurdle. He smiled and came to my rescue. He held my hand, I steadied my shaking legs as much as possible and crossed this stream to reach the tents. Two of the pilgrims had arrived before us. I was not feeling at all hungry. I had a glass of water and started the preparations for the next day. We would be able to stay one more day at Kailash. On 8th July, we were to go to Mansarovar and the other batch would come here.

In the morning, I got up and finished my morning prayers in front of Kailash.

I saw a building that was under construction near our camp for the future Kailash pilgrims. At 7.00 a.m., Mr. Saini and Miss Madhumohan trickled in. In our batch, Mr. Saini had always been the fastest. So I was surprised when I did not see him in the camp last night. When I asked him about this unusual delay, he told me that he had lost his way. He had climbed Dolma Pass as usual before the others but lost his way from there. After a strenuous search he located some of our friends at a distance of two kilometres, in terrain that takes very long to be traversed. As such the co pilgrims did not wait for him because they could not contact him. Finally, he came to the correct route but had fallen back. After crossing the pass, he found Miss Madhumohan who was also travelling alone, having got detached from the main party. Darkness came. They were worried about spending the night in open air. Such danger was again averted by the grace of the Lord of Kailash. They spotted a tent which belonged to some Tibetan shepherds, who were preparing for their night halt and had lit a fire. Mr. Saini and Miss Madhumohan requested them for a night's shelter. These simple men of Tibet immediately agreed and made their stay as comfortable as possible. In the morning, they thanked these folks of Tibet and returned to the camp. Around 11.00 a.m., some more people trickled in but there was no sign of Bhakti Baheen. The pilgrims reported that she had had a quarrel with the horsemen and they refused her the horse ride and she also did not follow the main party. Till evening there was no sign of this woman. All of us became worried. In the meantime, a Nepali sage named Ramananda Brahmachari came and reported that a gentleman of our party requested that we send him a horse immediately. We told Swamiji that one member was definitely missing, but the individual was a woman and not a man. Swamiji refused to believe that it was a woman. With a lot of persuasion he was finally convinced that it was a woman, not a man. He still had his doubts. However, a horse was despatched to bring her back.

Ramananda Brahmachari's guru is in Nepal, close to Muktinath. He had come for this pilgrimage with the consent of his guru and would return to Nepal after paying his respects to Kedarnath and Badrinath. He was a very well read and decent man, aged about 34-35. He came with little money from Nepal. He also told us that for the Nepalese, no passport or visa is necessary to visit Kailash.

We were all sitting outside the tent and gossiping when Dr. Laghu informed us that Dorji had taken him to a spot from where one gets the best view of Kailash. The moment I came to know this, I started pleading with Dorji to take me to that spot. Initially, he refused, but on my promising him a tip, he agreed to take me to that spot at 3.00 p.m.

Exactly at 3.00 p.m., we started for the view spot. I saw that Dorji had taken a gunny sack. Being curious, I asked him why he was taking that sack. He said that he wanted to collect some fuel to make a fire. Actually the Yakdung on the hill slopes makes excellent fuel for the people of this region. The ascent started, my God, it was steep. Yesterday's weariness was still lingering in my limbs. Therefore, the ascent seemed too difficult to negotiate. I carried on; rest and move was the motto. En route, Dorji kept on collecting the dung to be used as fuel. I also had a bag. It contained some flowers, some leaves of the 'bel" (a kind of shell fruit) tree and some sweets as my offering to Lord Shiva. The condition of these were quite bad because I had brought them from Calcutta. Still I shall offer them at His feet. I shall say my prayers with such offerings. Won't He accept? He does not see the quality or quantity of the flowers. He is only concerned with the devotee's faith and love for Him. The "Bhagwat Gita" says

"A pious and dispassionate devotee who devotionally offers me basil, a leaf of the bel tree, flower, fruit and water, I accept such offerings of that devout mind."

Offerings by a pure mind are accepted by Him. Ashutosh (Lord Shiva) is satisfied with very little. He has showered blessings on His followers whenever a pure mind has prayed to Him. I was sure that my humble offerings would also be accepted by Him.

On climbing up a hill the beautiful panorama of Kailash appeared before me, making me forget time and space. I went into a trance. I forgot to offer the flowers to the Lord. Swami Pranavanandji of Pithoragarh had told to us about this spot for viewing Kailash. I had not bothered to listen to him carefully, I had thought that the spot would be on our route of circumambulation but I was mistaken. Thanks to Mr. Dorji, thanks to everybody who brought me here, who asked me to come and see Kailash from here. I sat down to meditate, I sat down to offer flowers. My innermost mind started singing the praises of Lord Shiva.

A nudge from Mr. Dorji brought me to my senses. The sun was setting. We had to hurry back to the camp. I looked back to my Lord, my last glance and started my return journey; On our return I rewarded Dorji as promised.

The wind had picked up. The cold wind became unbearable and we took shelter in the tents. Suddenly I heard a noise. It was Bhakti Baheen. She had just arrived. She was yelling at the horsemen, but as they did not understand a word, they didn't reply. Seeing the adversary not replying, she turned her wrath towards our leader, Mr. Bhagwati. But there too was a stony silence. Finally, not getting a response, she gave up and went inside the tent.

* You are peace. You are happiness. In all troubles Your words remove sorrow. We all look up to You to see when this sorrowful night will end into dawn.

Ramananda Brahmachari came inside the tent to gossip. I pointed at Bhakti Baheen and asked him. "Is this the gentleman you met on your way"?

Brahmachariji looked at her and stammered incoherently, nodding his assent.

I told him, "At last you will believe us. I hope, it is a she and not he".

Bhakti Baheen did not know what we were talking about which made her stare at us blankly. A discussion regarding her and she did not know anything. She kept staring at us suspiciously.

This was our last night at Kailash. I had spent only four days here, but the mind refused to move away from the place. I knew I had to go, but the saving grace of the situation would be the view of Kailash from Mansarovar also.

My dream to come to Kailash had come true. Am I really blessed? It is believed that all the sins of a lifetime get washed away by one parikrama. Ten circuits wash away the sins of one Kalpa and 108 parikramas secure Nirvana in this very life. Pious and orthodox Tibetans do either 3 or 13 circuits. Some of them do the circumbulation of Kailash in a single day.

Rudra Yamala Purana (the mythological book) says, "The sages came to Kailash, bowed to Lord Shiva and said,' Oh Lord! To see You with physical eyes is impossible. Now we have come to You, we have seen You. Our lives entire religious urge has been fulfilled. Our penance, our worship, our urge for the fulfillment of this world has been satisfied. We have crossed this ocean of life and death. We shall not take rebirth again and come into the bondage of Maya. Your abode is beyond reach of Gods or mortals. No one except a few Mahayogis can come to this place. Even Brahma and Lord Vishnu kept a secret about the fact that rebirth ceases if one visits here.'

"Lord Shiva told Skanda the King, 'Oh! Skanda Very few out of a crore may come here. In Satyayug seven lakhs, in Treta five lakhs, in Dwapar three lakhs and in Kaliyug only one lakh mortals may be able to come here. Hara Gouri is ever present in Kailash. They are here to relieve a mortal from the cycle of birth and death. Whoever can visit this place takes the place of Gods.'"

Sages like Marichi, Vasistha and others did penance here for twelve years at a stretch. In Treta Yuga (the second age of the world, according to the Hindus), Ravana and Bhasmasura came to this holy place in order to propitiate Lord Shiva. The great sage Dattatreya also came to Kailash. Arjuna had to come here to recover the horse of the Rajsuya-Yagna (horse sacrificing religious ceremony to become the undisputed emperor of the land) by defeating the kings of this region. Among the other dignitaries who visited Kailash, Lord Krishna, Rishi Vyasa, Bhima, etc. are worth mentioning. From time immemorial, innumerable spiritual aspirants, including kings and sages, had been visiting this holy region.

I came to know Mr. Menon's predicament later from Dr. Verma. He could not move an inch and had become unconscious. Dr. Verma got worried seeing his condition. In the meantime, he saw a few Tibetan pilgrims and appealed for help for the ailing man. One of them took pity on him, and carried him on his back till Dolma top. The horse arrived at that point to rescue Mr. Menon. The Tibetan was rewarded handsomely for his magnanimity.

The transport arrived in the morning with the Manas batch. They got down with their luggage and we got in to go to Mansarovar, at a distance of 30 kilometres (18 miles). Two hours later, we reached our base camp at Mansarovar. The transport went back to Taklakot to return after three days to pick up both batches.

Wild flower near Mansarovar

Out of 14 pilgrims, only two wanted to go for the Manas Parikrama. A jeep picked them up from the base camp to drop

Manas Parikrama

them at the first transit camp. This arrangement had been made to help the pilgrims to cross a very fast flowing stream, which cannot be negotiated easily.

We were told that only three horses were available for the Manas Parikrama. For this journey, a horse is a must because a number of rivulets which have to be crossed cannot be negotiated on foot. I did not go for this parikarama because this half-hearted journey did not appeal me. The first few miles in a jeep, then on a horse, that is is not in the total spirit of prikrama. I stayed back.

At Manas, there were only two tents. One tent housed 12 of us. The other tent had place for 4 or 5. Our Tibetan Liaison officer stayed in this tent. Like at Kailash, here also there was a building under construction for future pilgrims.

On the Bank of Mansarovar

Tibetans call the holy Mansarovar Tso Navang or Tso Mapham. In the Mahabharat this has been called Bindu Sarovar. Situated in the South of Tibet, enclosed by the Kailash and Janskar mountain ranges, Mansarovar is at a height of 4,540 metres (4544 mtrs). To its North is Kailash, to the South is Garia Mandhata Mountain, to the West is Rakshas Tal or Ravana Lake and to the East are various other mountains. The circumference of this lake is 88 kilometres (54 miles), with an area of 200 sq. kms. The East, West, North and South coasts of the lake are 16, 13, 15 and 10 miles across. The deepest part of Mansarovar is about 90 metres, (90 mtrs). Generally, snowfall starts towards the end of October in this region, the water start freezing by December and slowly the entire lake freezes into a solid state. From the month of May, the ice starts melting slowly. At this time of the year, Mansarovar is totally clear of ice. This area is also known for its fickle weather. It is difficult to predict the weather pattern, which may change suddenly. You may be enjoying bright sunshine and a clear blue sky, and the next moment, hail and snow will force you to withdraw to a tent. There is a proverb in Hindi, "Mansarovar Kaun Barse, Bin Badal Heem Barse", that is,. "Who can approach Mansarovar where snow falls without clouds"?

Mythology has given appropriate attention to the sanctity of this place. Lord Brahma created this lake by his Manas (thought process), hence it is called Mansarovar. The saying goes that King Mandhata discovered this lake first and sat for tapasya (penance) for a long time, that is why the adjacent mountain is known as the Mandhata mountain. In the Vishnu-Purana it is written that Mandhata was the son of King Jubanaswa of the Surya dynasty. The incident of the birth of Mandhata is a fascinating story. Having no son by his queen for a long time, King Jubanaswa started practising yoga in an ashram of sages with the sole desire of being given a son. Seeing the penance of the king, the sages were pleased and they started a yagna for the birth of a son to the king. After the conclusion of the yagna, the sages placed a sanctified pitcher full of water on the altar and went to sleep. They told the king that his queen, after drinking the sanctified water would give birth to a son. At night, the king felt very thirsty and finding no other water nearby, drank the sanctified water meant for his wife. When the sages learnt about it in the morning, they told the king that as he had drunk the sanctified water, he himself would give birth to a son but without suffering any labour pain. After a lapse of a hundred years, a son with a dazzling appearance came out piercing one side of the belly of Jubanaswa. But the king was worried at the thought of how the baby would live without mother's milk. At that very moment, Indra, the King of Gods appeared before him and assured the king that the baby would live and sustain itself with His (Indra's) help. Having said this, Indra thrust one of his fingers into the mouth of the baby who started to suck it. For this reason, he was given the name of Mandhata. Afterwards, Mandhata established himself in his father's kingdom and then set out to conquer the world. On the Sumeru mountain, he fought with Ravana, but ultimately they became friends as both of them were equally strong and brave. When Mandhata next went to conquer the kingdom of Heaven, Indra told him to come back after conquering the world. At this, Mandhata told that there was no one on the earth, who could challenge his supremacy. Indra replied : "You have not yet conquered Labanashur, the mighty son of Madher. "Mandhata then had a fight with Labana and was killed by the demon. Mandhata married Bindumati, the daughter of King Sasabindu. He had three sons—Purukutsa, Aurbarish, Muchukunda and also five daughters.

While talking about the flora of this region, the great sage Pranavananda said that in some villages of the lake region, the grass is smooth like velvet with a carpet of brilliant tiny flowers in rose, violet and yellow colours; at other places it is sharp and cuts like a steel blade. In the upper parts of some valleys are countless types of flowers of various hues over which botanists could very well devote some time to find out new material for research. There are Dama bushes which provide the people of these parts with firewood, since Dama burns even when green and freshly cut. These apart, there are Umbo (red barked tree) and Pema (a variety of Deodar), 8 to 10 feet high, which grow in Shar village. A plant called Jumbo or Jimbu, the Tibetan onion, grows wild in abundance near the hot springs of the Tag Tsangpo at Tirthapuri, Nabra, Dapa

Thuling and at several other places in Western Tibet. On the shores of Mansarovar, a plant called Thuma can be found. It is a marvelous drug specifically for spermatorrhoea and an excellent aphrodisiac. Thuma is the root of a creeper thriving at a height of 4560 feet above sea level[5] .

Mansarovar is the source of four mighty rivers. From the North the Indus, from the East, the Brahmaputra, from the South, the Karnali, and from the West, the Sutlej come out of this lake. The Tibetan names of these rivers are Senge Khambab, Mapcha Khambab, Tamchok Khambab, Langchen Khambab respectively. However, according to some scholars, Manasarovar is the source of only two rivers and not four. Swami Pranavananda is also a believer of this theory.

I sat next to this holy water. I tried to spot the mythological swans and lotus but apart from some unknown birds I could not spot any swan as such. It disheartened me because I had heard so much about them. The expanse of the water is crystal clear and blue. Fish could be seen playing in the deep water. The fish were not very big, at the best they could be termed as medium sized trout.

The swan, the birds that I could see, are known as Ngangha in Tibetan. In Uttar Pradesh, they are called Sawan. They are of two types: Ngaru Serchung and Chakerma. In October-November they can be found in Surat and Chilka Lake in India. I believe they fly upto Siberia in Russia.

---

5 Pp64-65 (Exploration in Tibet)

The cold did not affect me much because by now I had become acclimatised. A new problem started troubling me. My nose started bleeding. At about 11.00 am, I got up to collect my bathing kit and decided to have a bath before noon at least. Otherwise, the wind speed would pick up, making it impossible to have a bath.

I went to the tent and collected my bathing things and also my dismal lunch. The aim was to have a bath and food on the bank of Manas before retiring to the tent in the evening. I wanted to build up friendship with Manas. What is the use of wasting time in the tent. I have come all the way from Calcutta to be with this holy lake, the abode of the gods and sages. I did not want to waste a second anywhere else.

I got ready to get into the water. The sun was playing hide and seek with the clouds. It was quite cold. The water was ice

On the Bank of Mansarovar

282

cold. I touched the water to check the temperature. It could have been a degree or a half above zero. Gradually, I descended knee deep into the water. I dipped myself thrice. Oh God! it was not a wise decision, I was frozen. My blood circulation seemed to have stopped. I got out of the water, rinsed myself and got into warm clothes. The warmth of the body came back slowly. The sun also helped

I finished my food and sat down on a big rock facing Manas. The fish were playing, the birds were singing, the small waves of the lake rippled to the shore. Total silence, total serenity, no sound apart from the musical notes of the waves of Manas could be heard. All around I could see the gorgeous mountains standing as the guardians of this exquisite lake. My mind was immersed in the beauty, my mind wanted to pick up the jewels from such depth. Oh my Lord! My mind wanted to drink the nectar of Your beauty. But I remembered the sad story from the book of Prnavananda. He found that "hundreds of fish frozen and crushed in the swimming posture under the transparent ice or a whole flock or a line of ducks with their young ones frozen to death and sandwiched on the surface of the ever-changing mysterious lake or scores of new born lambs and kids frozen to death in a shepherd camp on single cold night[6]." Thank God I didn't see anything like it.

Three hours passed like this. Suddenly a voice startled me. I saw that Ramananda Brahmachariji had come close to the spot

---

6 pp28-29 (Exploration in Tibet)

where I was sitting. He sat next to me.

I asked him, "Where are you coming from"? He said, "I have just arrived from Kailish on foot".

He took some food out of his bag and invited me to share it, which I declined because I had already had my lunch. He showed me a replica of Kailash, a small stone shaped exactly like Kailash. It was beautiful.

The sun was setting. The resplendent golden rays of the waning sun spread on the water of Manas. The sight was heavenly. "Incredible is the only word to describe this mystic charm. The ecstasy of my mind came out through a song. I sang in praise of the Lord. I sang in praise of the beauty of the Creator. I am really blessed to be able to see such beauty. Thou light my eyes. They beauty is in my heart. Ramanandji said, "I did not understand a word, but its tune is beautiful." I completed the last line of the song, "If I call not Thee in my prayers, if I keep not Thee in my heart, Thy love for me still waits for my love".

Hearing the last line of the song, he said that the composer of such a song must have been a great sage.

I said "Yes". It was written by a saint-like poet, Rabindra Nath Tagore. He has written and composed thousands of songs like this. He was an all time great composer and poet.

It was cold yet I wanted to enjoy the company of the colourful Manas. You have to have an eye to see such beauty, you have to have the mind to perceive it. So many pilgrims have come and gone. How many have seen such colour? That is why it is said that if you want to perceive the holiness of a place you must acquaint yourself with that place intimately otherwise you will be deceived. My abandonment of the Manas circumambulations was due to the same reason. From the spiritual point of view, anyone who wants to feel the enrapturing vibration of a holy place, to calm the wondering mind into sublime serenity, should be a loner.

The sun went down. The colours disappeared, and I returned to the tent. The scene started changing. As the sun went down, the moon came up on the horizon.

There was no Bengali gentleman in our batch, hence my conversation with the other pilgrims was limited. I was mostly a listener to all the heated conversations. As a result, I was friendly with everybody.

I got up from a peaceful sleep. One night had already passed. After the morning prayer and breakfast, I set course on a tour on the bank of Manas. The first day I went towards the South. I carried on walking on the rocky ground till I became tired. On this journey I suddenly came across a two feet beautiful Shiva Lingas made of black stone. Quickly I picked up some holy water from the lake and offered it to Lord Shiva, wondering who had built such a big Linga at this place. Who was there to reply? My question will remain unanswered forever. I also picked up a lovely stone, a small replica of Kailash, as shown to me by Ramanandji.

I looked at my watch. I had drifted too far. I had to return before noon. Otherwise bathing would not be possible due to the strong winds. I could come back to have a bath at 11.00 am.

My experience of the previous day made me careful. I descended into the water quickly, had one dip and ran out of the water. My food was with me. I sat down again on the same stone to enjoy the company of Manas.

Two hours later, I kept the dried clothes in the tent and the three of us set course to the North i e. towards Kailash. In the morning, on the southern side I spotted a destroyed Gumpha. Hoping for more such discoveries, we started walking. We could see the peak of Kailash at a distance, and a little further we came

A part destroyed Gumbha

across an abandoned cave. We left the bank of Manas, and started to climb a hill. With a little effort we climbed to the top. The panorama unfolded in front of our eyes. On one side,

Rakshas Tal and on the other Mansarovar, further away snow .covered Kailash was standing in full grandeur. I felt that the distance of Rakshas Tal was not much, and suggested to my

View of Kailash from Mansarovar

companions that we go up to that lake. But they refused so we returned. On this route we did not come across any Gompha There were eight Gumphas viz. (1) Gossul Gompha (West), (2) Chiu Gompha (North—West), (3) Cherkip Gompha (North), (4) Langpona Gompha (North), (5) Ponri Gompha (North), (6) Seralung Gomphas (East), (7) Yerngo Gompha (South) and (8) Jhugolho Gompha or Thoker (South) on the bank of Manas on the route of the circumambulation but all have been destroyed. The ruins of these Gomphas may still be seen.

The previous night I had fallen asleep, which deprived me of the beauty of Manas in a moonlit night. Now I was careful. After dinner I sat down on the bed and kept waiting for the moon to rise higher on the horizon. When the concert of snoring reached a certain pitch, I got up quickly and lifted the tent flap. What a scene exploded in front of my eyes. Manas in the moonlight was different. Hypnotising beauty surrounded that watery surface. The reflection of bright moonlight on the waves by strong winds had changed the face of Manas. As if Manas had got united with the moon through its soft rays. The

287

mountains were far away, and admiring the beauty in solitude, sharing such beauty with them was a sleepless traveller. How long I remained in such a hypnotic spell, I did not know. The moonlight started fading away into the horizon warning me of the onset of dawn. I went to bed for a while but my enjoyment was not fulfilled. I wanted to see Manas at sunrise. I changed quickly and came outside the tent, but the morning clouds did not allow the sun to come out and did not allow me to see Manas with sunrise as the background.

On the third day also, I finished my bath with one dip only. I sat on a big rock facing Kailash. I offered my prayers to Kailash and read the Gita for some time. At noon, I finished my lunch and went to collect a few colourful stones from the waters of Mansarovar.

The end of our stay at Manas had finally arrived. I wanted to stay on and see the ice on Manas breaking[7] as described by

7 The breaking of ice and its melting to clear blue waters are an even more interesting and awe inspiring sight than the freezing of the lake. A month before thawing sets in, along the West and South coasts, at the mouths of Ding tso and the Tag, ice melts and forms a fine and picturesque blue border 100 yards to half a mile in breadth, to the milk white garment of the lake. Here and there are seen pairs of graceful swans majestically sailing on the perfectly smooth surface of that border, setting up small ripples..... 11 days before the breaking, the disturbance in the lake becomes most intense between 6 and 10 am and terrible sounds, rumblings, groaning crashes resembling the roars of lions and tigers the trumpeting of elephants, the blowing up of mountains with dynamite and the firing of cannon are heard. One can hear all sorts of musical instruments and cries of all animal. ... Nine days before the breaking of the lake the coastward sheets of ice, ranging in length from a few yards to half a mile, get isolated from the main sheet of ice along the fissures and other lines of cleavage and are drifted by winds mostly to the Western southern and parts of the Eastern shores to be stranded there in part.... After thus exhibiting a series of interesting and versatile transformations all of a sudden one night the lake breaks into a clear beautiful and charming blue expanse to the surprise and joy of the villagers and pilgrims on the shores. Tibetans believe that the Holy Mansarovar breaks on the full moon or new Moon day or on the 10th day of the bright or dark half of the lunar month. ....One can forget oneself for hours altogether gazing at the beauty charm, and grandeur of the oceanic lake, teeming with pairs of graceful swans here and there merrily tossing up and down the waves. Pp50-52

Swamiji in his book but I was not that lucky. The next day we had to leave.

In the tent, the scene was similar. The conversation led to arguments between Dr. Verma and another gentleman. Their verbal duel started becoming acrimonious. However, they realised the difficulties of the others and went to bed. Dr. Verma slept next to me. This affected me the most. With Dr. Verma next to me my condition became critical. Every few minutes he would yell, "Om Nama Sivaya" (salute to Lord Shiva). At first, I thought that being in the kingdom of Lord Shiva, he was shouting his name loudly, before going to sleep. But I was mistaken. Dr. Verma carried on with this loud pronouncement for a long time. Even a request from me or the difficulties of the fellow pilgrims did not stop him. I understood that the momentary psychological imbalance caused by the argument had led to this dangerous reaction. He was trying to calm himself by taking the name of God loudly. My repeated requests were ignored. And I kept awake listening to this roar again and again, till midnight when he finally gave up, and I also slept.

Before dawn I was awakened by a dog barking incessantly. I had seen that dog during the day, most likely our caretaker was his master. The dog was black and hairy like any hilly species. I wondered why the dog was barking incessantly. It 1dining hall. I came back to my inviting bed for a good night's rest. Next day, after lunch, we were told to go to the Customs Office with our passport and luggage. After the Customs check, the luggage would be kept by the officials only to be handed over to us at Lipu Pass.

We received our passports. Luggage checking was carried out. Everybody cleared the customs quite comfortably except Mr. And Mrs. Rao. There was a store next to the

View of Kailash from Mansarovar

dining room where one could purchase goods like toffees, bed sheets, bedcovers, white plastic cans, handkerchiefs, various types of Chinese liquor and cigarettes, picture postcards of Tibet, crockery, etc. The prices of these articles were exorbitant in comparison with India, e.g. the cost of a plastic can in Indian currency was Rs.30, the cost of pillow cover Rs.100 etc. Mr. Rao had purchased a dozen pillow-covers and bed sheets. The Customs officer refused to release these articles because as per regulation only one pair of pillow-covers was permitted to be taken by any one person. Mr. and Mrs. Rao started pleading with him. The interpreter came. Mr. Rao told them that he was taking the articles as a token of gift for a large family. Finally the Chinese official agreed to release them on a special consideration. He must have taken into consideration the Indo-China friendship angle. Mr. Rao heaved a sigh of relief. The customs officer saw Mr. Bhagwati outside and let him off without checking his luggage.

There is a small market at Taklakot. We wanted to buy some souvenirs, but the market was closed because it was a Monday.

Everything settled, we were now directed to pay our bills. Mr. Bhagwati started calculating the total amount due to each individual. The amount was generally between 450 to 500 Yuan (Rs. 2250 to 2500). This difference was due to the differences in the mode of travel (jeep or truck), utilisation or non-utilisation of horses during the parikrama etc. Some people had to pay a little less as they did not eat at Taklakot. The liquor lovers had to buy liquor with hard cash which I have mentioned already.

We had exchanged dollar for yuans prior to our departure for Kailash at Taklakot. Now we changed the yuans to dollars after paying our bills.

After completing all the formalities, I went to Shankar's room to enquire about their Manas parikrama. Shankar said that it went off smoothly, except that two of them had slipped from the horses and Mr. Reddy along with Swamiji (Swami Gahananda) had taken a wrong route for some time. However, they soon realised their mistake and returned quickly to the correct route.

We were called for an early dinner. We had to go to bed early and get up at 1.00 a.m. for our journey to Lipu Pass. Before noon, we had to cross Lipu Pass, before the snow began to melt. The path becomes dangerous when the snow starts melting.

I went to bed after dinner. Early to bed may be good for health but too early to bed is bad for sleeping. This happened to me. I just could not sleep, and tossed in bed, the thoughts of Kailash-Mansarovar fleeting away. At last, I went to sleep only to be woken up by Mr. Bhagwati at 12:00 a.m. After visiting the hellish lavatory for the last time, I got ready and joined others in the dining hall. We were given tasteless breadrolls to eat, which we ate quickly.

The ponies were already announcing their loud presence. I quickly went and grabbed the reins of one of the ponies. My previous experience on this route prompted my alacrity. One by one, we all gathered. Our Chinese hosts came to bid farewell. The luggage carriers had already started off. We followed them to Lipu Pass.

We made enough noise to wake up the local inhabitants at that hour of night. The 26 cavalry men were on the move towards home by the same route which appeared different in the dark night. Ominous looking mountain ranges all around were looking at these travellers with sharp eyes and as if pleading and saying "Do not wake up the earthly beings, they are all asleep now, go quietly."[1]

The time passed slowly. Sitting in one posture and the slow progress of the pony made me sleepy. I struggled to keep my eyes open so that the flying horse of mine would not drop the load from his back majestically. What irony! Last night, I had tried very hard to go to sleep, and now I was fighting to keep sleep away from me. The eastern horizon became red. The morning light greeted me with a smile. But the path was unending. We reached Pala, a small place. The cavalry halted for rest. The stiff bodies of the cavalry men alighted from the ponies in different poses and stood on the ground in different poses. Such living dolls could be stowed away in a museum. There was hardly any resting place. There were a few shelters, made of stone. We took shelter in those stony cubicles to save ourselves from the onslaught of the cold winds. Our faces were already numb due to the cold. After resting for half an hour, we started again. The sun came up cheerfully. It was a clear sunny day. We had been blessed with clear weather during the entire period of our pilgrimage apart from the rain we faced in the nights during the early part of our journey.

We spotted Lipulekh from a distance, and reached the foot of Lipulekh Pass after a while. The ascent started through narrow pathways. My earlier comment regarding the weather became uncalled for. The clouds started gathering, obscuring the sun.

We reached a place from where the ponies could not carry us further. We got down and started on foot. Earlier, we had faced the descent. Now it was a steady ascent, but the snow was much less.

At about 10.00 a.m., I could see our luggage carriers waiting at the top of the pass. They would return with the luggage of the next batch.

We had progressed a little further when drops of water began falling from the sky. I looked up for the blessings. Instead, snow flakes came down. The sky became dark, the snow started falling like puffed up cotton wool. It reduced visibility to a few feet only. The Indian border was not far away. Before the visibility reduced, I saw a few jawans of the ITBP. standing at the border.

The snowfall carried on. Nature was now dressed in white. Every open place got covered with snow. Snow started gathering on our clothes and parts of the body even though we were moving. What a novel experience for a man from the plains. I had seen snowfall on my way to Manimahesh but that was not as dangerous as this. However, we climbed to the top through this blizzard and met Dr. Tripathi of the ITBP who was waiting for us.

The third batch of pilgrims was waiting for us to return, In this batch, I was very happy to spot the familiar face of Mr. Sarkar. Finally, he had made it. I wanted to talk to him but our leader goaded us to get down from the pass quickly. So after exchanging pleasantries I started my downward journey. Looked around, I found no one, except Shankar waiting for his mother. I found out later that it would be impossible to progress in this weather without help. All my co-travellers had already disappeared. I went back to the horseman and engaged him and his horse to take me back to safety. Till 2.00 am I was on the horse. Thereafter, I travelled for some distance on foot. Again, I had to mount the horse. This decision to engage a horse was correct, as I realised later.

Two of my companions had gone down. One of them got

caught in knee deep, soft snow and while trying to pull himself out of snow he descended further into it. The second gentleman dragged him out to safety. This could have been a calamity for that pilgrim. My horse took me down effortlessly upto Navidhang (Sangchim). We had our lunch here and after a little rest, my flying horse brought me to Kalapani. Here I parted company with the horse after paying the horseman's dues.

By now, everybody had arrived and everyone was happy. No untoward incident occurred in the blizzard. The successful trip to Kailash-Mansarovar made everybody happy. Again our night halt was at Kalapani.

We were busy gossiping in the tent. In the meantime Mr. Pal called me aside to narrate his supernatural experience during the Kailash circumambulation. He said, "Mr. Ghosh, you must be remembering the crossing of the fast streams on the second day of our Kailash circumambulation. You and a few others stopped short of it. The riders crossed effortlessly. Some crossed through the water with difficulty. Without trying to cross the current, I started walking upstream towards the snow bridge. My intention was to cross early over the snowbridge. This decision was most dangerous. I reached the snowbridge. I had only normal shoes. No sooner I got on this bridge, my legs became numb. I could not move even an inch. From the heel downwards, there was no feelings left. I tried my best to move but without any response from my feet. I started weeping thinking about snow-bite.

"I started praying to Lord Kailash, to my deity, Lord Mahavira. I could do nothing but pray. Suddenly, a gust of gentle wind blew. It sent a tremor of happiness in my body. I cannot explain this feeling to anyone. Suddenly I felt that sensation had returned to my feet. I quickly walked across the snowbridge and came abreast to all of you. You saw me walking naturally."

After listening to this surprising anecdote, I told him, "You are really blessed. Such occurrences cannot be explained by modern science, logic or intelligence."

From Kalapani we came to Gunji. After spending a night at Budhi we came down to Malpa. On our way to Kailash, we had spent a night at Malpa. From Jipti we went to Budhi via Malpa. On our return journey from Malpa, we came to Sirkha via Jipti.

From Sirkha, we started very early. Two ladies had gone to the nearby Narayan Ashram and as such they did not come with us. They planned to spend the night at the Ashram and join us at Tawaghat.

The rain started from early morning. We set off in the rain. I was slightly handicapped because my raincoat did not have the head cover. But I thought, why not walk in the rain? Already I had walked in a blizzard, so why not in the rain too, to complete the cycle. I was having difficulty in walking with snow boots. I put on a pair of sandals at Kalapani. The slippery path due to the rain water was creating a lot of problems for me. I got wet. The last 2 kilometres were almost a steady descent. The feet could not be steadied in the rain. A little carelessness and you could roll down to reach the bottom at a very fast speed. Such descent had to be negotiated slowly.

I walked slowly for another 8 kilometres. Only a kilometre away, I could see Tawaghat. If I could reach Tawaghat, that would be the end of the foot slogging. But on reaching Tawaghat we came to know that the bus had been caught up in a landslide, so we had to walk another 2 kilometres to catch up with the bus. I reached the bus quickly to occupy a front seat. The road clearance was in progress, After an hour, the road was cleared and the bus brought us to Tawaghat. All the pilgrims arrived except the two from Narayan Ashram and the luggage carriers. We waited till 2.00 p.m. for them. Everybody became ravenous. At last, we decided to go to Dharchula from where the bus would return to pick up the luggage and the two stragglers. But fate was against us. Only a kilometre later the bus had to stop because of another landslide. We got down. Hunger made us desperate enough to help in clearing the way of boulders. We came to Dharchula. The bus went back to Tawaghat.

Everybody charged into the dining hall. Our hunger was satiated, and the rain had slowed down to a drizzle. Our clothes were wet but we could not change because our luggage had yet to arrive.

I joined the others to cross the bridge over the Kali river to go to Nepal. The place is very small. There are a few shops and houses. We wanted to buy some souvenirs, but hardly anything was available. We returned after a small tour of the area. An hour later the bus arrived with the two stragglers but it did not bring our luggage. We sent the transport again to collect our luggage, because without the luggage, we could not have started out from that place.

By this time, our clothes had dried up on us. However, on reaching Tawaghat, we saw that the luggage had arrived. With the help of the porters, we loaded the luggage and returned to Dharchula. We started for Pithoragarh. We crossed Jauljibi, Ascot, Ogla, Kanalichina. We reached Pithoragarh at night. I wanted to meet Pranavanandji to inform him about our successful trip, but because of the undue delay, I could not.

Again the July rain came down pouring. The drumming of raindrops woke me up. We ate our breakfast and got into the bus in the rain.

Our programme to have lunch at Rudrapur had to be altered. Two tyres of the bus got deflated, luckily close to some shops that could provide us with food.

The rain stopped. The sky became clear of clouds. We got down from the bus. We had to be satisfied with tea, milk, biscuits, etc. for lunch. Some pilgrims became restless and left by a minibus. By evening, the bus became roadworthy and we started for the Rudrapur P.W.D. Inspection Bungalow. We were supposed to reach there for lunch, but we reached at dinner time instead. The caretaker refused to provide this hospitality. He said that he could not cater for so many at such a short notice. He also informed us that we could get a place to stay at the local Dharamsala.

We arrived at the Dharmasala to find a 'no-vacancy' notice. We ate something and decided to travel by night to Delhi. But all were worried about reaching Delhi at midnight, because Delhi by night does not have a very good reputation.

The journey was coming to an end. My co-pilgrims with whom I had spent so many days, shared both sorrows and happiness, had become a part of a large family. This family would disintegrate tomorrow. A family consisting of members from different parts of India had come together, become a unified body. We may not meet each other again. Who knows?

I am grateful to God. You allowed me to go to You. You allowed me to live in Your abode, You allowed me to touch Your feet. I am blessed.

I fell asleep in the running bus, my head banging against the obstructions around. The bus stopped for few hours due to mechanical trouble. But it did not bother me. I had a peaceful sleep for two hours.

I did not know when the bus started. Dawn woke me up. We were in the outskirts of Delhi. We reached the doorstep of Chandralok Bhavan in Delhi. We had worried unnecessarily. Again the Almighty Lord had brought us, to safety. Exactly

28 days earlier we had started at the same time for our pilgrimage, from the same place.

Note: Cost indicated in the entire journey is of the year 1983.

Everest

Everest Base Camp
And Kalapathar

On the scheduled date, we reached the airport at 5.30 in the morning, much ahead of the time of departure of our flight. Two hours went by without any sign of activity at the airport. At 7.30, the announcement came to check in, much to our relief. It took us a long time to sort out our luggage problems. Finally, taking the Lord's name for a safe flight, we boarded the plane. It was a small plane with five seats. All the baggage was put inside by removing the seats. The passengers were also dumped inside in a similar fashion, leaving no space for limbs. Four passengers sat down on the baggage and the fifth one, a hippy lady, occupied the co-pilot's seat much to everyone's amusement.

The plane took off without any trouble and began to gain height. The scene outside, with snowy peaks glittering in the morning sun, the green fields and the river Dudkoshi looked

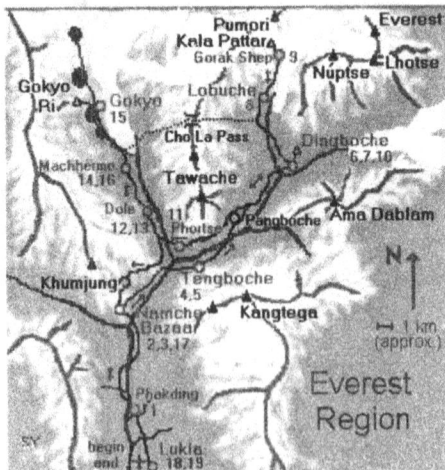

Everest Trekking Route

magnificent. We landed soon after at Lukla airstrip. From here we would be walking to our destination.. The aircraft was surrounded, as soon as it stopped, by a cartload of sherpas and porters. We were lucky to be able to hire a Pasang Sherpa, a veteran of several expeditions and also of very strong build. The Sherpas normally carried a load of 25 to 30 kg, and the rest of the load had to be carried by us.

On the first day, we walked quite easily on the trek and within two hours. reached Ghatchatti around noon. We had our meals in a hotel. In Nepal, men work in the fields and the women run wayside hotels, tea-shops, etc. These women are very efficient.

After lunch, we resumed our journey on foot, keeping the Dudkoshi river to our left. The path was all going down but being sandy it was difficult to walk. On the road, we met a few people going up, but most were coming down; as such, the hotels were not crowded and we faced no difficulty in getting accommodation.

By about 4.00 pm, we crossed the river on the Banker Bridge and rested for tea. One hour from this place we crossed Chuma village. At this village, we were surprised to find a Japanese lady who had set up a vegetable farm to supply vegetables to the Japanese hotel – perhaps the world's only hotel in the high mountains. I almost fell in love with her, watching her fanning herself.

It took us seven hours to reach Jorsale after crossing the

Dudkoshi river timber bridge - an engineering marvel. It was already evening, and we decided to halt there instead of proceeding to Namche Bazar. Jorsale is within the Sangarmatha National Park developed around Mt. Everest as the centre. The authorities have banned the hunting of animals and the cutting of trees, much to the annoyance of the locals. The problem was of getting fuel at that height. The authorities had imposed a tax of Rs.60 on every person entering the area other than Nepali citizen. We did not agree to pay the tax, and got into an argument with the guard, because we were Indian citizens and India does not pick on the Nepalese and impose taxes. Probably the argument had some merit. The guard decided to take up the matter with his boss at Namche Bazar, and left us in peace for the time being.

We stayed the night in the hotel run by a middle aged lady. The lady took care to keep the place spick and span, and supplied us with plenty of firewood and chulli. I noticed that she was worried about her young child who had fever. She brought the baby to me but unfortunately we did not understand each other's language. I gave her some safe medicine from my stock with a hope that the child would be cured. And by God's grace, on our return journey we were informed by the lady that the medicine had worked wonders and cured the child. I don't take the credit of being a doctor. But I accepted the heartfelt thanks of this lady with embarassment. The thanks should have gone to the Parcetamols.

The hotel was almost hanging on the Dudkoshi river,

surrounded by the mountain peaks, covered with thick Deodar forests almost touching the sky. There were many also wild flowers. It gave the impression of a 'hermitage' where old hermits and their consorts were engaged in meditation on the Lord and serving the guests. There was a lot of cultivation in the area, particularly of potato.

At some places, in the centre of the road, a few stones were put together in the form of a stupa with few 'mantras' inscribed; I became curious. I was told that these were erected by devotees of Budhha. When the local people cross a stupa, they keep it to the right. We saw several such stupas, and we followed the custom.

In the morning we woke up our Didi. In Nepal, women are addressed as Didi and they like it. We fell in line and called her out to pay our dues and set course on our journey. We began to walk by the side of Dudkoshi river towards Namche Bazar.

The journey was charming through the fields. Namche Bazar had its importance because every expedition team rested there to get acclimatised for the higher altitudes. The place had plenty of hotels to suit different pockets and was also well supplied with necessary provisions, good and cheap. Hindu temples and Buddhist vihars could be seen. In totality, the valley was picturesque, with the background of the snow-clad Kwangde peak .

Namche Bazar can be reached on the same day after landing at Lulka. But this is tiring and leaves the trekker with no energy or time to enjoy the all pervading heavenly beauty. Therefore, my suggestion would be to stop over at Jorsale for the night.

On the road beyond Namche Bazar, my friend was finding it difficult to walk due to the heavy weight of the baggage. I wanted to arrange for another porter but he didn't agree. We kept on going but the pace was slow. Ultimately, we decided to leave the extra load at the hotel where we had our meal.

The post lunch journey was pleasant and the famous bazaar was left behind. Every Saturday, the village market assembles. But, unfortunately, during our journey, there was no Saturday. The Police Check Post at the bazaar required every foreigner to get his passport checked. Due to shortage of time, we hadn't collected the permits . So we were worried that we would be sent back. Fortunately the police didn't create any problem for us.

A little further up we came to a tri-junction. One of the roads proceeded to Seanghoche, (a famous Japanese village); the other went direct to Thyangboche. We preferred the direct road and found the road smooth and less steep. Soon the roaring Dudhkoshi river could be heard and then seen. It was like a silver path flowing in a serpentine manner between the two hills that were almost touching the sky; the green Deodar trees on both sides of the river created a beautiful scene.

We carried on, keeping the river on our right and after walking a while we had the first glimpse of the famous Buddhist temple, the Thyangboche monastery, on the top of a hill, surrounded by green wood and snow-clad mountains. Our hearts leapt with joy. We crossed a group of Sherpas, Sherpa women with yaks and also two hippies, coming down from base came.

By about 2.30 p.m. we reached a place called Pungi Tamge, a beautiful place on the bank of the river, surrounded by forest. In our journey to the above place, we had passed through a real 'tapovan' with an abundance of flowers of various shapes, sizes and colours. The rhododendron was in full bloom in various colours. Bhuj, pine and other trees added to the beauty. Unfortunately, we could not spend much time here to enjoy the scene.

Beyond Pungi Tange, we crossed the Dudkoshi river again and out of the two hotels run by two brothers we selected one. The husband and wife with one child comprised the hotel owner's family. After about six days we got the opportunity to cook our own food, since firewood was available. We enjoyed hot khichuri flavoured with Australian butter, topped with potato and cabbage curry. But after the meal, as we were about to retire, the lady of the house asked us to march out of the accommodation to the other house. We didn't understand why and were most perplexed. We quickly paid her and got out.

The night was comfortable. I got up in the early hours of the morning for attending to Nature's call and went to the forest close by. I was surprised to see a man coming out of the side room of the house. He appeared to be searching for something. I thought that he had come out to give me company but I was mistaken when he flashed his torch on my face, I decided to challenge him.

He did not say much except to inform me that he was from Kathmandu. Thereafter, I finished my rituals and went to my room. As soon as I entered, the same person entered the room again and started inspecting my sleeping bag which was quite costly and not easily available. I tried to question him but he refused to reply much. This made me worried . What could it be?

After the morning meal and coffee, we began our journey through the deep forest in a calm atmosphere. We looked up to see the sunlight caressing the peaks that seemed immersed in meditation They could smile and cast rays of hopes and encouragement to a traveller like me.

As we proceeded, we suddenly came across a caravan of porters and yaks, all loaded and obstructing the narrow path completely. We didn't have even a foothold on the narrow path. We came to know that 600 porters and 200 yaks were with the Yagoslav Everest Expedition team comprising 25 members. They were returning from the base camp with the expedition material. We happened to meet two members of the expedition party – one was lean and thin and the other was healthy, with the skin of their faces cracked due to snow. We were informed that only five members of the expedition team could reach the summit and the lean man was one of them.

The other person could not go further than the 5th camp. Towards the top, they faced terrible Tibetan winds, which carried away their tents and equipment. Some of the equipment which we saw with the team was extremely light and attractive..

The walk in the morning was through the forest, and in the cold it was difficult but not tiresome. With sun coming up on the horizon, the dull and drowsy scene changed into one with bright smiles. The famous Amadablam peak dressed in white snow from top to bottom was shining like silver. Gradually, we reached Thainagboche Monastery. I remembered that strange visitor who had searched my room in the hotel and felt very uneasy. because he had asked me about my destination and I found him waiting here.

The fear became real, as the unknown individual and four uniformed policemen advanced towards me as we walked to the gate of Thiangboche Monastery. I went cold and got scared thinking of the many evils that could befall me in that strange land. I was suspecting trouble, and did not know what to do. One policeman enquired about my identity, the purpose of my visit and my destination. I gave them all the details very politely. I think he believed me and let me off, accepting my innocence. I was not a trouble maker, in any case. Later, I discovered that the plain clothed person was a police officer from Namche Bazar.

I thanked God that I had not got into trouble with the police, and began to pay attention to the monastery. The building was not very impressive. Around the wall of the shrine the

accept it.

It was snowing outside but the lady put her baby in a basket, wrapped in a blanket and went out in the snow nonchalantly. We got scared and thought of dissuading her from doing so, but she was quite bold. She prepared a fire, and sitting by its side we warmed ourselves and also prepared some nice khichuri.

A remarkable thing that I noticed about the Sherpa villages was the cleanliness. Probably this was due to the influence of a large number of expedition teams from Europe and other Western countries. Unlike Indian villages, where any place in the open may be used as a toilet, thus, spoiling the whole place, each house in the Sherpa village has at least one small wooden enclosure around a deep pit, which is their toilet. Each house has a basket for waste matter and this is emptied into an enclosed pit. The villages in our country could learn this profitably from the Sherpa villages. The villagers, besides their own language, could understand and speak a few English words but no Hindi. The night was very cold with temperature below zero. Even in my sleeping bag of goose feathers, I kept shivering .In the middle of the night, I went outside to relieve myself and found a white sheet spread from one end to the other. The yaks were sleeping in the snow. The black ones had turned white due to the snow covering them.

In the morning, we began to walk. The cold was intense.

We crossed Thukla village and had some tea at a wayside shop. Changing shoes, stockings or wearing double stocking – nothing was of any help against the cold. At Thukla village, we met a Sherpa who had lost eight fingers of his hands due to frostbite in an expedition where he was working as a porter. The cold was truly unbearable.

After toiling for five hours, we reached Lobuje at a height of 5167 mtrs, and stayed there for the night. There were three small stone huts covered with plastic sheets with plenty of holes. Of these, two huts belonged to an old lady and a boy of 13 years. Unfortunately, both were not available. A young girl owned the last hut. I was very hesitant to be her guest and specially to share the room with her but there was no alternative. We prepared a little 'khichuri' for ourselves by paying Rs.10/- for the fire, and enjoyed it. The cleanliness of the Sherpa villages could be seen here also.

We set off at 6.00 a.m. Everything was covered with snow. It was a wonderful sight to see Peoli kak and also 'Moral' birds having fun in the snow

The track went further up the glacier. Since the area was extremely busy on account of a large number of trekkers going across, employing an equally large number of porters and yaks to carry their loads, the path had turned into a beaten track, and even on the snow it was clearly identifiable and we could follow it without difficulty. On our way, we came across 16-20 graves of the trekkers who had gone to that area but unfortunately lost their lives. The graves were very simple. We stood by them with a prayer for peace for their souls.

By about 9.00 a.m., struggling for about three hours, we reached Gorak Shop (5167mtrs). On our way we crossed a very swift shallow stream. Taking a great risk, we crossed it and were told that Gorak Shop had no arrangement for huts or food. We were prepared for this eventuality, but fortunately we got shelter as well as a meal of hot rice, dal and potato, which tasted like nectar at that height. The so-called hotel was made by piling stones upon stoves without any plaster, and on the roof there was only a simple plastic sheet. There were lots of perforations in the sides.and the roof. It had begun to rain, things would have been very difficult. The hotel could protect against light snowfall but during heavy snow , the locals moved down to the lower altitudes.

In the same hotel, there was a hippy couple, who had pitched a tent. There were four trekkers from Holland also but they had gone to Kalpathar. The Dutch were going to leave the place, and the owner promised us accommodation when the Dutch vacated the place. The arrangements in the hotel were very austere. Just a stone bench by the side of a wall. Since we were hungry, we ordered for food to be prepared and in the meantime, started calculating the chances of the Holland party vacating the hotel.

Soon, the party, consisting of medical students, came back after visiting Kalapathar. In no time we became good friends.

The students had spent plenty of money and gone through great trouble to come all the way from Holland just to see the Himalayas of India and Nepal. They were very satisfied with their trip and unable to find words to express their joy. They insisted on our going up to Kalapathar immediately without wasting any time. We had planned to finish our meal and then proceed. But since the Dutch were so insistent, we decided to go right away and have our food on our return.

Keeping Mt. Everest on our right, we started walking on the sandy soil of the dry river. After a while, we kept a hill on our left and came across with a number of paths to climb. We were told to follow any one of the paths and seemed to have selected an easier one. But soon we faced problems. The problem was to reach the Kalapathar summit. It was immaterial which path we selected. All the paths led to the same point. The path was very uneventful and every time we felt that the summit was close, our expectations proved to be wrong. Without the end in sight, the climb became stiffer and stiffer.

At one point, being tired, we sat down to rest and ate the snacks we had bought with us. We looked back and what a majestic scene accosted our eyes. Mt. Everest (Sangarmatha) in the centre with Nupts and Lhotse on the side in the bright sunshine, spreading their radiance all around. A little away, Pumori and Chanji peaks of Tibet were also clearly visible. Not a cloud was visible anywhere in the clear blue sky, which is considered to be a rare event at that altitude. The Sagarmatha peak, partially white and black, was a sight to see. It looked very much like Kailash.

There were three summits and gradually we reached the lower one. Some trekkers had to be satisfied with going up to this alone and then had to return. We were determined to reach the top-most. One by one we scaled them and standing at the summit we felt as if someone had lifted a veil and we could see an absolutely unobstructed distant horizon. We got absolutely lost in the all-pervading infinity and for a moment our individual existence was obliterated. A boundless joy engulfed us. We started shouting at each other and went under a spell of hypnotism deeply drunk with the sight.

As we came on the top-most summit we had to bear the onslaught of the terrible Tibetan winds, which in the past have defeated many trekkers. Against the wind, our progress was almost impossible. However, we continued our progress and ultimately reached 5867 mtrs and from there enjoyed the view. But it was nothing compared to the Everest group and Khambu glacier. It appeared that all had emerged from the heart of Khambu, which, therefore, stood erect with pride.

As I was enjoying the majesty of Mt. Everest, right in front, surrounded by Nuptse and Lhotse on two sides, I visualised Mt. Kailash the lord of the Universe with his Shakti Sarada and Annapurna. With such imagination, the view became absolutely motionless and in a moment forgetting every other thing, the mind got deeply absorbed in it. I could have

continued in that state, for any
length of time but the terrible
wind and biting cold made it
impossible. With tears and a
sorrowful mind we started
going down after eating some
snacks and collecting
mementoes.

Kalapathar

As soon as we started preparing to go down, the clear blue
sky changed colour and clouds started gathering, bringing in
more cold and unbearable icy winds. At high altitude normally
the weather is good in the forenoon, and deteriorates later. For
visiting the Kalpathur summit, had we not listened to the
advice given by the Dutch trekkers, we would have failed in
our attempt in the afternoon. It was only due to them that we
reached the summit and enjoyed the unforgettable scene.

Coming back from the summit, since the road was downhill,
we didn't have much difficulty. In fact, we were almost running
a race and thus were separated from each other. Immediately I
cautioned my friend and Pasang (our porter) to stay close while
walking. This was necessary to ensure safety for all of us. We
reached our hotel by 2.30 p.m. completing the round in 4 to
5 hours. We had not eaten anything since the morning.
Therefore, immediately on our return, we ordered food which
took about an hour to prepare. Hot rice and potato curry tasted
like nectar. Due to fatigue, my friend sufferd from nausea while

returning and took some time to recover.

The Holland party returned to the hotel by about 4.00 p.m. after visiting the Everest Base Camp. They were very happy to see us, particularly the gentleman who had particularly forced us to leave immediately, without wasting any time. We thanked him profusely for the timely suggestion, and also narrated our indescribable experience and supreme joy. The Holland party covered the Kalapathar summit and the Base Camp in one day, which was possible for them due to their youthful strength, but was impossible for us. Our age was against us. Since we were also visiting the Base Camp, we obtained all the details from the Hollanders and they suggested that we should attempt the Base Camp only in the morning since the ice would not melt at that time.

After visiting the summit we returned to the hotel but were still not sure of our accommodation. Only one member of the party had returned and unless the others also returned we could not be sure about the accommodation. I was anxious so ultimately I asked the Holland party about their programme and came to know that under no circumstances would they stay back.

The hotel proprietress then served us lunch consisting of many dishes. One of them was Sherpa soup. I tried to make it out what this was. It turned out to be a simple mixture of rice and dal, what we call 'khichuri'. The Holland party left at 4 o'clock; by that time, it had started snowing, which is called

'Murga Dome'. The Hollanders were well equipped, so it was no problem for them to be out even in the snow.

They left and we were thankful to get the vacated accommodation. Without wasting time, we opened, our sleeping bags and got inside to save ourselves from the freezing cold. I had to leave my bag a number of times, thus disturbing my sleep. Early next morning, I was the first to get up and prepared hot coffee for my two companions to warm them.

In the morning, the sky was clear, but everything was under a thick blanket of snow. The morning sun over Huptse and Pumeri was exquisite. With a hotel boy as guide we started at 6.30 a.m. for the base camp. The road was by the side of Ghumbu glacier and thereafter by the Chukarma glacier of solid snow with stones here and there. Due to the passage of many many expedition parties, their huge porter and yak teams, a regular path had formed, which could be clearly seen. So we had no difficulty in following it. On our way, we crossed the Shahid Stambha, a memorial errected in memory of some important persons who had lost their lives during a Mt. Everest expedition. We stood in silence for a minute and offered our prayers in their memory. Two Sherpas had also lost their lives at the 4th camp and were buried there.

Our guide was quite an experienced chap and had assisted a German party on Khumila Peak a short time earler. He had sound knowledge of the peaks and paths. The expedition party had given him some useful clothing. Wearing these, he looked very smart and in comparison we looked shabby.

The sun rose a little after we began to walk. The base camp was straight ahead of us at the base of the Tibetan peaks, Ghanje, Nuptse Thotse, Sanche, which with expanded hands were welcoming us like a mother anxiously awaiting her child. We too, with great joy, were running forward carefully, selecting every step lest we tumble on the slippery stones. As we looked at the snow-capped towering peaks, various designs, carvings and creations of fantastic beauty could be perceived which equalled the Ajanta-Ellora creations. Plenty of snow tables, pillars of various sizes and dimensions could be seen. We came to a beautifully decorated garden with benches, trees, bushes, figures of different size and shapes, pairs holding each others' hands and dancing, some figures were sitting, busy combing their hair, small boys and girls playing with dolls. Every imaginable thing was created in the garden out of the snow. We on our part simply enjoyed it and were amazed at the dexterity of the master sculptor.

Enjoying the wayside beauty, at last we reached the base camp of Mt. Everest. A long-standing desire was fulfilled. From that point at 5806, mtrs we had an exquisite view of Mr. Everest (Sangarmatha) standing majestically attended by Nuptse (7855 mtrs.) and Lhotse (8478 mtrs.). With folded hands, we offered our prayers to Lord Shiva in the form of Mt. Everest. It was only by His grace and mercy that humble trekkers like us could touch His feet. We were extremely blessed and fortunate in that respect. I had no words to offer and prayed in silence and in tears. The scene which I witnessed was beyond description, particularly as I am not a poet. The Master Sculptor's every creation is perfect and I attempted to engrave it in my mind to last me for the rest of my life.

The base camp was littered all over with empty tins and garbage left by men and animals. Nature creates beauty and man only defiles it. We had been fortunate to get a guide to bring us here. Usually, there is such a rush of visitors, and guides are in great demand. I had a great desire to cross the Khumbu glacier but without proper equipment and aid, it was risky.

With a heavy heart we took leave of that blissful place, and started going down. The sun had come up and due to the heat, the frozen snow had liquified, creating streams and rivulets which we found difficult to cross. We had no ropes or any other aids so necessary for scaling mountains. As such, we attempted every possible improvisation. Taking risks, we reached our base by about 1.00 p.m., covering the trip in six hours. Due to the prolonged exposure in the snow, we were suffering from headache, nausea and breathing problems. But with a little rest and food, we recovered our normal state at Hotel Gorakshop.

By about 3.30 p.m, we prepared to go down. Snowfall had

already started and we were a little hesitant but the locals encouraged us, that snowfall in the afternoon was a routine affair. Within two hours, in a great hurry we reached Lobuje (4864 mtrs.). At Loubuje, we could not get accommodation in Lucks Hotel as it was full and a hippy was lying ill with altitude sickness. We took shelter in the hotel boy's shop, which had been closed when we were on our way up. For a change, here we had chappatis and cabbage which were prepared by the hotel boy and, which we enjoyed immensely after eating rice and dal all these days.

After a night's rest, we moved down on the following morning. Before leaving, we had a last look at Lobuje. The beauty of the place was indescribable and we also knew that we would never return to the place. Hence, we felt very sad. On our way, we crossed a placed where seven mountaineers lay buried in peace. They had lost their lives while attempting to go up the Himalayas. The lord of Everest claims some human sacrifices every year.

Walking through the blanket of white, we reached Thukla, walking by the side of Khumbu rivulet on the bank of Lobuje Khola. We had come down to the grass line, leaving the snow line behind. Gradually, we were observing the presence of vegetation in the form of grass and Juniper bushes and also some animals. The height of the trees in the area did not exceed two feet and the locals used the leaves for firewood.

It took us five more hours to reach Pheriche (4257 mtrs.),

the last tiny village en route to Mt. Everest. At Pheriche, many hotels were available, Also, the Himalayan Rescue Association Hospital had a volunteer physician stationed during most of

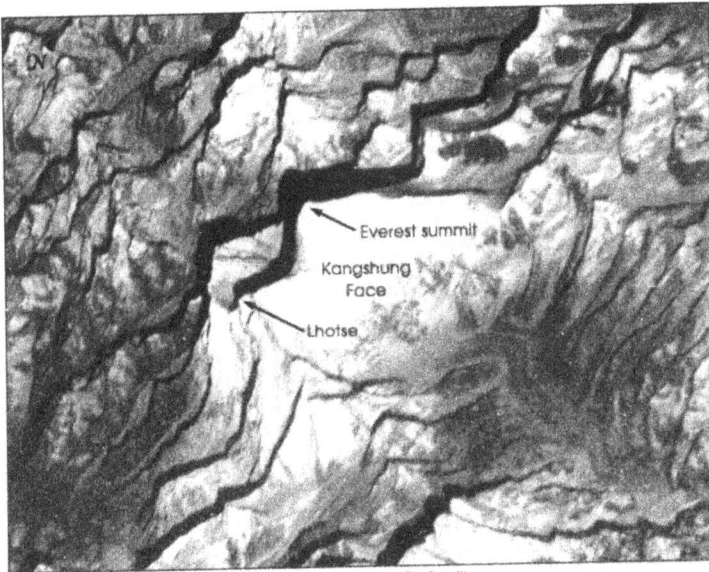

Everest a view from NASA Satellite

the trekking season. The length of the village took about half an hour to cover. The village had green surroundings everywhere, which for us, after living in snow for three days, was a great relief to the eyes. The Sherpas of the village mostly worked as porters for the expeditions, and the mountaineers, at the end of their expeditions, often gave some of their clothes to the porters. My friend was on the look out for a rucksack if available. Unfortunately, he couldn't get one.

One person had accompanied us from Gorak shop to

Pheriche and had asked us to meet him there. We came to know that he had two wives and also owned two hotels, one each at Gorak Shop and Pheriche. The two wives managed these hotels and the fellow enjoyed life with the expedition teams. At Pheriche, just in front of his hotel, a board indicated the distances: Lobuche (4,930 metres) 8 kilometres and Thyangboche (3,867 metre) 10 kilometres. On reaching Pheriche, we went to our old hotel and reclaimed the things we had left behind. We came across plentry of yak and nuks (female yak). They are known as chamari gai also, since their tails are used as 'chamar' in temples. These fetch a good price. In the high altitude area of Nepal, they use them as beasts of burden, as well as their milk for tea, etc. We also thought of tasting the same and ordered a cup of yak milk, but due to its awful smell and taste, we could not swallow it.

We continued our trek down and by about noon we reached, at a height of 3922 mtrs, a beautiful Sherpa village, situated at two levels. One portion of the village had a Gumpha in a grove of cedar trees containing a so-called Yeti scalp. While crossing to the lower half of the village, we noticed a man and a woman washing clothes. The lady was hotel keeper; therefore, we asked whether she could provide us some food. She readily agreed and after a while served us with hot rice and potato curry. It was delicious. The husband was a high altitude porter. He had been to the last camp with a Yugoslavian expedition to Mt. Everest and told us that that had he been given the chance, he would have scaled the summit. We inspected his collection of mountaineering equipment but nothing interested us.

After finishing our food, we began to walk again and crossed the bridge on the river Imje Khola. The river originated from the Khumbu glacier a little below Thyanboche at Pungitenga, and the river originating from Cokeo Lake joined it and got the name of Doodkoshi, a name, well known to the people. On our way, we crossed a rhododendron forest with yellow flowers and green leaves which looked like an artist had painted it.

We passed through Chiyang and through the biggest Sherpa village of the region, Khumjung (3773 mtrs.). The Gumpha of the village preserved a relic of the skull of a Yeti. Close to the village, was the Himalayan Trust Hospital of Khunde. From the village 'View Point' we could see Kangde and Amdablam peaks, side by side. A little further down was the location of the famous Japanese hotel. The hotel was like a glass house, where one could be comfortable in bed and enjoy the beautiful scene of the snow clad peaks. People liked to stay in this hotel although the tariff, compared to other wayside hotels, was too high. We also could not resist the temptation of seeing the hotel; but it was closed for the rainy season. There were only a few servants who couldn't help us. We came down to the airstrip, which looked like a postage stamp covered with grass from the top. The strip had a gradual slope and we ran down on it. There were number of trekkers from Kathmandu. After leaving the hotel, we reached Namche Bazar by about 5.30 p.m. and decided to take refuge in our old hotel. We also collected our extra luggage, which we had left behind on our journey to the top.

At Namche Bazaar, I was scared of the Pungitenga police who had questioned me on my upward journey. And within a few minutes, as luck would have it, we met the same policemen on the road. An unknown fear gripped my heart. We were expecting an unpleasant situation. But we were surprised when the same man greeted us with a smile but said nothing. One of them even invited us to have tea with them. We were more than surprised by this unexpected hospitality. I ventured to ask them why he had suspected me. He admitted it had been a case of mistaken identity, "We found the man we were looking for." I heaved a sigh of relief.

We continued our return journey and met a stream of porters and yaks engaged in carrying the loads of expeditions in the Himalayan region. We came to know that the Schwabesche Mt. Everest Expedition party, with a view to undertake a post-monsoon expedition, was dumping their equipment. Mt. Everest is a popular place for trekking, as such, booking is done in advance for five years. This is no doubt a valuable source income for the Nepal Government.

After walking for about 11 hours we reached Banker Bridge and rested for a while. A cup of tea brought in the extra energy required. We met some small children crying 'Bhom Bhom' and begging. I offered them some money which made them very happy. They left us and began to play.

We were on the last lap of our journey to Lukla and expected to be there by the evening. I kept my fingers crossed so as to not to miss the flight. I prayed to God to help us in getting a flight. Although normally there were no flights in the evening, I was banking on a miracle.. The road was through the dense forest of Chir trees, and the morning calm, and the fast flowing Doodkoshi cast a spell on me. I heard a noise at a distance, looked up but could not see anything as we approached the airstrip. The noise grew and I knew that it was an aircraft It was an odd hour for a plane to arrive. The morning flight had already left. We increased our pace to avail of the flight if it had come.

We ran, stumbled and again ran to cover the distance as quickly as possible. On the way, we met two trekkers who had landed by the flight. They gave us hope and asked us to hurry up. But the faster we walked, the more difficult the way became and our legs refused to move. We were almost nearing the airfield when we heard the sound of the plane. We ran up the rest of the distance. And with great difficulty I reached the aircraft with my friend and the Sherpa being left behind.

There were many passengers for the flight. I asked for two seats. My request was rejected. I approached with folded hands but it was of no use. After much pleading and persuasion, the man demanded to see our tickets. The reservation was for June. He shook his head and refused almost in finality. I was persistent and told him that I had hurried all the way from the base camp for this flight. At last, he took pity on us and asked us to produce our luggage. But he agreed to take only one of us since five passengers had already boarded the aircraft. It became a battle of wits. He was determined not to take us and I was determined to go by that flight only. After lots of arguments, pleading and requests, he pulled out some luggage and arranged for the two of us to get in. I thanked him and we made ourselves comfortable in that cramped space.

The plane took off. But as we got air borne problem began. Due to the brisk walk and the lack of space inside the aircraft, I began to feel very uneasy. I was sure to get nausea and vomiting. The immediate requirement was to take off my shirt and allow the body to cool. But since I was sandwiched from all sides, I could not take off my shirt. Luckily, my co-passenger came to my help and I got saved for the time being.

I looked at the snow peaks in the distant horizon, the green fields below on Mother Earth, dotted with a red hue and the serpentine roads. It looked good to me. By about 1.00 p.m. we landed at Kathmandu. It normally takes 12 to 13 days with all modern aids and equipment to go to the Everest base camp and return. But we had done it in just nine days and completed our visit to Kalapathar and the base camp. Was it an achievement? The next day we bid good bye to Kathmandu.

Trekking Routes

Most often than not trekking is confused with mountaineering. But actually they are not the same. Mountaineering is an organized affair, requires careful preparation. On the other hand trekking can be extremely enjoyable if done in a group. It does not require as much planning and preparation like mountaineering activities. Himalayas may be the only hill ranges where there are immense opportunities for trekking despite the inherent dangers in certain routes. But it is a common knowledge among the lovers of mountains that don't try to navigate through the hilly tracks unless you are brave and adventurous. That is why one must remember the following:

- Enjoy trekking through the mountain tracks. The great Hindu gurus like Sankaracharya trekked through these mountains and left his unmistakable footprints.
- Carry sufficient good and light clothing
- You must wear a well fitting boot and carry few pairs of woolen socks.
- Don't forget to carry medicines for minor ailments.
- To battle the uncertainty of the weather a raincoat will be a great help.
- To avoid becoming a pray of the hypoglycemia carry sufficient quantities of chocolate, lozenges, glucose and dry fruits.
- Learn a little about Hypoxia and its effects to avoid being a pray to this unknown troubles.

- Presently very good GPS (Global Positioning System) receivers available. It would be a good idea to carry one of this modern generation equipment for you to know exactly where you are.

- Carry a good map before you venture into an unknown route.

- Trekking is possible upto 4628 Mtr from April to October and in from Nov to Mar upto 2500 Mtrs.

- Most of the trekking routes do not have accommodation. It would be better to hire alpine tents.

- Mountaineering and Trekking Division of Garhwal Mandal Vikas Nigam Ltd has a well-equipped trekking equipment division.

ROOP KUND
(5029 Meters)

N

NANDA GHUNTI & TRISHUL PEAKS

SHAIL SAMUDRA GLA.

TO JOSHIMATH

TO KAURI PASS

NANDPRAYAG

NANDAKINI

HOME KUND
4061

ALA KHN ANDA

ROOP
KUND
5020

KARAN
PRAYAG

SUTOLA
18

BADNI KUND
26

BISTOLA
4667

TO SRINAGAR

TO SIMLI

BEDNI BUGYAL
3354

GHAT
1331 LOHAJANG PASS
2133

MAND
OLI

BAGRIGAADH
1845

PINDER

DEBAL
1218
13

TO RANIKHET

THARALI
333

21

GWALDAM
1929

TO BAIJNATH

Human
skeleton
and
remains of
horses were
found

Distances in KM. Not to scale

Motorable Roads

Trekking Routes

Rivers

Tourist spots   O

Religious Place   ●

Lake

Mountain Peaks   ▲

VALLEY OF FLOWERS AND HEMKUND
(3658 to 3962 Meters)

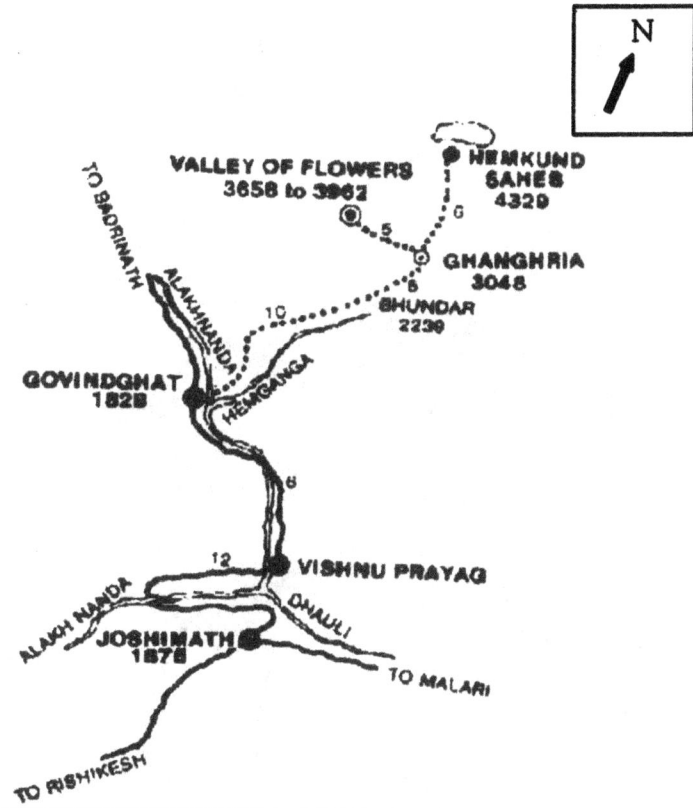

PANCH KEDAR
Kedarnath, Madmaheshwar, Tunganath,
Rudranath, Kalpanath
(Distances in KM) Not to scale

KAURI PASS TREK
(4268 Meters)

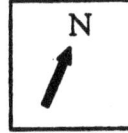

Distances in KM. Not to scale

Motorable Roads ⌒	Trekking Routes ⋯⌒	Rivers ⌒
Tourist spots ○	Religious Place ●	Lake ⬭
	Mountain Peaks ▲	

HAR-KI-DOON
(3568 Meters)

Distances in KM. Not to scale

Motorable Roads	Trekking Routes	Rivers
Tourist spots	Religious Place	Lake
	Mountain Peaks	

KEDARNATH-VASUKI TAL
(3584 Mtrs – 4135 Mtrs)

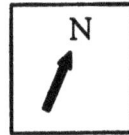

Distances in KM. Not to

Motorable Roads	Trekking Routes	Rivers
Tourist spots ○	Religious Place ●	Lake
	Mountain Peaks ▲	

337

NANDADEVI SANCTUARY

Distances in KM. Not to scale

Motorable Roads	Trekking Routes	Rivers
Tourist spots ○	Religious Place ●	Lake
	Mountain Peaks ▲	

GANGOTRI-GAUMUKH-NANDANVAN TAPOVAN TREK

(3048 Meters)

N

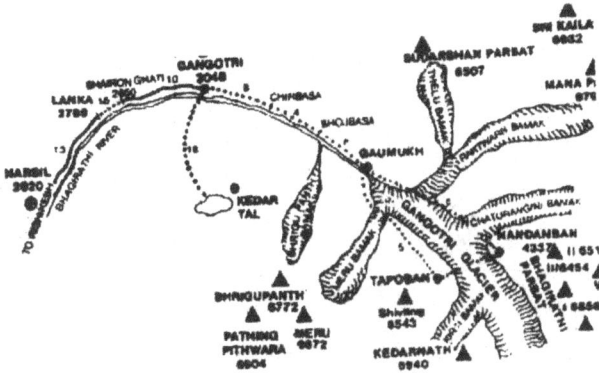

Distances in KM. Not to scale

Motorable Roads

Tourist spots   O

Trekking Routes

Religious Place   ●

Mountain Peaks   ▲

Rivers

Lake

RISHIKESH-PAURI-BINSAR

N

TO BADRINATH

MANDAKINI
TO KEDARNATH
RIVER
PINDER

ALAKHNANDA

ADIBADRI

17
KARAN
PRAYAG

48

GAIRS/
165(

32

12

RUDRA PRAYAG

PANCHOYA

32

DHUDHATOLI

SRINAGAR

8

30

BRAHMAD HUNGI
3020

BHAGIRATHI

38

30

2

PAURI
1814

134

BINSA
2980

DEOPRAYAG

72

THALI
SAIN

7

13

PIERSAIN
2372

70

GANGA

EAST NAYAR

21

13

26

LANSDOWN

RISHIKESH

50

16

KOTDWARA

DELHI

TO NAJIBABAD

TO KALA GARH

Distances in KM. Not to scale

Motorable Roads ⌒   Trekking Routes ⌒   Rivers ⌒

Tourist spots ○   Religious Place ●   Lake ⌒

Mountain Peaks ▲

340

KHATLING-SAHASTRATAL-MASARTAL
(3717 Mtrs – 4572 Mtrs – 3675 Mtrs)

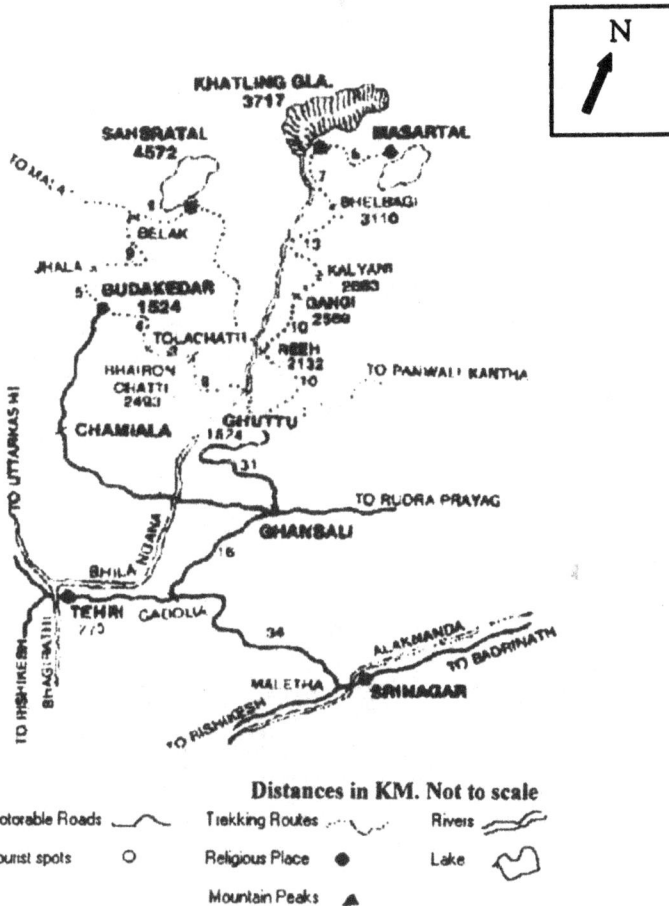

Distances in KM. Not to scale

Motorable Roads	Trekking Routes	Rivers
Tourist spots O	Religious Place ●	Lake
	Mountain Peaks ▲	

RISHIKESH-PAURI-BINSAR

N

SWARGA ROHINI
▲▲▲▲ **& BANDAR PUNCH**
PEAKS

DEOBAN
10 12
NADA VILLAGE
CHAKRATA
.... 10
39 11
GORAGHATI
IDUNGYARA
7
BAHUNTHA
5
KUWA
11
MAGTI
6
GHURANI
BIJNATH
BARATKHOI
R 44
NAGTHAT
42
22
DAUNDILANI
8
DAMTA
LAKHWAR
6
KALSI
25
YAMUNA BRIDGE
CHAKARATA
DEOBAN
LAKHA
MANDAL
KUWA
TO BARKOT
YAMUNA
BRIDGE
MUSSOORIE
TO TEHRI
OAK
PATHAR
KALSI
VIKAS
NAGAR
TO MLA
HARBURT
DEHRADUN
TO RISHIKESH
TO DELHI

Distances in KM. Not to scale

Motorable Roads	⌒	Trekking Routes	⋯
Tourist spots	○	Religious Place	◆
		Mountain Peaks	▲

Rivers ~
Lake ⬭

342

MUSSOORIE-NAGTIBA
(2250 Mtrs & 3048 Mtrs)

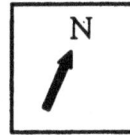

Distances in KM. Not to scale

Motorable Roads ⌒   Trekking Routes ⋯⌄⋯   Rivers ≈

Tourist spots ○   Religious Place ●   Lake ⬡

Mountain Peaks ▲

GANGOTRI KEDARNATH
(3048 Mtrs & 3548 Mtrs)

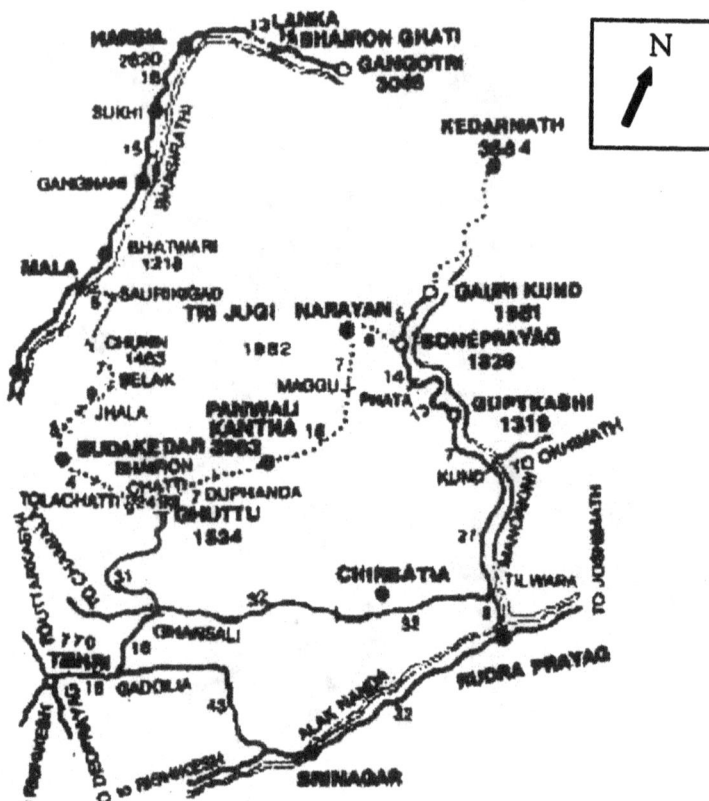

Distances in KM. Not to scale

Motorable Roads ⌒

Tourist spots ○

Trekking Routes ⋯⌄⋅

Religious Place ●

Rivers ⌇

Lake ♡

Mountain Peaks ▲

DODITAL
(3024 Mtrs)

Distances in KM (Not in scale)

Motorable Roads	⌒	Trekking Routes	⌁	Rivers ≈
Tourist spots	○	Religious Place	●	Lake ⬭
		Mountain Peaks	▲